MOZA

H. C. Robbins L ... oston, Massachusetts, in 1926. In 1949 he founded the Haydn Society, which began to issue the Collected Edition of Haydn's music and also made a number of gramophone records. Later he was a Special Correspondent of *The Times* for which he wrote mostly from Eastern Europe. He has published books on Haydn, Mozart and other composers of the eighteenth century, and was also responsible for the first edition of all Haydn's symphonies as well as the editions of many of his other works. In addition, he has shared in the editing of the new Collected Edition of Mozart's works.

He has received honorary doctoral degrees from Boston University, Queen's College, Belfast, and Bristol University. He is at present honorary Professorial Fellow of University College, Cardiff.

H. C. Robbins Landon lives near Toulouse with his wife Else Radant, an Austrian historian and writer.

1791
MOZART'S LAST YEAR

H.C. Robbins Landon

THE SUNDAY TIMES
THE TIMES
Mozart
BICENTENARY FESTIVAL

FLAMINGO
Published by Fontana Paperbacks

For Albi Rosenthal
Old friend and dedicated fellow Mozartian

Note for the Second Edition

The publishers have kindly allowed me to make some factual corrections for this new edition. Since its initial publication, an important book by a Viennese doctor has appeared: Anton Neumayr, *Musik und Medizin* (Vienna 1987) in which the author tends to support Dr Bär's theory of the medical reasons for Mozart's death (see pp. 187ff. below) rather than those of Dr Davies (188ff.). For particular corrections I am indebted to Monsieur P. A. Autexier (Poitiers), Dr A. Hyatt King (London), and Dr Eric Offenbacher (Seattle, Washington).

H.C.R.L.
Foncoussières, July 1988

Emily Anderson's translation of the letter from Sophie Haibel to Georg Nikolaus von Nissen of 7 April 1825 is reproduced from *The Letters of Mozart and His Friends*, ed. E. Anderson (Macmillan, London, 1938; 2nd edn 1966) by kind permission of Macmillan, London and Basingstoke.

First published by Thames and Hudson 1988
Second edition 1989
This edition produced exclusively for The *Sunday Times* in 1990 by Harper Collins Publishers Limited, London

ISBN 0 00 654 432 0

Printed and bound in Great Britain by
William Collins Sons & Co. Ltd, Glasgow

Contents

Appendices

Note on Currency

In Austria in 1791, the principal currency was Gulden, abbreviated 'fl.' or 'f.' (florins); the words 'Gulden' and 'florins' are used interchangeably. The Austrian currency was, like the British pound before decimalization, based on a system of six and twelve. The smaller denomination was Kreuzer (abbreviated 'kr.' or 'xr.'), and sixty Kreuzer made one Gulden. Another term widely used was ducat (a silver or gold coin), one ducat being equivalent to four-and-a-half Gulden. In 1791 £500 transferred to 4883 Gulden. At the *Tonkünstler-Societät* concerts of 16–17 April 1791, when Mozart conducted one of his last three symphonies (possibly K.550), a box in the Burgtheater cost 4 fl. 30 kr.; the best seat in the pit cost 1 fl. 25 kr. (a 'locked' seat 1 fl. 40 kr.). Tickets for Haydn's benefit concert of May 1792 in London cost half a guinea each (10s. 6d.), about the price of a whole box for Mozart's concert. (One can see how dear London was compared to Vienna.) In his four seasons in London between 1791 and 1795, Haydn reckoned that he earned £2400 – some £50,000 or $85,000 today.

Foreword

to *The Sunday Times* edition

When my modest little book *1791 Mozart's Last Year* became a best seller it would have been difficult to say who was more surprised – my faithful and loving publishers Thames & Hudson or myself. Up to then we had collaborated on numerous projects, the most extensive being the five-volume life and works of Haydn (*Chronicle and Works*, 1976–80). They had always treated me as if I had been Harold Robbins Landon instead of the very slow-selling H. C. Robbins Landon – and there was certainly no idea of a *Carpetbaggers* in sight.

Possibly none of us was aware just how profoundly Mozart had entered the consciousness of men and women all over the world. A friend recently returned from Shanghai told me that the classical music station there plays (literally) 'mostly Mozart' all day long – and *Amadeus* has never entered the market in China. As one foreign-language edition after another appeared, and *1791* was translated into French, Italian, German, Portuguese, Norwegian, Spanish, Dutch, Japanese and, most recently, Hungarian, we shook our heads in disbelief. And now it is to be turned into a television film, directed by Christopher Swann (for Granada TV).

Being an American, I am all for mass diffusion of culture: I abhor the idea of music, especially classical music, being a creation for the élite. Now, with the advent of the CD, classical music is reaching millions of people for whom Mozart was scarcely a name, if that. So I welcome this special edition of *1791* for *The Sunday Times*: I hope it encourages each reader to go forth and buy a CD of Mozart's music – the most humane, civilized and perfect music ever written by anyone.

Château de Foncoussières,
Ascension Day (24 May) 1990 H.C.R.L.

Preface

I was thirteen years old, and a pupil at Asheville School, North Carolina, when I discovered Mozart. The school had a fine music teacher by the name of Matthew Cooper; I studied piano with him and sang in his church choir. One of the first works we performed was Mozart's *Ave, verum corpus*, which I found mysteriously beautiful. But the greatest incentive, in those spring days of 1939, for a music-lover without access to chamber music, or a symphony orchestra, much less an opera house, was the exceptional library of gramophone records – many European – which Asheville School housed in a building specially endowed for that purpose and which we boys were allowed to use. There were many rare Mozart recordings, including Richard Strauss conducting the Symphony in G minor (K.550) and an even greater rarity conducted by Paul Sacher (who would one day become a friend) – the choruses from Mozart's *Idomeneo*, then as good as unknown in America. (There was also the Overture, on a German recording, which I found equally astounding: this was my first inkling that a brilliant key like D major could be made to sound so sombre and dark-hued.)

Two years later, in 1941, we celebrated the sesquicentenary of Mozart's death, and for the first time in its history the Boston Symphony played a whole series of concerts devoted exclusively to Mozart at its summer home in Tanglewood. Serge Koussevitsky conducted, and we were introduced to works like the then hardly known Symphony in C (K.338), which the Boston Symphony played with matchless brilliance. It was at this series, in which the orchestra appeared in white dinner jackets, that I first became aware that textually all was not simple with Mozart: Koussevitsky played the Concerto for two pianos (K.365), with clarinet, trumpet and kettle-drum parts which were not in my Eulenburg miniature score and, when I crept up to the conductor's podium in the interval, I saw with astonishment that these parts were not in the Breitkopf & Härtel conducting score either: where did these beautiful parts come from? I was sure, even then, that they were by Mozart, and I note with delight that they have now been included in the score of the complete edition, the *Neue Mozart Ausgabe*. They were not in the original score, but Mozart added them later, for a performance in Vienna.

As it was, I had in 1939 decided to dedicate my life to Haydn, of whose music there was, in those days, no collected edition; indeed, only one-tenth had ever been published at all. Yet I always considered Mozart something quite alone and beyond any other music, including Bach, Beethoven and Wagner. I ought to say that this view was then considered not merely eccentric but almost lunatic. I could hardly attribute to a thirteen-year-old schoolboy a special prescience concerning Mozart and the fact that, one day in England, at least, he would become the most popular composer in the concert hall, topping Beethoven's pre-eminence (which had lasted for a generation). But I did sense that there was a curiously unsettling ambivalence in Mozart's musical language which I found at once compelling and of immense emotional satisfaction.

I had about this time in Lancaster (thirty-four miles west of Boston), where my parents lived, a friend, Millard Gulick, who shared my profound enthusiasm for Mozart and especially for the piano concertos, which I was then playing myself and also collecting on gramophone records: a surprising number were available, some in great performances (by Edwin Fischer, Robert Casadesus, and Artur Schnabel). But in those days it was very difficult to hear such works as the C major Concerto (K.503) in the concert hall, especially in Boston. Soon gramophone records were to become a necessity for Mozartians: where in America could one hear *Così fan tutte*?

In our age, Mozart's spectacular rise to fame has been a continuous process since the 1941 sesquicentenary celebrations – there were, that year, my wife tells me, magnificent performances of all Mozart's great operas at the Staatsoper in Vienna, which she attended. (She, too, has always had a special affinity for Mozart.)

Then, in 1955, three things happened which brought me to Mozart and his music directly. The first was that the late Karl Vötterle and the late Ernst Fritz Schmid, the owner of the Bärenreiter-Verlag and the general editor of the *Neue Mozart Ausgabe*, came to Vienna (where I was then living) to ask me to contribute to this new edition (in the event I edited the last three symphonies and the *Maurerische Trauermusik*). The second Mozartian project was to edit the Mass in C minor (K.427) in a new scholarly edition for C. F. Peters and Eulenburg; we had prepared the first complete recording of it in 1949 with Meinhard von Zallinger in Vienna. And the third Mozartian operation was the editing, with Donald Mitchell, of a symposium on Mozart's music which was issued for the bicentenary celebration of his birth in 1956. I had meanwhile become a member of the Zentralinstitut für Mozartforschung in Salzburg, which concerned itself primarily with the new edition. Mozart's music began to thrive as never before. (I have a little vignette before my eyes: it is January 1956, and we are celebrating Mozart's birth in Salzburg. It is the eve of his birthday and Salzburg is in the grip of a violent snowstorm. A BBC wireless crew has arrived and I take them across the river to the Residenzplatz. From the tower, the top of which can scarcely be seen through the snow, music starts to float across the very silent town, in the streets of which the traffic has disappeared. The music is Mozart's arrangement of ballet music (K.187 and 188) scored for two flutes, five trumpets and four kettledrums.

The BBC crew, like everyone else, is enthralled. It is a magic scene and we might be in the Salzburg of 1776.)

Then in the 1980s came Peter Shaffer's *Amadeus* – play and film, but especially film: a huge, international success, the sound-track for months on the best-seller list in America. All of a sudden, Mozart's name was on every tongue. This is not the place to discuss the faults and merits of *Amadeus*, which has already become a myth (in Italy, the young make a speciality of imitating Mozart's laugh from the film). As a film it was superb entertainment, but of course it had little enough to do with Mozart's actual life. All during its filming, my late friend Roland Gelatt of Thames and Hudson was trying to persuade me to write a book on Mozart's 'decline and fall'. I hesitated, but then, upon considerable reflection, I thought that it might be useful to Mozart's many new friends and admirers to write about his last year, basing the account upon the authentic and contemporary documents at our disposal: there are many more of these than one might dare to expect, and in their totality they certainly bring us nearer to Mozart and his wife Constanze than does fiction, even at its most inspired.

* * *

In this book I have been obliged, given the nature of the project, to treat the music somewhat fleetingly, but here I would like to say a few words on a subject about which, admittedly, much – perhaps too much – has been written.

Haydn, Mozart's greatest contemporary, has often been compared to his younger colleague, generally to Haydn's disadvantage. This is because Haydn's music has something very self-contained about it; he does not invite you to share in his problems because he has reduced these problems to a brilliant intellectual *tour de force*. His great quartets, symphonies, and religious music unfold before us like a pageant which we watch with fascination but which does not necessarily require our personal participation, our immediate emotional involvement. With Mozart, on the other hand, the relationship is entirely different: he invites us to share his emotional world, he takes us by the hand, as it were, and leads us, ultimately requiring us to follow wherever he goes. Hence his joys are our joys, his sorrows our sorrows; and the hauntingly beautiful autumnal world of the music written in 1791, where the sun's rays are slanting sharply and are soon to turn into sunset and twilight, is peculiarly our own, perhaps on a massive scale (given the world's present situation). Mozart probably did not intend to portray this, but it seems to accord better with our pessimistic view of life than the optimistic self-enclosed comfort of Haydn, or the life-asserting triumphs of Beethoven. Like Wagner's *Ring* cycle, which becomes more important to humanity every year, its truths more compelling (possibly because *Götterdämmerung* is a closer reality than it ever was before), Mozart's music becomes increasingly an essential part of our lives. The drama in his operas, his revelation of truth and beauty, has always been perceived in *Figaro* and *Don Giovanni*; now it is also strongly felt in *Così fan tutte* and *La clemenza di Tito*, while *The Magic Flute*'s mystery and majestic solution of seemingly incompatible stylistic elements appear to us with ever greater relevance. The Mozartian legacy, in brief, is as good an excuse for mankind's existence as we shall ever encounter and is perhaps, after all, a still small hope for our ultimate survival.

H.C.R.L.
Château de Foncoussières,
Christmas 1986

I
Coronation in Frankfurt

By the autumn of 1790, Mozart's financial situation was becoming desperate. He was not earning as much money in Vienna as he required for his standard of living, and he had lost a substantial part of his former public. Times were changing dramatically, not only in revolutionary France but also in Austria: there was a new Emperor, Leopold II, and he was about to be crowned Holy Roman Emperor of the German Nation at St Bartholomew's Cathedral in Frankfurt-am-Main on 9 October. Mozart had not yet come to the new monarch's personal attention, but hoped to achieve this by appearing in Frankfurt. On 22 September, therefore, the composer pawned his silver to pay for the trip[1] and set forth with Franz Hofer, the husband of his sister-in-law, Josepha.

Only an incurable optimist could have expected much from the journey. Laying siege to Leopold II was a dubious operation for a composer, and in any case the Emperor had more pressing matters in hand. He had acceded to the Imperial throne upon the death of his brother, Joseph II, on 20 February 1790, and had inherited from him an empire deeply divided by his well-minded but over-hasty reforms. The kingdom of Hungary was seething with revolutionary ideas, actively fomented by Austria's old enemy Prussia; unruly Austrian Netherlands (today's Belgium) had recently declared itself independent; and the Austrian army was bogged down in a seemingly interminable war with the Ottoman Empire. Fortunately, Leopold was a skilled and experienced administrator: as Grand Duke of Tuscany he had managed his Duchy wisely, introduced many successful reforms, and was much loved by his subjects. Now, as Emperor, he moved quickly to resolve his country's pressing problems. By September 1790 he had concluded an armistice with the Porte (the Ottoman court at Constantinople), negotiated the future of eastern Europe with Friedrich Wilhelm, King of Prussia, and gone unopposed to the coronation at Frankfurt. By December, with Prussia's tacit agreement, the Austrians had reoccupied Brussels. Leopold was equally successful dealing with the proud and intransigent Hungarians, and he had begun to make significant progress unravelling the chaotic mess of internal affairs – agricultural, ecclesiastical, administrative – that had been Joseph II's principal legacy to Austria.[2]

All this left little time for music – or for Mozart. To begin with, the court theatres in Vienna were closed for several months after the death of Joseph II and did not reopen until the official period of mourning ended early in June. Thereafter, if he had wanted to, Leopold could have attended performances of *Così fan tutte* in the Burgtheater on 12 June, 6 and 16 July, or 7 August (the final performance, after which the opera was dropped from the repertoire during Mozart's lifetime). And he could also have seen the revival of *The Marriage of Figaro* which remained in the repertoire until February 1791. But he did not. His first appearance at the Burgtheater[3] was on 20 September 1790, and the work performed was Antonio Salieri's *Axur, re d'Ormus*. Leopold timed his first public entrance in a Viennese theatre carefully: Count Carl Zinzendorf, in Imperial Royal service, reports in his important (and still largely unpublished) Diary that day: 'Our king arrived when Axur is on his throne and was warmly applauded.' So Salieri was, for the moment, the conqueror (but he, too, was to fall from grace and to fall heavily); nor is there any evidence that Leopold was much concerned with Mozart at all. He did confirm Mozart's not very brilliant position as Imperial Royal Chamber Composer, a sinecure Joseph II had conferred on him in 1787, but the principal music post had gone to Salieri, who succeeded old Giuseppe Bonno as *Kapellmeister** (the musical director as well as principal composer of the court theatres) in 1788; and Leopold confirmed that position too.

An appearance at the coronation festivities in Frankfurt could serve to counter this neglect, or so Mozart hoped. It was thus that he and Hofer set off from Vienna. There were several ways to travel from Vienna to Frankfurt. One was to take the public coaches, which were costly, uncomfortable and rather tedious; another was to hire a postchaise, changing horses at the post stations; the easiest, most comfortable and by far the most expensive was to travel in one's own coach – and that is what Mozart did. We do not know if he owned a coach – which seems unnecessary and unlikely, since he lived in town – or whether he bought one specially for the journey to Frankfurt. At any rate, he writes from Mainz on 28 September 1790:

> The trip was very pleasant and we had fine weather except for one single day – and this one day didn't cause us any discomfort because my carriage (I would like to give it a kiss) is so wonderful. – In Regensburg we had a splendid lunch, a divine Tafel-Musick [music performed during dinner], ate as well as the English, and drank a superb Mosel wine. – We had breakfast in Nuremberg – an ugly city – We strengthened our worthy tummies with coffee at Würzburg, a beautiful, magnificent city – the expenses for living were everywhere passable – except that 2½ post stations from here in Aschaffenburg, mine host was graciously minded to fleece us horribly . . .[4]

*The *Kapellmeister* was responsible for the music of a court chapel and the term was translated in the eighteenth century as Chapel Master. However, the post also involved conducting, usually composing, and administrative duties.

In the event, Mozart had a quick journey. 'We only took six days,' he told Constanze, adding that they were 'mighty pleased to have found a room' at an inn in the Frankfurt suburb of Sachsenhausen. The coronation town was bursting with visitors.

How Mozart spent the first two weeks in Frankfurt is not recorded, but we know that he gave an academy (concert) on 15 October at the City Theatre. That same day he reported to his wife:

> today at 11 o'clock was my academy, which was marvellous as far as honour is concerned but brought little money . . . It was unfortunate that there was a big déjeuner given by a prince and also big manoeuvres by the Hessian troops – and thus there was always a hindrance every day during my stay here . . .[5]

It is thought that Mozart performed two piano concertos at this concert, a new one in D (K.537, later known as the 'Coronation' Concerto) and an older one in F (K.459, perhaps in the lost 'larger' version with trumpets and kettledrums).[6] Probably one of the newer symphonies was also planned – K.504 ('Prague'), 543, 550, or 551 ('Jupiter'), none of them yet in print.

We have an interesting and 'professional' description of Mozart, his playing and his concert in the diary of Count Ludwig von Bentheim-Steinfurt:

> Friday the 15th at 11 o'clock in the morning in the room of the National Theatre was a *grand concert by Mozart.* It began with that beautiful 1) Symphony by Mozart which I've had for a long time. 2) Then a superb Italian scena 'non so di chi' which Madame *Schick* sang with infinite expression. 3) Mozart played a concerto of his *composition* which was of a *gentilesse and an extraordinary charm* [K.459?], he had a forte piano by Stein of Augsburg which is supposed to be foremost of its kind and which costs 90 to 100 ducats, that instrument

belonged to Madame Baronesse de Frentz. Mozart's playing resembles slightly that of the late [composer Johann Friedrich] *Klöffler* [who had been *Kapellmeister* in the service of the Bentheim-Steinfurt family] but infinitely more perfect. Mr Mozart is a little man, with an agreeable figure, he was wearing a navy-blue[7] satin suit richly embroidered, he is engaged at the Imperial Court. 4) The soprano castrato *Cecarelli* sang a beautiful Scena and Rondeau, but the bravura airs do not exactly seem to be his strong point; he possesses grace and a perfect technique, an excellent singer but his tone is declining a bit with that of his unbecoming presence; as for the rest his passagework, ornaments and trill are admirable, must see if I can get him for the summer months to give lessons to [my daughter] Henriette. Perhaps he could come with Edom or someone else; because he ought to be free, not being attached to the theatre like Madame Schick who in the summer will be in Francfort. *In the second part* No. 5 another concerto by Mozart [K.537?] but which did not please me as much as the first. 6) A Duo which we own and of which I recalled the section 'Per te, per te' with the passage that goes up right afterwards . . . 7) *A Phantasie* with no notes [*i.e.*, played from memory] by Mozart, most charming, *in which he was infinitely brilliant, displaying all the force of his genius.* 8) The final symphony was not even given because it was already 2 o'clock and everyone was going to be exhausted after the dinner. The music hence lasted three hours and what happened was that there were very long intervals between each piece. The orchestra could only be feeble with five or six violins and moreover not very precise, but that which enraged and saddened me was that there were not very many people and I was seated next to a young singer called Succarini, her German quite good. Mr Westerhold, that grand amateur of music, was behind me.[8]

On the way back to Vienna, Mozart stopped at Munich, where the Elector Carl Theodor, for whom *Idomeneo* had been composed in 1780, asked him to participate in an academy for the King of Naples, Ferdinand IV, and his consort, Archduchess Maria Carolina of Austria. They had just been to Vienna to marry off two of their daughters. 'That is a real distinction,' wrote Mozart to his wife at the beginning of November, and added acidly: 'A fine honour for the Viennese Court, that the King must hear me in a foreign country . . .'[9]

Towards the middle of November 1790, Mozart returned to Vienna and the ever-present need to earn more money and reduce his debts. Since financial worries are to hover so balefully over the composer's last year, it might be as well to pause here for a moment and examine why his money problems had become so acute.

Mozart's financial situation had appeared most optimistic in 1785 when his father came to visit him in Vienna and wrote to Wolfgang's sister Maria Anna (Nannerl) on 12 March, 'your brother made 559f. in his academy', and a few days later (19 March), 'I think that my son, if he doesn't have any debts to pay, could deposit 2000f. in the bank: the money is surely there, for the household, as far as food and drink are concerned, is economic in the highest degree!'[10]

But despite the success of his subscription concerts in 1785 and 1786, and the success of *Figaro* (May 1786) in Vienna and, half a year later, in Prague; despite the success of *Don Giovanni* in Prague and the large sums Mozart was able to command for the few works he decided to publish (*e.g.*, the six quartets dedicated to Haydn, sold to Artaria in 1785 for 100 ducats or 450 fl.);[11] despite all this evidence of growing affluence, Mozart's popularity in Vienna, and with it his financial security, had begun to wane by 1788. *Don Giovanni*, when revived in Vienna that year at the express instigation of Joseph II, was (as Lorenzo da Ponte, its librettist, related many years later), 'not a success'.

To be sure, Mozart's fame abroad was growing steadily, especially in German-speaking countries, where his operas in the vernacular, such as *The Abduction from the Seraglio* and also *Figaro* and *Don Giovanni* (soon translated into German), proved to be extremely popular despite their technical difficulties, both vocal and instrumental. All this 'foreign' popularity, however, did not improve Mozart's finances except indirectly, in the sense that it created an ever-increasing desire on the part of the public to hear his music. A composer could command a fee for playing or conducting his music; but as there were no 'performance rights' as such those performances of Mozart's operas in Germany brought fame but not florins. Similarly, there was no copyright law, and German publishers were free to print or reprint Mozart's music at will. The time when a composer could earn at least a modest living by his own efforts, without the support of aristocratic patrons, was drawing near, but it had not yet come, and the consequences for Mozart were to become increasingly evident.

By the middle of 1789 he was painting his situation at its blackest to his Brother Mason Michael Puchberg, treasurer of the Lodge *Zur wahren Eintracht*:

> God! I am in a situation in which I wouldn't wish my worst enemy, and if you, my dear friend and Brother abandon me, *unhappy and innocent* though I am, I and my poor sick wife and child are lost . . . My fate is alas, *but only in Vienna*, so against me that I can't earn money even if I wish to; for the last fourteen days I have circulated a list [for a new subscription series] and there is only one name on it, Swieten . . .[12]

Even allowing for a certain amount of exaggeration, it seems clear that Mozart's finances were in dire straits, partly because Constanze was constantly pregnant and often in need of expensive cures at Baden (a spa near Vienna), and partly because Mozart's subscription concerts had come to halt. These were series of private concerts, organized by Mozart himself, for which subscribers paid a certain sum in advance. Puchberg, who knew the Mozarts well, must have agreed with the composer's need for money because he continued to send some whenever he was asked.

This, then, was the state of affairs when Mozart set off for Germany to introduce himself to the new Emperor. In the same letter of 28 September 1790 in which Wolfgang apprised Constanze of his safe arrival in Frankfurt, we have the first reference to a complicated financial transaction which the composer hoped would help him to deal with his debts:

> I await news from you with longing – of your health, of our circumstances, etc. – Now I firmly intend to conduct my affairs here as well as possible, and then I heartily look forward to returning to you – what a marvellous life we shall live! – I will work – and work hard – only so that through unexpected circumstances I won't again be forced into such a fatal position. – I would be pleased if you could have Lackenbacher [name later rendered almost illegible] come to you via Stadler and deal with all that. – His [Stadler's] last idea was to have someone advance the money using only Hofmeister [*sic*] as security – 1000 fl. in cash, the rest in credit – [two words cancelled] in that way, everything could be paid for with money to spare, and upon my return I would only have to work. Using a blank power-of-attorney [*carte bianca*] in my name, a friend could put the whole thing into operation. – Adieu – I kiss you 1000 times.
>
> Always your Mzt

Constanze seems to have taken matters in hand and to have organized the loan of 1000 fl. in Mozart's absence. She was by no means ungifted in money matters, as she was to demonstrate after his death. The arrangement she made with Heinrich Lackenbacher, a Viennese merchant, was to advance Mozart 1000 fl. in cash against all his furniture. According to the original idea, Mozart was to supply his friend and Brother Mason Franz Anton Hoffmeister (the correct spelling) with a series of compositions, the proceeds from which would be used to pay off the debt. Hoffmeister, apart from being a composer himself, also directed a very successful publishing firm to which, just at the end of 1790, Haydn was in the process of selling his latest string quartets, known as op. 64.[13] But in the end, Hoffmeister's name does not appear in the document, dated 1 October 1790, which Mozart signed when he returned from Germany. The composer was to pay 5 per cent interest for the loan, and the principal became due for total repayment in two years, *i.e.*, 1 October 1792. Inasmuch as Lackenbacher's name does not appear in the list of Mozart's creditors drawn up after his death, it would seem that this debt was repaid with interest before December 1791.

The new chamber music works that Mozart composed, with the idea not only of performing them at concerts but of selling them to a publisher, were the three 'Prussian' quartets (K.575, 589 and 590)[14] and two string quintets (K.593 and 614). All five works were first published not by Hoffmeister but by Artaria & Co., the firm that had also issued the six quartets dedicated to Haydn.

Temporarily relieved of money worries, Mozart could rejoice in the unexpected appearance in Vienna of his best musical friend, Joseph Haydn. The doyen of Austrian composers had suddenly, through the death of Prince Nicolaus Esterházy on 28 September 1790, become a free man. The new Prince Esterházy did not require the active service of his *Kapellmeister*, though he retained the title and also a yearly pension of 1000 Gulden from the late Prince Nicolaus. Haydn quickly set off for Vienna, where King Ferdinand (to whom Mozart had not been presented) tried to induce him to come to the Neapolitan court.

At that time, however, the elderly composer's life was

suddenly and dramatically changed by the arrival in Vienna of a persuasive German violinist and impresario named Johann Peter Salomon, who was living in London. Born in Bonn and a friend of the young Beethoven, Salomon had moved to England some seven years earlier and had established himself there as a composer, violinist and, particularly, as an entrepreneur of extraordinary gifts. He was in Cologne to engage singers for his next season when he read in the newspapers of Prince Esterházy's death. He made straightway for Vienna and arrived on Haydn's doorstep one evening with the announcement, 'I am Salomon of London and have come to fetch you. Tomorrow we shall come to an agreement.' Haydn was at first reluctant to make the long trip, but Salomon (with whom he had had dealings for some time) made financial proposals, including a large advance, which he found difficult to turn down. He secured the new Prince Esterházy's permission and began to collect his luggage for the journey.

Salomon had actually set off for Vienna with two purposes in mind. One was to engage Haydn: in that he was brilliantly successful. The other was to engage Mozart. This is made clear in an obituary of Salomon printed in a British newspaper:

> in 1790 . . . he determined to engage Haydn and Mozart, not only to write exclusively for him, but to conduct their compositions in person. For this purpose he went to Vienna, where after several interviews with both these great musicians, it was mutually agreed that Haydn should go to London the first season, and Mozart the next. They all dined together on the day fixed for the departure of the travellers; Mozart attended them to the door of their carriage, wishing them every success, and repeating, as they drove off, his promise to complete his part of the agreement the following year.

Haydn was to leave with Salomon on 15 December 1790 for England and for the greatest adventure of the composer's quiet and retiring life. His biographer G. A. Griesinger had the following information from Haydn's own lips:

> Mozart said, at a merry meal with Salomon, to Haydn: 'You won't stand it for long and will soon return, for you aren't young any more.' 'But I am still vigorous and in good health,' answered Haydn.

Another biographer, A. C. Dies, to whom Haydn granted a whole series of interviews, tells us:

> Especially Mozart took pains to say, 'Papa!' (as he usually called him), 'You have had no education for the great world, and you speak too few languages.' – 'Oh!' replied Haydn, 'my language is understood all over the world.' [The travellers fixed the date of their departure] and left on 15 December 1790 . . . Mozart, that day, never left his friend Haydn. He dined with him, and at the moment of parting, he said, 'We are probably saying our last adieu in this life.' Tears welled in both their eyes. Haydn was deeply moved, for he applied Mozart's words to himself, and the possibility never occurred to him that the thread of Mozart's life could be cut by the inexorable Parcae [Fates] the very next year.[15]

One of Haydn's favourite pupils, Sigismund von Neukomm, related in a letter:

> For some time Mozart had a kind of premonition of his death. I remember my master Haydn told me: towards the end of 1790, when he undertook his first trip to London, Mozart said farewell and, with tears in his eyes, said, 'I fear, my Papa, this is the last time that we shall see each other.' Haydn, who was much older than Mozart, took this to mean that his [Haydn's] age, and the dangers which he faced with his last journey, gave rise to this fear.[16]

Haydn was then fifty-eight, Mozart not yet thirty-five. Who would have suspected that the elder composer was to outlive the younger by more than eighteen years? Mozart came from sturdy stock. His father died at sixty-seven, a ripe old age in the eighteenth century; his sister survived into her seventy-ninth year. There was no reason to think that Wolfgang's life was hanging by so frail a thread and that he would be gone within twelve months. No evidence from this period, as the new year of 1791 began, points to any alarming symptoms or signs of fatigue. Mozart was seemingly his usual effervescent and energetic self.

And so, as Haydn's coach rolled off towards England, Mozart stayed behind, ready to cope with his debts, the bewildering incomprehension of the Viennese nobility who had once been his principal support, and the frigidity of the Austrian court that provided the only regular financial basis for his precarious existence.

II
Mozart's Vienna

The city to which Mozart returned, and which he obviously loved, had a population in the last decade of the eighteenth century of about 210,000. Today people think of Vienna in terms of the Ringstrasse, the magnificent boulevard lined with imposing edifices in a variety of styles, which encircles the old city. Until the middle of the nineteenth century, however, this area was occupied by impressive walls and fortifications, sloping down from which was the *Glacis*, a large, grassy expanse on which it was forbidden to build. Beyond lay Vienna's prosperous suburbs, the Danube and several beautiful parks and gardens, including the famous Prater. Within the city walls were some 5,500 dwellings, mostly tall and nestled together in the habit of the Middle Ages. Although erected many years previously, the houses had been partially rebuilt in the Baroque manner. In the case of palaces, the interiors included at least one grand salon with marble decorations, tall windows and gleaming parquet floors.

Vienna was an elegant city and generously proportioned. The ancient Romanesque and Gothic Cathedral of St Stephen's dominated the skyline, but there were many other noble churches, some of great antiquity, such as St Michael's, near which Haydn had lived as a young man. St Michael's faced the Burgtheater, where, in 1782, Mozart had conducted his first operatic triumph in the city – *The Abduction from the Seraglio*. The Burgtheater was adjacent to the Hofburg, where the Emperor Joseph II resided. In the streets, to judge by contemporary accounts, wind and dust were a perpetual tribulation and pedestrian traffic was hampered by the enormous number of carriages and wagons of all kinds – some 4,000 of them.

The upper classes of Vienna at the end of the eighteenth century were fascinated by the English way of dressing: it was less constricting (literally) for the ladies and less formal than the French manner, which had been the rage in Mozart's youth. The army officers' uniforms in the Imperial Royal regiments ranged from the elegant white jackets with red facings to the fantastic uniforms of the Hungarians (widely imitated abroad).

Although it may not have seemed so to Mozart at the time, the Vienna of 1791 appeared to a later generation to have been a musical paradise.[1] The reason for this was that in the years of Schubert's and Beethoven's maturity, around 1820, the situation for composers became much worse. Anton Schindler, Beethoven's biographer, summed it up admirably:

> A cultured and enlightened upper class that also possessed tremendous wealth will certainly be in a position to serve both science and the arts. This state of affairs prevailed among the Viennese nobility who had a special penchant for music. There was a preference for music without ostentation – music which, whether performed by four voices or a hundred, would work magic on the listener, cultivating his mind and his senses, ennobling his emotions. It was characteristic of the whole German people to respond to the unpretentious greatness, true feeling, and pure human emotions that were inherent in its music. This people also knew how to derive from the mystery of musical tones their inexpressible meaning and lofty spirit. And yet this was not a time of philosophical sophistication; it was rather a period of uninhibited enjoyment whose purity lasted well into the first decade of our century.

Such nostalgia as Schindler's may be exaggerated, but as far as the nobility in Vienna is concerned, and also the upper bourgeoisie, we have confirmation of their abilities by an unprejudiced foreigner, the Swedish diplomat Fredrik Samuel Silverstolpe. Silverstolpe arrived in Vienna in May 1796 as chargé d'affaires to the Imperial Court; he made an early study of musical life in the city and became a personal friend of Haydn's. On 20 September 1797 he wrote back to his family in Stockholm:

> Everywhere I have been in Germany the middle class [*Mittelstand*] among the population is very cultured. I think that among the so-called better classes one seldom meets complete idiots as with us [in Sweden]. The officers of this day and age are supposed, however, to be the exceptions to this rule . . . The women are much better read than ours, [but] . . . in Vienna it is rare to encounter domestic virtues among that sex . . .[2]

In the next twenty years, most of the private orchestras maintained by the Austro-Hungarian nobility had to be disbanded as a result of rising costs caused by inflation, but in 1791 several of the wealthiest Viennese houses still boasted a full orchestra. Apart from Prince Esterházy, the Princes Lobkowitz, Schwarzenberg and Auersperg – all of them patrons of both Haydn and Beethoven – kept an orchestra and gave regular concerts in their Viennese palaces. Prince Grassalkovics, who had wanted to engage Haydn as *Kapellmeister* in 1790 after Prince Nicolaus I Esterházy died, supported what was called a *Harmonie-Musique*, a wind band, which consisted of two oboes, two clarinets, two bassoons, and two horns. This popular combination was sufficiently small to enable the patron to take it with him to the country in summer, where he and his guests could hear arrangements from the latest operas. Count Zinzendorf had twice heard a wind band arrangement of Mozart's *The Marriage of Figaro* while visiting various Bohemian castles in September 1787. Prince Nicolaus II Esterházy also liked a wind octet, and much of the music played in the 1790s and early 1800s is still preserved in the Eisenstadt archives, including arrangements of numbers from Mozart's operas. If the family could not afford a whole orchestra or even a regular *Harmonie-Musique*, they could perhaps support a string quartet, as did Prince Carl Lichnowsky, Beethoven's patron; and almost anyone could work up a piano trio at short notice. The famous *Briefe eines Eipeldauers*, written in the local Viennese dialect by Joseph Richter, includes the following characteristic statement for the year 1794: 'There's not a noble maid, not even a burger's daughter, who can't play the piano and sing as well.'

There was still a vast social gap between the upper and lower classes. A visiting Englishman might observe that 'The Emperor appeared abroad without any ostentation; riding in His carriage or on Horseback, with a servant or two, like a private gentleman, and no guards or parade of any kind', but in the next sentence he noted: 'The Nobility are not, as in England, "Peers" (pares or equals), but are divided into classes: the higher orders such as Prince Esterházy, – the Prince de Li[e]chtenstein, &c. only receiving other Classes as Inferiors.'[3] A similar observation was made by the German *Kapellmeister* and composer J. F. Reichardt in 1808:

> The higher nobility here [in Vienna] entertains rather a high opinion, a very high opinion actually, of its own nobility, and even for foreign nobility of very good houses it is not at all easy to penetrate the inner circle and intimate family parties.[4]

The same opinion is expressed by the Duchess Hedvig Elisabeth Charlotte of Södermanland, who with her husband visited Vienna in 1798 and 1799 and wrote in her diary:

> Altogether here [in Vienna] there reigns an unbelievable

> haughtiness in the highest circles. They think of nothing else but their ancestors and are so precise about it that untold difficulties can occur when someone is presented at Court.

The musical strength of Vienna lay not only among the nobility and whatever public concerts there were but also, of course, among its private citizens. In this connection may be cited the Vienna correspondent (anonymous, as always) of the *Allgemeine Musikalische Zeitung (AMZ)*, who, in an article published in October 1800, discussed this aspect of musical life in the city:

> There are few cities where love of music is so widespread as it is here. Everyone plays, everyone learns music. . . . So-called private 'academies', that is, music in the fine houses, are given here in numberless quantity throughout the winter. There's no nameday, no birthday, on which music is lacking. There is not much to be said about such occasions, and nothing at all if it is not to sound ridiculous. Most of them resemble each other rather closely. This is the way they look: first a quartet or a symphony, which is seen as a necessary evil (you've got to start with *something*), and during which one chats. Then comes one Fräulein after another and rolls off her piano sonata – probably not without charm and grace – as best she can. Then others appear and sing some arias from the newest operas, in the same kind of performance. People are pleased, well, why not? And who has the right to mix in it, so long as the thing remains in the family? . . . Every proper girl, whether she has talent or not, has to learn the piano or singing; first, it's the mode; secondly (and here business enters into it) it's the easiest way to produce oneself in society and thus, if one is lucky, to attract attention and perhaps make a good match. The sons also have to learn music; first, because again it's the mode; secondly, because it helps them in fine society, too, and experience shows not a few (here,

at least) have by their music caught a rich wife or a very satisfactory position.

The article concluded that the economic situation of a musician in Vienna was not at all rosy. Musicians had a bad name which they earned for themselves with their crude manners, lack of education, and so on; thus they were often treated as inferiors in the great houses. Of course there were exceptions among the musicians, and, the writer added, among the great houses too. Times had changed, naturally, since Mozart's youth, when musicians had often been treated like servants, but it was still possible to find, in the *Wiener Zeitung* for 23 June 1798, the following notice:

> *Musical* valet-de-chambre *wanted*
>
> A musician is wanted, who plays the piano well and can sing too, and is able to give lessons in both. This musician must also perform the duties of a *valet-de-chambre*. Whoever decides to accept the post is to ask in the first floor of the small Colloredo house No. 982 in the Weihburggasse.

So long as advertisements such as this could be printed, and the position filled, as it presumably was, it was difficult for a professional musician to escape being treated as a servant. The continual mixing of professional and amateur status, as happened at the Augarten (a pleasure garden on the far side of the suburb of Leopoldstadt, where concerts were held in the summer), and also in many private salons, greatly helped to make the social status of the professional musician less lowly.

If the *AMZ* writer was less than wildly enthusiastic about the state of amateur music-making in Vienna, our Swedish diplomat Silverstolpe had some devastating comments to make concerning the first musical impressions he received in the city. On 4 June 1796 he wrote:

> I have seen several *spectacles* [operas, plays] here, but

> without pleasure, for here they act very indifferently, horribly recited for a Swedish ear, tasteless and often miserably sung, and moreover the orchestra does not fulfil its duties well.

Silverstolpe soon noticed the vast gap between the fashionable society and the dialect-speaking plebeian world that flocked to Emanuel Schikaneder's Theater auf der Wieden. On 24 August 1796 he reported:

> . . . now I have seen *The Magic Flute* on the stage and also the subjects for whom Mozart wrote this piece. The music is excellent. However, the whole opera is put together in such a way that it would certainly have no success in a Swedish theatre. I do not wish that any effort along these lines be expended. We're not German enough (*i.e.*, for the theatre) . . .

The *AMZ* correspondent also had some hard things to say about operatic life in the city. Although his article was published in 1800, much of what he wrote will obviously have applied to 1791 as well. After discussing the Italian soloists, he comments:

> The orchestra is not lacking in good people, but it very much lacks good will, unity, and love for the Art. . . . The director, Herr Conti, is not up to his job; it often happens that half the orchestra are substitutes, sent by the gentlemen when they have other engagements or pleasures: the effect can be imagined. The choice of operas is certainly not good: the old ones which are known to be good are seldom played, while the new ones, which as is well known could not be called good *en bloc* by any connoisseur, are often given. They procure them from Italy, on the recommendation of this or that member of the company, often because of a pretty role or even because of one brilliant aria. There are many operas given of which they are convinced during the first rehearsal that they can't succeed.

On the one hand we have the enthusiastic description from Schindler of musical life in *fin-de-siècle* Vienna; on the other, the negative comments of Silverstolpe and the *AMZ*. Probably the truth lay somewhere in between.

* * *

The Viennese lived in houses where the infant mortality rate was appallingly high: of Mozart's six children, only two survived. Children were brought up in rooms overlooking stinking courtyards, and altogether hygiene was not a strong point with the middle and lower orders. The ground floors of most houses were used for shops and businesses; this was the case with the Mozarts' house in the Rauhensteingasse, where we possess (by some miracle) not only a handsome view of the now demolished house but also the groundplan of their apartment. More than that, we can reconstruct precisely how the rooms were furnished and what Mozart wore. In fact, we know much more about Mozart's daily life than we do about the largely secret processes of thought that gave us *The Magic Flute* and the Requiem.

From all the evidence, it is clear that Mozart's financial situation was rapidly recovering throughout the second half of 1791. The reason that there were only 60 Gulden in cash in the Mozarts' house on 5 December 1791 right after his death was certainly that they had used the fee for *La clemenza di Tito* to pay off some of their pressing debts, and no doubt the advance payment on the Requiem had been put to similar use.

Mozart's expenses were heavier than those of many other Viennese musicians: his obligations included appearing at court functions (*i.e.*, conducting the orchestra in the many court balls when they were playing his own compositions), appearing in the elegant salons of people such as Johann Tost and Court Councillor Greiner, and mixing in court circles and receptions in Prague as *Hofcompositeur* (court composer). In many of these his wife took part, and in

Baden she was also expected to be nicely turned out in the evenings. This means that the Mozarts had to be well dressed and Wolfgang's hair attended to regularly. For evidence of the latter, we actually have an eye-witness account from his hairdresser:[5]

> As I was doing Mozart's hair one morning, and was just occupied with completing his pigtail, M. suddenly jumped up and, despite the fact that I was holding him by his pigtail [Mozart wore his own blondish hair, not a wig] he went into the next room, dragging me along with him, and started to play the piano. Full of admiration for his playing and for the lovely tone of the instrument – it was the first time I had ever heard such a one – I let go of the pigtail and didn't dress it until M. got up again. One day when I was rounding the corner from the Kärntnerstrasse into the Himmelpfortgasse in order to serve M., he arrived on horseback, stopped, and as he rode on a few steps, he took a little board out [of his pocket] and wrote some music. I spoke to him again, and asked if I could come to him now, and he said yes.

We have no idea what Constanze Mozart wore: there is not a single eye-witness account of the period telling us what kind of dresses she owned. But we do know what Mozart wore in 1791, for the simple reason that his clothes were listed with his effects, in a document called the *Sperrs-Relation* (Suspense Order), when he died.[6] The list is impressive:

> 1 white frock coat of cloth, with Manchester [cotton] waistcoat
> 1 blue ditto
> 1 red ditto
> 1 ditto of nankeen [*i.e.*, of yellow or pale buff colour]
> 1 brown [braun=brune de marine?] satin ditto together with breeches, embroidered with silk[7]
> 1 black cloth whole suit

1 mouse-colour [*i.e.* dun, greyish-brown] great-coat
1 ditto of lighter material
1 blue cloth frock coat with fur
1 ditto *Kiria* with fur trimming
4 various waistcoats, 9 various breeches, 2 plain hats, 3 pairs of boots, 3 pairs of shoes
9 silk stockings
9 shirts
4 white neckerchiefs, 1 nightcap, 18 handkerchiefs
8 underdrawers, 2 nightgowns, 5 pairs of stockings

Such a wardrobe was equivalent to that of a well-to-do merchant. Even from this dry list, it can be seen at once that these are expensive, not to say luxurious clothes. They suggest that Mozart attached considerable importance to his outward appearance. Presumably Constanze's dresses were no less elegant.

The house ('Small Kaiser-Haus') in Rauhensteingasse,[8] to which Constanze Mozart had moved while her husband was away in Frankfurt, contained four rooms, plus kitchen and vestibule all on the first (US second) floor: this was the part of the house the Mozarts rented. It was by no means a step towards poverty. Although it was certainly less grand, it was not much smaller than the previous apartment in the Camesina House in the Domgasse; this latter apartment – which also had four principal rooms – was the one where *Figaro* was composed, where Leopold Mozart lived in 1785 and where Haydn heard the quartets dedicated to him. The rent of the apartment had been excessively high: 450 Gulden p.a. but in the Rauhensteingasse, there was space (although in a room with not much else) for Wolfgang's billiard table (both he and Constanze were very fond of the game). The total floor space was about 145 square metres (173 square yards), and in December 1791 it included a substantial amount of linen (5 table cloths, 16 napkins, 16 towels, 10 sheets), with the furniture and furnishing arranged as indicated on p. 222.[9]

The official value placed on such property can be misleading, since in the interests of the heirs, who were required to pay probate duty, it was traditionally estimated as low as possible. The total assets were accounted as follows:[10]

	fl.	kr.
Ready cash	60	
Collectable debts [salary from court due]	133	20
[Debts listed elsewhere as uncollectable – 800 fl.: Anton Stadler 500 fl., Franz Gilowsky 300 fl. of 1786]		
Silver [rest pawned for Frankfurt journey and not redeemed]	7	
Clothes and linen	55	
Table linen and bedclothes	17	
Furnishing	296	8
Books and music	23	41
Total	592	9

Mozart owned in 1791 a small number of books, including German literature, poetry, history, travel books, philosophy, plays and (of course) libretti. Some of these were in English and Italian, but none in French (except libretti). One has the impression that he must have rid himself of many books[11] and even more music – the officials were not counting Mozart's autographs – before December 1791.

Among the outstanding debts (totalling 918 fl. 16 kr.) there were three substantial bills: a tailor's bill (for 282 fl. 7 kr.), an upholsterer's (for 280 fl. 3 kr.) and the Imperial Royal Court Apothecary's (for 139 fl. 30 kr.) There was another, smaller apothecary's bill for 40 fl. 53 kr., and there were more from another tailor, a cobbler, and so on. The Mozarts had evidently either redecorated the apartment or re-upholstered some of the furniture: both the tailors' bills and the upholsterer's show that the couple felt it important to keep up a good appearance. There is every reason to believe that they were handsomely dressed; and that they lived in a very comfortable, attractively furnished apartment with (usually) two maidservants (Wolfgang let one go when his wife was in Baden and used a man, Joseph 'Primus',[12] to bring in meals from outside). There is not the faintest indication that Mozart gambled (except in the usual small way with billiards or private card-games), and certainly not in the famous gambling dens which actually existed in Vienna but which he could never have afforded even for ten minutes.[13] There is, in fact, no sign that either of the Mozarts was in any way extravagant. They were certainly care-free and generous with their hospitality and, indeed, with their money: they could ill afford to lend Anton Stadler 500 Gulden in 1791, for example. But such magnanimity is a far cry from the recklessness and irresponsibility with which they have often been charged. They appear not to have been particularly interested in money as such; yet they were hardly scatter-brained in the spending of it.

III
Concert Life in the Austrian Capital

The first work for 1791 that Mozart entered into his thematic catalogue was the Piano Concerto in B flat (K.595), under the date 5 January. The autograph manuscript of this work has fortunately survived and its watermarks suggest an interesting chronology: the concerto was first drafted not in 1790 but in 1788, the year in which Mozart composed his last three symphonies, K.543 in E flat, 550 in G minor and 551 in C ('Jupiter').[1]

By 1791 Mozart was no longer giving subscription concerts; but contrary to what is generally believed, there is evidence that he did give a final series of subscription concerts in 1788. Since the matter is of considerable importance, and has a direct bearing on this final piano concerto, I propose to examine the evidence once again.[2]

The crucial works in question for the 1788 season are not only the three symphonies, but also the 'Coronation' Concerto K.537 (it derives its title from the first edition published posthumously by André), which, like the Concerto in F (K.459), was listed above as having been played at Frankfurt in 1790. Let us start with the problem itself, *i.e.*, the subscription series.

Our knowledge of such concerts – insofar as we have any information at all – comes mostly from Mozart's letters to his father; they were not announced in the local papers, nor did Count Zinzendorf (a valuable source) write about them in his Diary. After Leopold Mozart's death in 1787, our principal source for details of these concerts dries up.

The evidence we have is in a letter from Mozart to Puchberg, which is, alas, undated and has been, possibly without sufficient reason, dated June 1788.[3] In this letter Mozart asks for 100 fl., 'but only until next week (when my academies in the Casino begin) . . . ; by then, my subscription money must necessarily have come in, and I can then quite easily repay you 136 fl. with warmest thanks.' (Mozart notes earlier in the letter, 'I still owe you 8 ducats' *i.e.*, 36 fl.) In a following paragraph, we read something which most Mozart scholars have overlooked or deliberately ignored: 'I take the liberty of offering you 2 tickets which I ask you, as a Brother, to accept without any payment, since in any case I shall never be able adequately to recompense the friendship you have shown to me.'

The chronology of the Casino series hinges, of course, on the date of the letter. Let us suppose it was written not in June but much earlier (perhaps in March). Then it might refer to a Lenten subscription series and could have included the new 'Coronation' Concerto in D, which is entered in Mozart's catalogue on 24 February 1788. But there is something very odd about the scoring of the new concerto, in that all the wind instruments and kettledrums are marked *ad libitum*. This precautionary measure seems to suggest not a grand subscription orchestra but rather a small chamber-music band without wind instruments, by which, perhaps, the work was really played. In any case it is exceedingly unlikely that its first performance occurred, as has been hitherto assumed, at the Dresden Court on 14 April 1789, before Elector Friedrich August III of Saxony and his consort, Amalie von Pfalz-Zweibrücken.

And what if the letter was written in June 1788? That would refer to a subscription series occurring in, perhaps, summer. However, the chronology of the last three symphonies is: the E flat, 26 June; the G minor, 25 July; the 'Jupiter', 10 August. The letter suggests that the subscription series is imminent, hence June is probably too early a date; perhaps the beginning of August would be more plausible. And a summer subscription series is unlikely, since most of the aristocracy would have been away in their country homes. On the other hand, an autumn subscription series would have been entirely possible.

Again, the actual presence of the autograph of the G minor Symphony (K.550) helps us to establish an interesting chronological fact. It used to be proposed that the added clarinet parts (and some changes in the slow movement to simplify the woodwind writing) were specially made for a public Lenten concert in 1791; but the watermarks of the additional sections in the autograph are, with one exception (sheet 7 of the clarinet-oboe parts – Mozart had to rewrite the oboe parts when he added the clarinets), the same as those in the main body of the work. All this suggests that Mozart made the revisions almost immediately after completing the autograph proper; and that he made them for a concert in 1788; they were surely not made for the desk drawer. The fact cannot be overstated: Mozart was a supreme pragmatist and finished his works exclusively with a specific performance in view.

As for the public concert in 1791, we must examine it next; for in it one of Mozart's last three symphonies was assuredly performed. We have seen that his subscription concerts came to an end probably in 1788, but there was another yearly concert series in which he frequently participated: the two pairs of annual concerts given by the *Tonkünstler-Societät* (the Society of Musicians, formed in 1772 to aid their widows and orphans – Mozart should have been a member but could not find his birth certificate which it was necessary to present).[4] He had contributed *Davidde penitente* (K.469)[5] in 1785 and had played the piano and offered other music, vocal and instrumental, in the course of the last decade. Now, in 1791, Court *Kapellmeister* Antonio Salieri conducted the annual Lenten concerts, which took place on 16 and 17 April and began with 'Eine neue grose [*sic*] Simphonie von Herrn Mozart'. Which symphony did Mozart offer? Myths die hard, and writers have always preferred to imagine that Mozart never heard his last three symphonies of 1788. Even if we assume that the 1788 subscription concerts never took place (which as we have seen is unlikely), it is obvious that Mozart will have taken his last four unpublished symphonies, *i.e.*, including the 'Prague' (K.504), with him on his German tours of 1789 and 1790. There is even a distinct tradition of manuscript parts of the last four symphonies which derive, obviously, from the first manuscript performance material rather than directly from the autographs themselves.

Each of the last three symphonies is scored for a different wind band: K.543 has 1 flute, 2 clarinets, 2 bassoons, 2 horns, 2 trumpets and kettledrums; K.550's first version has 1 flute, 2 oboes, 2 bassoons and 2 horns (originally there were to be four horns); the second version has 1 flute, 2 revised oboe parts, 2 clarinets, 2 bassoons and 2 horns; K.551 has 1 flute, 2 oboes, 2 bassoons, 2 horns, 2 trumpets and kettledrums. As it happens, the manuscript list of the Society's performers for 16 and 17 April has survived, and includes flutes, oboes and 'Clarinetti:/ Stadler/Stadler jun.', *i.e.*, Anton and his younger brother Johann. The only work with flute, oboes and clarinets among the last three symphonies is the revised version of K.550.[6]

In a sense it hardly matters: a vast and elegant Viennese audience heard one of the last three symphonies by its Imperial Royal Chamber Composer directed – irony of ironies – by Antonio Salieri, who, whatever else he may or may not have been, was hardly to be considered Mozart's friend. It was probably the last time that Mozart heard a huge orchestra: the Society's concerts usually boasted a band of well over 100 players. The musicians were expected to donate their services to the Society, so that all Mozart would have reaped was more celebrity.

If the symphonies were dependent upon public concerts for their survival, this was even more crucial for the piano concertos, which, of course, Mozart himself not only composed but also performed. Perhaps the 1788 subscription series turned out to be smaller in scope (three concerts rather than six?); that might explain why in that year Mozart started to write the B flat Piano Concerto (K.595) in *particella* form (*i.e.*, an incompletely realized score)[7] and then shelved it for three years. But the 'official' arrival, as it were, of K.595 in Mozart's catalogue on 5 January 1791 raises another thorny question. Scholars have realized for some time that these dates do not always indicate the completion of the work in question. Sometimes Mozart simply used a date which he had entered for another work: in the case of K.595, the entry might have indicated the day on which he began work again on the *particella* sketch. But on the whole, Mozart probably entered a new work in his catalogue when he actually completed it. It seems, moreover, unlikely that he put unfinished works into this catalogue. When a work was completed, Mozart entered it; hence K.595 would not have been entered in 1788 but in 1791, when it was (presumably) completed. As a concrete illustration, we may take the case of the final work of the six string quartets Mozart composed for and dedicated to Haydn, the 'Dissonance' Quartet (K.465). Leopold Mozart, in a letter dated Salzburg, 22 January 1785, writes to his daughter in St Gilgen, 'this very moment I've received ten lines from your brother, who writes . . . that last Saturday [15 January] he arranged for a performance of his six quartets, which he has sold to Artaria for 100 ducats, for his dear friend Haydn and other good friends . . .' The final quartet (K.465) was entered into the catalogue on 14 January, a day before the first performance (the parts had, of course, to be copied and the complicated new work rehearsed at least once before the actual première).[8] Thus, by analogy, it may be supposed that 5 January 1791 indicated the actual date when the new piano concerto was completed.

But if, as seems likely, the new concerto was ready early in January 1791, why was Mozart so anxious to complete it if there were no actual performances in sight? In fact, to the best of our knowledge the work was first given not in one of Mozart's own concerts – he had no such series any longer – but as part of a benefit concert on 4 March for a clarinettist named Joseph Bähr or Beer at the so-called 'Jahnscher Saal' (Jahn Rooms) in the Himmelpfortgasse, a few yards away from Mozart's quarters in the Rauhensteingasse.[9] This concert was the last one at which Mozart appeared in public in Vienna;[10] hence K.595 marks the end of the long, brilliant series of piano concertos with which he had begun his career in Vienna so auspiciously ten years earlier.

One curious footnote to this affair is that Mozart sold the new work to Artaria, who announced it on 10 August in the *Wiener Zeitung*;[11] curious because most of the earlier concertos of 1785–88 were unpublished during Mozart's lifetime – the great C major K.503, for example, was published posthumously by Constanze, in 1798, as 'Nr. 1 del retaggio del defunto publicato alle spese della vedova' ('No. 1 from the effects of the late composer published at the widow's expense').

Being much more of a pragmatist than is generally realized, Mozart was quick to shift his emphasis as circumstances required. If public concerts were now scarce, why not concentrate on music for private concerts? Towards the middle of 1791 that is what he proceeded to do.[12] In that year, there were two families for whom we know Mozart composed. The first is associated with the composer's final String Quintet in E flat (K.614), which was entered in his thematic catalogue on 12 April 1791. When it was posthumously published in 1793 by Artaria, it was entitled 'Composto per un Amatore Ongarese'. It has always been thought that the 'amateur Hungarian' was the businessman Johann Tost, the ex-leader of the second violins in Haydn's orchestra at Eszterháza, who had married a rich wife and commissioned chamber music from leading composers. A letter from Constanze to J. A. André of 26 November 1800 supports this view. She writes:

> There is a Herr v[on] Tost here – he lives in the Singerstrasse – who says he has autograph scores by Mozart. It is true that M. worked for him. He has promised me the themes . . .[13]

Considering that the quintet was finished on 12 April, I would suggest that there was a musical soirée at the Tosts' about 14 April, at which this work, the last in another noble series, received its first performance. Naturally Tost paid Mozart a fee for having composed the quintet and also, one presumes, for organizing a performance in which Tost himself participated.

We may note, then, a distinct shift from public concerts – the *Tonkünstler-Societät* was one of the last of its kind to survive at the end of the eighteenth century in Vienna – to private soirées. The aristocracy, of course, continued to give elaborate musical evenings all during this period, but Mozart's letters show that he definitely was not frequenting any aristocratic salons at that time; he never mentions one to Constanze. In Mozart's life, at any rate, bourgeois society and the Schikaneder theatre were slowly beginning to replace court opera and aristocratic salon. The Schikaneder theatre was in Mozart's mind not only because of *The Magic Flute*; there were also two other works connected with it, and both seem to have been commissions. The first is the amusing concert aria (entered in Mozart's catalogue on 8 March), *Per questa bella mano* (K.612), composed for Franz Gerl (the first Sarastro in *The Magic Flute*), with a virtuoso solo part for the double bass (intended for Friedrich Pischlberger, a member of Schikaneder's orchestra in the Freyhaustheater). The second is the piano variations on a song entitled *Ein Weib ist das herrlichste Ding* (K.613),[14] taken from an opera currently enjoying a great success in Schikaneder's theatre. Mozart was evidently growing steadily closer to the personnel of

Schikaneder's successful little theatre (in the suburb of Wieden, now the Fourth District of Vienna), for which he was soon to begin to compose *The Magic Flute*.

Mozart's correspondence has only partially survived, and the first letters known to us from the year 1791 are to his friend and fellow Mason Michael Puchberg. As might be expected they concern a loan, but also – more importantly for us – news of a quartet party at Hofrat Greiner's:

Most worthy friend and Brother!
on the 20 inst., that is in 7 days, I shall receive my quarterly salary[15] – can and will you lend me till then some twenty odd Gulden, if so I would be most obliged, best friend, and as soon as I receive my money you shall have it back again with many thanks; – till then I remain – always

Your
most obliged friend
Mozart

13th April 1791[16]
[Michael Puchberg's hand: 'sent 30 fl. 13th April']

Pour/Monsieur de Puchberg/Chez Lui
I hope Orsler[17] will have returned the keys; so it wasn't my fault. I also hope that in my name he will have asked you meanwhile for *a violin* and 2 *violas* – they are for an à quatro at Greiner's; you already know that it is *important* to me – if in the evening you want to come along to the music, you are most cordially invited by him and me.–

Mozart

P.S. Please forgive me that contrary to my word I didn't return the certain thing [the 30 fl.], but *Stadler* who instead of myself (because I have so much to do) was supposed to go to the pay-office, forgot to go for the

whole of 20th April – hence I have to wait for 8 days [to collect my quarterly salary].[18]
[After 20 April 1791]

Franz Sales, Hofrat von Greiner (1730–98),[19] had been a protégé of Empress Maria Theresa. He served as Court War Secretary in the Bohemian-Austrian Court Chancellery, was ennobled in 1771 and given the title of *wirklicher* [actual] *Hofrat* in 1773. He was of assistance to the government in the importation of foodstuffs to Vienna, and as a trained lawyer he was put to work on problems of inflation, initiating a tax on alcohol and the abolition of statute-labour in Bohemia. He was a member of the Imperial Royal Study Society (*Studiengesellschaft*), which organized *inter alia* the school system, and has been described as a typical enlightened civil servant. A contemporary called him 'a smooth, right-thinking, understanding, active man, worthy of respect; protector of the sciences and the Enlightenment, enemy of hypocrisy and bigotry, and the warm friend of all those who display talents and ability . . .'[20] Greiner's daughter, Caroline Pichler, a poet and diarist of local distinction, related in her memoirs that 'everything in the way of new poetical works that appeared here or abroad was at once known to us, read and discussed.'
Another contemporary, Joseph von Hormayr, wrote that

> His house in the Mehlgrube on the Neuer Markt was a temple of music, a collecting place of *le bon ton* and everything that was excellent from local and foreign artists, whether of equal or higher birth. No excellent foreigner was refused the house's noble hospitality, its encouraging and educated circle of friends.[21]

Caroline Pichler recalled that Mozart, after improvising on *Non più andrai* (*Figaro*, Act I), jumped up from the piano, sprang over chairs and tables and miaowed like a cat. 'Haydn and Mozart', Frau Pichler noted primly,

> whom I knew well, were persons who displayed in their

> contact with others absolutely no other extraordinary intellectual capacity and almost no kind of intellectual training, of scientific or higher education. Everyday character [*Sinnesart*], silly jokes, and in the case of the former [Mozart] an irresponsible way of life, were all that they displayed to their fellow men, yet what depths, what worlds of fantasy, harmony, melody and feeling lay hidden in that unlikely outer shell. Through what inner revelation came their understanding of how to bring forth such gigantic effects, and to express in notes such feelings, thoughts and passions that every listener is forced to feel with them, that his very soul is so profoundly touched?[22]

The Hofrat, though a bad amateur poet himself, had good taste, and among those who frequented his hospitable house was Lorenz Leopold Haschka (secretary to the Hofrat from 1777), who was the author of the text of Haydn's Austrian national anthem *Gott erhalte* of 1797, which alone would have made his name immortal; and 'with him', wrote Caroline, 'the Muses entered our house.' (It was rumoured by Vienna's evil tongues that Haschka enjoyed more than the literary favours of Frau von Greiner.) Poets, playwrights, scientists, scholars and doctors frequented the salon. The Hofrat was an ardent Freemason and a member of Haydn's Lodge *Zur wahren Eintracht*. Many of his brother Masons were welcome guests: Johann Baptist von Alxinger (the poet), Freiherr von Gebler (of Mozartian fame – he had written the play entitled *Thamos, King of Egypt*, for which Mozart wrote his brilliant instrumental and vocal music K.345), Freiherr von Jacquin (also Mozart's friend), Gottfried van Swieten (not a Mason), and of course Mozart himself. In the summer, the 'at home' took place in Greiner's house in the nearby countryside (Hernals).

To a considerable extent, the face of Viennese society was changing: Greiner's was a bourgeois salon, replacing

Mozart's own subscription concerts of the early 1780s as well as the grand aristocratic salons. The gradual failure of Mozart's own subscription concerts must be explained in terms more realistic (and less romantic) than the composer's increasing lack of contact, and hence lack of success, with the Viennese public. The war with the Turkish Empire was bleeding Austria: Count Zinzendorf in his Diary listed with horror the astronomical war expenses year after year. Many of the men among the great families of the nobility were in what we would call the 'reserve' and joined their regiments as soon as war broke out. The war was neither popular nor successful:[23] the siege of Belgrade in 1787 cost the Austrians dear, especially in terms of disease. Many aristocratic families left their Vienna palaces and went to their country estates. Money was short, and there is no doubt that one reason for the failure of Mozart's subscription concerts was simply the lack of aristocratic and bourgeois money. The large orchestras of the nobility began to disappear. Chamber music, on the other hand, was not only cheaper but became fashionable among bourgeois families. The grander of them, like the Greiners, paid for professional musicians to come and give quartet parties; the more modest played the music themselves and invited their friends to come and share a good meal afterwards (like Haydn's friend, Dr Peter von Genzinger, whose wife, Maria Anna, was a good amateur pianist and whose children were also musical: one was sufficiently proficient to sing Haydn's cantata *Arianna a Naxos* in 1790[24]). Naturally Mozart received a fee for organizing a quartet evening at the Greiners', though we have no idea of the amount involved.

We shall pass over the many smaller commissions for 1791: songs, pieces for mechanical clock (Mozart hated the squeaky little thing) and one small masterpiece: the Adagio and Rondeau for glass-harmonica, flute, oboe, viola and violoncello (K.617) for the blind harmonica-player Marianne Kirchgessner.[25] It was almost impossible for Mozart to do anything but write perfect music: even the other, unaccompanied Adagio (K.356 [617a]), composed for her this same year, is of an unearthly beauty. But none of it is fundamentally what he wanted to do and what he should have been doing – creating large-scale masterpieces.

IV
Dance Music for the Imperial Court

Mozart's musical career now began to take a curiously oblique turn, one that was a direct consequence of his contract with the Viennese court. Emperor Joseph II had engaged Mozart in 1787 for what one might term negative reasons. When, after Mozart's death, Constanze attempted (with success) to secure a pension from the court, the authorities sought the advice of various court officials. The position Mozart held was by then considered superfluous; and in a letter of 5 March 1792 Johann Rudolph, Count von Chotek – director of the new financial section of the ministry – wrote to the Court Exchequer-Chamber that Mozart had been engaged 'simply in view of the fact . . . that such a rare genius in the field of music should not have to seek his bread and butter in foreign countries . . .'[1]

One of the genres which the Vienna court needed regularly and in large quantities was dance music for the court balls given during Carnival-time in the large and small halls (known collectively as the *Redoutensaal* or, lumping both rooms together, *Redoutensäle*) of the Imperial palace in Vienna. Balls in 1791 started on Epiphany (6 January), for on that date Count Carl Zinzendorf notes in his Diary '. . . from there home, then to the *court ball*. The confusion bored me. The Queen of Naples greeted me graciously. The Empress gambled.'[2]

The peculiar aspect of Mozart's position within the court was that one of the few duties it involved was the composition of such dance music. In 1791 he furnished the court with a whole suite of the greatest dance music written hitherto; it was the beginning of a grand line that was to include the late dance music of Joseph Haydn (1792 and later) and, as it happened, Beethoven's first orchestral compositions for Vienna, the *Redoutensaal* Dances of 1795[3] – magnificent and until recently much neglected minuets and German dances; and that culminated in the waltzes of Lanner and the Strauss dynasty. There is no question that the Austrians were always mad about dancing – Mozart himself included.

The court balls were famous even outside Austria and were regularly reported in travel- and guidebooks. The audience came masked, there were delicious things to eat and drink, and gambling tables were available. The Austrians were tremendous flirts and the masks encouraged daring conversations and *Così fan tutte* situations. The *Redoutensäle* could accommodate up to three thousand people, but, according to an Italian guidebook of 1800, 'it is much more diverting when there are only 1500 persons present.' The Carnival season began on the first Sunday after Christmas, and in the last two weeks of the season there were two balls, on Thursdays and Sundays. During the year there were also balls on some saints' days (for example St Theresa and St Catherine) and also on the Sundays after Easter and Pentecost. The balls started at nine o'clock in the evening and continued until five o'clock the following morning. The Italian guidebook noted that despite the vast numbers of people from different classes, there were hardly any disturbances, and the guards and police officers were really superfluous. At these balls, said the guide, you could find in elegant profusion love, youth, beauty, good taste, magnificent dresses; and you could observe 'the pacific character of this well-behaved [*brava*] nation.'[4] (It was elsewhere noted, however, that 'many of the maskers take the liberty, in the press of the crowd, of touching and pinching the ladies, and that the desired delicacy is not always observed in the choice of expressions;

such behaviour is, at express Royal command, prohibited.' In the year 1800 this notice (His Majesty's Admonition) was attached to the playbills on which the balls were announced, but it is likely that similar liberties were taken nine years earlier too.)

Mozart's thematic catalogue for 1791 (see Appendix B, p. 225) lists strings of minuets and German dances. Of course such dances were *pièces d'occasion*, but clearly Mozart took them seriously, lavishing on them the same care, particularly as regards orchestration, that he took with his larger instrumental works. The brilliant instrumentation reflects the excellence of the court orchestra, for which, of course, Mozart's operas were composed, and many members of which were engaged to play at his own subscription 'academies'. Some of the players were distinguished composers in their own right and others were celebrated virtuosi in their respective fields, such as the clarinettist and basset-horn player Anton Stadler, for whom Mozart composed the Clarinet Quintet (K.581) and Concerto (K.622). One of the Hungarian Guard's trumpeters, Joseph Zahradniczek, a member of Mozart's Masonic Lodge *Zur gekrönten Hoffnung* in 1790–91 engraved music for Viennese publishers such as Christoph Torricella.[5] In the large *Redoutensaal*, the orchestra, which (as was customary for dance bands at the time) contained no violas, consisted of some forty players; that in the small hall had about twenty-seven (these figures are from the St Catherine's Day balls of 1792 but probably apply to the year before as well).[6]

It was not usual to publish such dance music in full orchestration, and Mozart sold many dances in piano reductions to the publisher Artaria that year; one year later Haydn also found it profitable to make piano reductions of his St Catherine's Day dance music, which was published by Artaria along with arrangements for two violins and bass (useful for private balls). The Viennese had another tradition for the dissemination of dance music, however, and that was through the professional copyists. Right up to the end of the eighteenth century, these copyists continued to make a living selling manuscript scores and parts of operas, symphonies, concertos, dance music, arias – anything that could easily be marketed. It was, on the whole, cheaper to buy a manuscript score of an opera than the engraved edition of the same work. Music printing, although flourishing in Holland and France by the middle of the eighteenth century, and shortly to take off in Germany and England, did not arrive in Vienna on any great scale until about 1780. In the 1760s and 1770s Austrian music was circulated throughout central Europe by means of manuscript copies prepared by various Viennese scriptoria. Dance music, although particularly ephemeral, was a lucrative field for the copyists because a set of dances could become extremely popular for a season. Some of Mozart's dances were so well-liked that they continued to be played even after his death, for instance in the small *Redoutensaal* in 1793 (along with Haydn's dances for the 1792 season).[7]

In March 1791, no fewer than three Viennese houses offered the latest dance music by Mozart for sale in manuscript copies: K.599, 600, 601, 602, 604 and 605 could be purchased at Lorenz Lausch's (a famous Viennese scriptorium), Johann Traeg's (who also published music) and at Artaria's (the leading Austrian music publisher). Some of these great minuets and German dances have survived only in these manuscript copies, which were sold at a fixed price determined by the number of bifolii[8] (six *Bogen* or *Bögen*, as they are termed in German, at 5 Kreuzer each would make 30 Kreuzer, twelve bifolii 1 Gulden [60 Kreuzer]). In the case of the operas, the manuscript rights for those performed at the Imperial and Royal theatres in Vienna reverted to the official court theatre copyists. The rather substantial fee that the composers were paid in Vienna for their operas included the rights for the theatre to market copies; one such copy of *Così fan tutte*, produced in 1790, recently turned up at a Viennese antiquarian bookshop and is now in English private possession. We do not know the relationship between the court's dance music and the Viennese copyists; but it appears that the composers could make their own financial arrangements, and that the sale of the rights to Lausch, Traeg and Artaria gave Mozart an additional source of income which was most welcome.[9]

Mozart scholars have wondered what fees the composer can have commanded for the works he published in 1791, and have been unwilling to risk even an approximate figure. I believe that we are in a position to supply some of that information from two unimpeachable sources. The principal publisher in 1791 was, as far as Mozart was concerned, the firm of Artaria & Co.: as the name indicates, it had been founded by north Italians and by 1791 it was the leading (but by no means the only) Viennese music-publishing house. Artaria was also Haydn's principal publisher, and a great deal of the correspondence between them has survived.

As recorded in the last chapter, Mozart received 100 ducats (450 Gulden) for the publication of the six string quartets dedicated to Haydn (K.387, etc.), which Artaria issued as Opus X in 1785. It has always been assumed that this honorarium was especially high, but it can be shown that Haydn received the same fee from Artaria for the 'Prussian' quartets of 1787. A year later he wrote to Artaria as follows from Eszterháza (10 August 1788):

> Since I am now in a position where I need a little money, I propose to write for you, by the end of December, either 3 new Quartets or 3 new pianoforte Sonatas with accompaniment of a violin and violoncello. . . . Of course it is understood that I shall then complete the other 3 Quartets, or pianoforte Sonatas, so that the edition will comprise half-a-dozen, as usual. NB. – For 6 Quartets the previous sum of one hundred ducats, for 6 pianoforte Sonatas [Trios] 300 fl . . .

Haydn's letters also give us concrete information about his fees for other kinds of music:

January 1789: works for Breitkopf & Härtel in Leipzig, suggested fees–
one piano sonata: 10 ducats (45 fl.)
six piano sonatas: 60 ducats (270 fl.)[10]
March 1789: Fantasia for piano (Artaria): 24 ducats ('the price is rather high')
January 1790: Twelve Minuets and Trios for Orchestra (Artaria): 12 ducats
Piano Trios 'as usual': 10 ducats each
January 1790: receipt from Artaria for three piano trios: 135 Gulden[11]

Using these figures as a basis, we may calculate with some certainty the kind of fees Mozart could have collected from Artaria for his 'Prussian' quartets, which were announced in the *Wiener Zeitung* on 28 December 1791 and entitled *Tre Quartetti Op. XVIII.* On 12 June 1790 Mozart had written to his friend Michael Puchberg: 'Now I am forced to give away my quartets (this laborious work) for a ridiculous sum of money [*Spottgeld*].'[12] This can hardly have referred to the publication rights to Artaria, who would certainly not have taken a year and a half to issue them, but rather to manuscript rights to one of Mozart's patrons.

The great Mozartian corpus of dance music was issued during the year 1791 in two ways: first in manuscript copies, as we have seen, and secondly in piano arrangements, published by Artaria.[13] Again, we have Haydn's correspondence with Artaria as a guideline to the prices for dance music. Unfortunately, we have no records of the rights to the copyists for the full orchestral versions, but if we use Haydn's price of 1 ducat (4½ fl.) per dance from Artaria, a conservative estimate of the kind of fees Mozart might have expected from the copyists would be a minimum of 3 Gulden (fl.) per dance.

It is slightly confusing that Artaria not only published the piano arrangements of no fewer than forty-eight Mozart dances in 1791, but also issued – along with its rivals Johann

Traeg and Lorenz Lausch – the full orchestral versions in manuscript at the usual fixed price per bifolium. It should be noted that all the issues ran into several editions – further evidence that Mozart's music was becoming increasingly popular with a new public. It was music, moreover, that appealed to all classes of Viennese society: the rich nobility could buy and perform the orchestral versions, the cultivated shopkeeper's wife the piano reduction.

Haydn, in 1792, sold the rights of his latest twenty-four *Redoutensaal* dances to Artaria for 24 ducats[14] – the same scale of price which he had unsuccessfully demanded in 1790, but which he had undoubtedly received from Artaria for the publication of his earlier dances, either for full orchestra or in reduction. For his forty-eight dances in 1791, Mozart would probably have expected and received 48 ducats (216 fl.).

For the Piano Concerto in B flat, which Artaria published in August 1791, Mozart might have expected the 24 ducats (108 fl.) that Haydn received in 1789 for a piano fantasia. There must also have been smaller fees for the following publications: K.613 issued by Artaria in June 1791 (*Ariette*, Pub. no. 341); the songs, K.596–98 (*Sehnsucht nach dem Frühlinge, Im Frühlingsanfange, Das Kinderspiel*), issued by Mozart's Brother Mason Ignaz Alberti (a member of *Zur gekrönten Hoffnung*) in his collection *Liedersammlung für Kinder und Kinderfreunde am Clavier*, Vienna 1791; as well as more small fees for the various commissioned pieces for musical clock and glass harmonica. Hence we arrive at the following figures:

Quartets (Artaria)	225 fl.
Manuscript rights for 30 *Redoutensaal* dances	90 fl.
Publication rights (Artaria) for 48 ditto	216 fl.
Piano Concerto in B flat (Artaria)	108 fl.
	639 fl.

If we add a further sum of a conservative 100 Gulden

for the Variations (*Ariette*), songs, musical clock and glass harmonica pieces, we have a rough estimate of 739 Gulden for performance and/or publication rights in 1791.

When one examines the list of music that Mozart composed in these first three months of 1791, it is the lack of symphonies, quartets, quintets, masses, operas – in fact any of the large forms except the piano concerto – which is curious and depressing. Is that all the court expected from its official chamber composer – minuets and German dances, however magnificent? Some such frustration was in Mozart's mind, too. The Nissen biography refers to a receipt (now lost) for such dance music, on which the composer wrote: 'Too much for what I did, not enough for what I could do.'[15] It was a shocking, even a criminal, waste of music's greatest genius.

V
New Directions: A Cathedral Appointment?

Suddenly it appeared that everything was about to change. Mozart learned that Leopold Hofmann, Haydn's old rival and *Kapellmeister* of St Stephen's Cathedral in Vienna, was mortally ill. This important position, which paid an annual 2000 Gulden and the usual, very plentiful emoluments (firewood, candles, etc.), was not for the court to bestow, but the Vienna City Magistracy. Mozart thought that he had many friends among the general population of his beloved city, and applied for the position, requesting to be made an unpaid assistant to 'the present Herr Kapellmeister of St Stephen's Cathedral Church.' In this proud letter, written at the end of April 1791, we read that Mozart had decided to apply at a time 'when Herr Kapellmeister Hofmann was ill, because my musical talents and works . . . are known abroad, and my name is everywhere referred to with some respect.' 'But Kapellmeister Hofmann recovered,' adds Mozart, and then requests the Magistracy to appoint him as 'adjunct with no salary' to Hofmann, 'who is now rather elderly.' Mozart particularly draws attention to his 'knowledge of the church style', in which, quite rightly, he considered himself especially competent.[1] As Constanze related many times, he had a particular affinity for and devotion to church music; he had particular ideas not only about grand masses and requiems but also about smaller, *volkstümliche* (popular) pieces of church music.

The City Magistracy made a favourable decision with

regard to Mozart's petition on 28 April 1791. He would in time have become Cathedral *Kapellmeister* of St Stephen's, and the history of church music would have taken a very different course. In the event, old Leopold Hofmann recovered and continued to live until 1793.

Recently, a fascinating work has come to be associated with Mozart's new interest in church music: it is the sombre and dramatic Kyrie in D minor (K.341), of which the autograph has long since disappeared (so that we cannot examine its watermarks, etc.). It is known to us from a copy made by the Leipzig musician, A. E. Müller (Berlin State Library), and from the first edition in score, published from the autograph by J. A. André about 1825. This extraordinary work, which can be compared stylistically only to the Requiem (whose principal key it shares), is scored for a very large orchestra, with two flutes, two oboes, two clarinets, two bassoons, four horns, two trumpets, kettledrums, organ and strings. Hitherto, and for no reason except the large size of the scoring, this work has been assigned to the Munich period of 1780. (Mozart had no clarinets at Salzburg and this large orchestra also figures in *Idomeneo*, composed for Munich.) But it seems much more likely that Mozart intended to compose a large Missa solemnis in D minor to celebrate his new position at St Stephen's, and completed the Kyrie before Hofmann recovered.[2] That Mozart was preoccupied with church music at this period is attested by the following letter, written about the end of May 1791 to his and Haydn's friend Anton Stoll, schoolteacher and director of music at the parish church of Baden.

> 1mo I would like to know if [Anton] Stadtler [*sic*] was with you yesterday and asked for my Mass [Mozart then quotes the opening of K.317, the 'Coronation' Mass]. Yes? I therefore hope to receive it still by today; if not, please be good enough to *send it immediately NB with all its parts*. I will return it soon.
>
> 2do please order a small apartment for my wife [in

Baden]. – She only needs 2 rooms; – or a room and a small chamber [*Kabinetchen*]. – But the main thing is that it's on the *ground floor*. – should prefer it to be the one that Goldhahn had on the ground floor at the butcher's. – I would ask you to go there first – perhaps it can still be had. – My wife will come out on Saturday or at the latest on Monday. – If we don't get that one, the important thing is to have it near the baths – but more, that it's on the ground floor – at the Town Clerk's where Herr Dr Alt lived on the ground floor would be fine, too – but the one at the butcher's would be preferable to all the others.

3tio I would also like to know whether the theatre season at Baden has started? – and please may I have a very quick answer and news concerning these three points.

Mozart mpria

P.S. My address is: in the Rauhensteingasse im Kayserhaus N° 970 first floor–

P.S. This is the most stupid letter that I've ever written in my life, but it's just right for you.–[3]

Wolfgang was anxious to secure a ground-floor apartment for Constanze because she was pregnant and having trouble with her feet. In this connection appears the first reference to Joseph Odilio Goldhahn (or Goldhann), who witnessed the document of Mozart's effects after his death. For some reason the name was later made illegible (by Constanze or Nissen?); Mozart himself seems to have referred to him as 'NN' in his letter to Constanze of 12 June. It appears almost certain that Goldhahn was involved in the Mozarts' financial affairs.

The main point of Mozart's letter is that he intended to perform his already celebrated 'Coronation' Mass – so-called because it was given at the Frankfurt coronation in 1790 and a year later in connection with the coronation ceremonies at Prague[4] – probably at St Stephen's in Vienna. In the event the performance did not take place.

Because of the Emperor Joseph's edict of 1783 restricting the performance of *figuraliter* church music (*i.e.*, with orchestra) in the churches, orchestral masses had rather languished in Austria in the 1780s. Haydn composed only one mass in that period, the so-called *Mariazellermesse* or *Missa Cellensis* (1782), and Mozart's last large-scale mass, or indeed any kind of church music, had been the Kyrie, Gloria, Sanctus and Benedictus of the Mass in C minor (K.427), performed at Salzburg in October 1783 (the work was never completed and Mozart later salvaged the Kyrie and Gloria by turning them, with two additions, into the Italian oratorio called *Davidde penitente*). Under Emperor Leopold II, these restrictions were largely dropped, and for rich churches like St Stephen's they had never been strictly enforced anyway.

Mozart wrote affectionate letters to his wife, now at Baden with their son Carl; one was delivered by their chambermaid Sabine (they always spelled her name 'Sabinde'), who stayed with Constanze at Baden and remained with her until Sabine's death in 1806. Mozart's other maid was called Leonore ('Lorl'), but he dismissed her during the summer. 'Tonight I shall sleep at Leutgeb's', he wrote on 5 June, referring to his friend Joseph Leutgeb, a cheese-monger but also a magnificent horn-player, and a former member of the archiepiscopal band at Salzburg, now living in Vienna. Mozart had a special regard for Leutgeb, and had written a number of horn concertos for him. Now he started a new one, a Concerto in D (K.412 [376b] + 514): two movements (lacking a slow middle Andante) which remained a fragment and were later completed (orchestrated) by Süssmayr and dated by him on the Rondo's autograph, 'Vienna Venerdi Santo li 6 Aprile 792' (Good Friday, 6 April 1792).[5]

The correspondence with Constanze is delightful:

This very moment I received your dear letter and see from it with pleasure that you are in good health and well – Mad.[e] Leitgeb [*sic*] put on my neckerchief today, but how? – dear God! – though indeed I kept saying, *that's the way she* [Constanze] *does it*. That didn't help. – I am pleased that you have a good appetite – but if you eat a lot, you've got to sh – a lot – no, I wanted to say, walk a lot – though I would like it if you didn't take *long walks* without me – Do everything I suggest, it certainly comes from the heart. Adieu – dear – my only one – take them as they fly through the air – 2999 and ½ kisses are flying, waiting to be snapped up. – Now I'm going to tell you something in your ear. – – – – now you to me. – – – – now we open and shut our mouths – – ever more-and more – – finally we say; it's because of Plumpi-Strumpi – – you can think what you like during it all, that's what's so nice – adieu – 1000 tender kisses from

always your
Mozart

6 June 1791.[6]

Mozart hoped to be able to visit Constanze in the second week of June but the concert given by the blind glass-harmonica-player Kirchgessner, in which Mozart was obviously going to participate, had to be postponed. Wolfgang told all this to Constanze on 11 June, adding that he would surely arrive the next Wednesday.[7] He continues:

I must rush, because it's 6:45 o'clock – and the coach leaves [for the Leopoldstadt] at 7:00 – – Be careful not to slip in the baths and never stay there alone – also if I were you I should skip them for a day so as not to force things too quickly. I hope that someone spent tonight with you. – I can't tell you what I would give if instead of being here I could be with you in Baaden [*sic*]. – Out of sheer boredom I composed an aria for my opera [*The Magic Flute*] today. – I already rose at 4:30

– my watch, imagine! I've pried it open; – but – because I've no key, I can't wind it up, isn't that sad? – schlumbla! – That's another word to think about – I've wound up the big clock instead – Adjeu – dear! – today I lunch at Puchberg's – I kiss you 1000 times and in my thoughts I say with you: Death and desperation was his reward![8] [from *The Magic Flute*, no. 11 Act II].

Your ever loving husband
W. A. Mozart

Carl [their son] should behave himself,
kiss him for me.
(take an electuary if you're constipated – but not otherwise)
(take care of yourself in the mornings and evenings when it's cold.)

The next day, 12 June, another letter went off to Baden:

Dearest, best little wife!
Why had I no letter from you yesterday evening? So that I had to live in fear because of the baths? – that and something else ruined the whole of yesterday for me – in the morning I was with N.N. [Goldhahn] and he promised on his parole d'honneur to come here to me between 12 and 1 o'clock, in order to clear up everything. Therefore I couldn't eat at Puchberg's but had to wait here. – I waited, it struck 2:30 – he didn't come, so I wrote a little note and sent the maid to his father, – meanwhile I went to the Ungarische Krone, because it was too late everywhere else – even there I had to eat *alone* because all the guests had already left – in the fears that I had because of you and the annoyance because of N.N., you can imagine what my lunch was like – if only I had had some soul to comfort me a little. – For me it's not good to be alone when I have something on my mind, – at 3:30 I was back home again – the maid wasn't back yet – I waited – waited – at 7 o'clock she came with

> a note. – Waiting is surely unpleasant at best – but much more unpleasant when the result does not justify the expectation – I read a lot of excuses, that he hadn't yet been able to hear anything definite, and a lot of assurances that he has certainly not forgotten me and will quite surely keep to his word. – To cheer me up I then went to *Kasperl*,[9] which is creating such a noise – but there's nothing to it. – In the course of going there I looked in to see if Löbel[10] wasn't in the coffee-house – but he wasn't there either. – At night I ate (just so as not be alone) in the Krone again, – there at least I had a chance to talk – then I went straight to bed – up again at 5 o'clock a.m. – dressed at once – went to Montecuculi[11] – I found him at home – then to N.N. who had already flown the coop – I'm only sorry that because of unforeseen circumstances I couldn't write to you this morning – I would dearly like to have written!–

The rest of the letter goes on about his involved financial dealings with Goldhahn:

> . . . now I'm away from here tomorrow and off to you! – if only my affairs were in order! – who except me is there to give N.N. a push? – if he doesn't get a push, he cools off . . .

Mozart rushed to mail the letter ('now it strikes 11 o'clock! now I can't wait any longer').

In an undated letter to Constanze of about this time, he writes:

> Goldhahn [name rendered almost illegible] is off this moment to Baden – now it's 9 p.m. and I've been with him from 3 o'clock onwards. – I think now he'll keep his word . . . Greetings to your court jester [Süssmayr?] . . .[12]

Mozart went to join Constanze in time to compose one of his most beautiful and touching pieces – the *Ave, verum corpus* (K.618).[13] It was intended for a church ceremony which was, and still is, of particular importance in Austria: the feast of Corpus Christi.

The tradition of Corpus Christi included a procession that halted in front of four Stations, the number four having a symbolic reference, first to the four quarters of the globe to which the blessing was directed, and then to the recitation of the four Evangelists that accompanied it. The entire community took part in the procession, which also invoked a good harvest. It was a feast uniting Mother Church with Mother Earth.

Mozart's *Ave, verum corpus* celebrates this feast, but its significance goes far beyond the single ecclesiastical event for which it was composed. With this composition (as with the Requiem and – if my theory of its chronology is correct – the Kyrie K.341) Mozart was establishing what he considered to be the new style of church music. The style of the *Ave, verum corpus*, in its *Volkstümlichkeit*, its deliberate attempt to be unadorned, devotional and easily understood, is entirely in accord with the enlightened reforms of Emperor Joseph. To the connoisseur its one unusual modulation towards the middle to F – the work is in D major – and its canonic entries at the end reveal that a master hand is behind it all, but the dominant note is one of touching directness and simplicity. The Kyrie K.341 and the Requiem show the other side of the coin. Austere, even awesome, both of these D minor works nevertheless preserve a positively Josephinian sense of simple directness. Even in his church music, Mozart was an inspired product of the Enlightenment: *vox populi=vox Dei*, that is, a return to the voice of the people in its simplest and most basic form, implies a kind of truth which in turn was considered to have a touch of the divine.

Mozart composed the *Ave, verum corpus* for his friend Anton Stoll and it was first performed at the parish church of Baden on the feast of Corpus Christi 1791. Mozart's autograph is dated 17 June 1791 and the next day he entered the work into his thematic catalogue (from which we can surmise that he carried it about with him all the time). Its small orchestra (strings and organ) and its simple choral writing are all part of its Josephinian garb. Ever since its first publication in score by André about 1808 it has been one of Mozart's best loved works.

VI
Midnight for the Masons

Mozart joined the Freemasons in December 1784. His Lodge – always referred to with the sign □ in contemporary documents from Masonic sources – was named *Zur Wohltätigkeit* (Beneficence); its Master was Otto, Freiherr von Gemmingen-Hornberg, an old family acquaintance. He was Palatine Chamberlain and Privy Councillor, and Mozart had enjoyed his patronage at Mannheim in 1778. Gemmingen had moved to Vienna that same year and it was presumably he who first suggested to the young composer that he join the Craft.

Mozart's small Lodge had been formed on 2 February 1783, and its members found it expedient to work within the rooms of the larger, more influential Lodge *Zur wahren Eintracht* (True Concord); it and *Zur Wohltätigkeit* had been offshoots of the very influential Lodge *Zur gekrönten Hoffnung* (Crowned Hope). On 14 December 1784, Mozart was duly initiated in his Lodge as an Entered Apprentice.

In England, Freemasonry in an organized form began to spread its influence following the founding of the Grand Lodge in London on 24 June 1717, the feast of St John the Baptist, and it was under the flag of St John that the European Lodges were founded. In Austria the first was founded on 17 September 1742 by members of the Lodge *Aux Trois Squelettes* (Three Skeletons) in Breslau; it was called *Aux Trois Canons* (Three Canons). Freemasonry flourished in the Austrian Crown Lands and in neighbouring Bohemia and Hungary, not least because of the example set by Francis Stephen, Duke of Lorraine and the husband of the Archduchess (later Empress) Maria Theresa: he had become a member of the Craft in May 1731. A Papal Bull of 1738, which condemned Freemasonry, was simply suppressed in Austria, since Duke Francis Stephen (later Emperor) was able to persuade Emperor Charles VI to ignore it. Maria Theresa, however, did not approve of Freemasonry, and her son Joseph II, who co-reigned with her from 1765 (following the death of his father, Francis Stephen) to 1780, at first regarded the Craft with considerable, if tolerant, scepticism.

Most of the Austrian Lodges adhered to the English ritual and the ancient Landmarks, but on 26 March 1781 – by which time Joseph II reigned alone – an Imperial Decree prescribed that no spiritual or secular orders were to submit to a foreign authority, nor were such orders permitted to pay money to any body outside the Monarchy. Thus, on 22 April 1784, the *Große Landesloge von Österreich* (Grand Lodge of Austria) was constituted. This new Grand Lodge embraced seven provinces: Austria – seventeen Lodges; Bohemia – seven Lodges; Lemberg (Galicia) – four Lodges; Hungary – twelve Lodges; Austrian Netherlands – seventeen Lodges.

During the first half of the 1780s in Austria, Freemasonry became a meeting-point for the intellectual élite; it was also extremely popular. Our knowledge of the Masons in Austria comes largely from material collected by the Austrian Secret Police. But the papers of one famous Lodge, *Zur wahren Eintracht*, were hidden, and only discovered later when the city walls were razed in the middle of the nineteenth century. *Zur wahren Eintracht* was founded in 1781 and by 1785, when Mozart began to visit it, it comprised some 200 members under the Master, Ignaz von Born, a distinguished scientist, writer and mineralogist, whom Mozart and Schikaneder are purported to have used as the model for Sarastro in *The Magic Flute*. The surviving lists of the Viennese Lodges provide an impressive documentation of the Craft's importance at this period: they include the names of princes, counts, and barons, many senior civil servants, senior military officers, diplomats, writers, musicians, bankers, and merchants. In Mozart's Lodge, which was small but distinguished, were men like Carl, Prince Lichnowsky, who accompanied Mozart on his trip to Berlin in 1789 and was later famous as the patron of the young Beethoven in Vienna. Among the writers were Johann Caspar Riesbeck, whose book (first published in German) *Travel through Germany, in a series of letters* (London, 1787) contained bitter social criticism of, for example, the peasants' life near Haydn's residence, Eszterháza, in Hungary. It was no ordinary historian who could write: 'The clearest proof that a country is unhappy is the confrontation between the greatest magnificence and the most wretched poverty, and the greater the confrontation, the unhappier the country.' Was this not, *Figaro*-like, an extraordinary view of pre-Revolutionary Hungary, 'where the people live like animals in underground caves or like the Mongols in tents . . .'? This suggests that the conversations in the Lodge could have been, and probably were, political, and on the side of the Josephinian reforms. Among other writers belonging to *Zur Wohltätigkeit* were Ignaz de Luca, who published Haydn's autobiographical sketch in 1776, and Vienna's worthy chronicler, Johann Pezzl.

Haydn applied to join the Craft in December 1784 and became an Entered Apprentice in the Lodge *Zur wahren Eintracht* on 11 February 1785. Meanwhile, Mozart had been passed to the Fellow-Craft Degree on 7 January 1785 under the Master, Ignaz von Born. There is no surviving record of when Mozart was raised to the Third Degree, that of Master Mason.

Wolfgang's father, Leopold, arrived in Vienna on 11 February 1785 in time to hear the première of his son's D minor Piano Concerto (K.466) that night. Mozart *père* now joined the Craft – certainly at the instigation of his son –

and was rapidly (in view of the fact that he was only in Vienna for a short period and was to return to archiepiscopal Salzburg where there was no official St John's Lodge) advanced from Entered Apprentice (6 April), Fellow-Craft Degree (16 April), to Master Mason (22 April) – all except the first ceremony being conducted at *Zur wahren Eintracht*.

Wolfgang was a dedicated member of the Craft:[1] he supplied music for its ceremonies, his outstanding work being the astonishing and powerful *Maurerische Trauermusik* (K.477), written for a Lodge of Sorrows (memorial service) for two aristocratic Brethren, a Count Esterházy and the Duke of Mecklenburg-Strelitz. The heavy symbolism in the work (concept of 'three'), as well as its overall tripartite form (using the *Te decet* plainsong found in Michael Haydn's Requiem of 1771), reveal Mozart's total involvement with the Masonic theories and philosophies of death and their symbolic relationship to the Master Mason Degree. It is clearly and unmistakably to this symbolic passage from death to life in the Masonic ceremony that Wolfgang refers in a famous letter of 4 April 1787 to his father, who was on his deathbed:

> As death (considered precisely) is the real purpose of our life, for several years I have become so closely acquainted with this true and best friend of our life, that his image is not only no longer terrifying to me, but rather something very soothing and comforting! And I thank my God for affording me, in His grace, the opportunity (you understand me) of realizing that he is the key to our real happiness. – I never lie down in bed without thinking that (young as I am) I may not live to see the next day – and yet no one, especially among those who know me, can say that in daily life I am stubborn or sad – and for this happiness I give thanks to my Creator every day and wish every man the same from the bottom of my heart . . .[2]

We have a great deal of information about Mozart and the Masons – more than one would have dared to hope. From this final period we even have a complete list of the members in Mozart's Lodge which was now no longer functioning as *Zur Wohltätigkeit*. How did this change come about?

Emperor Joseph II, in a *Handbillet* of 11 December 1785, ordered the number of Viennese Lodges to be reduced to three. He obviously considered that the Masons had become far too powerful and that there was no control over their activities. He wanted their numbers drastically reduced, and it was rather clever to force a reorganization within the Lodges so that many members felt obliged to resign, or simply (like Haydn) no longer to attend. The Brethren themselves complied with this order earlier than required, and by 28 December 1785 the situation was as follows: the élite Lodge *Zur wahren Eintracht*, together with the *Palmbaum* (Palm Tree) and *Drei Adler* (Three Eagles), amalgamated as a new Lodge *Zur Wahrheit* (Truth); the Lodge *Zur gekrönten Hoffnung*, Mozart's Lodge *Zur Wohltätigkeit*, and the *Drei Feuern* (Three Fires) were fused into the principal Viennese Lodge *Zur neugekrönten Hoffnung* (New Crowned Hope), which opened its doors for the first time on 14 January 1786. Both these new Lodges voluntarily reduced their numbers to 180 members each. Two of the former Lodges, *Zum heiligen Joseph* (St Joseph) and *Zur Beständigkeit* (Constancy), disappeared entirely, but some of their members joined *Zur neugekrönten Hoffnung*. Ignaz von Born was elected Master of the reconstituted Lodge *Zur Wahrheit*, but in August 1786 he resigned. The Emperor also demanded regular information about the Lodges, with precise lists of their members, whether absent or present, and, as a result of this supervision, many Lodge lists, both manuscript and printed, were incorporated into the secret files of the Court Archives.

The last list of members of *Zur gekrönten Hoffnung* (the

neu had meanwhile been dropped) to include Mozart is that for the year 1790. It is important because it shows exactly who was and who was not (*e.g.*, Emanuel Schikaneder) one of the composer's Lodge Brethren. The most amazing discovery about the list, which was first published by this writer in 1982, is the presence of Haydn's Prince Nicolaus Esterházy as Master of Ceremonies, along with three other members of that illustrious Hungarian family. The Master was Johann, Count Esterházy, Imperial Royal Chamberlain, who had been the Lodge's Master in 1781 and would again fill that position in 1791: it was presumably he who led the Lodge when it moved quarters in November that year, for which occasion Mozart composed his swan-song, *Eine kleine Freymaurer-Kantate* (K.623). The third Esterházy was Count Franz Seraphin, the son of Franz, Count Esterházy (known as Quinquin and the co-recipient of Mozart's *Maurerische Trauermusik*), who followed his father's footsteps as Court Councillor in the Transylvanian-Hungarian Court Chancellery. The fourth was Johann Nepomuk, Count Esterházy, at this period in Transylvania where he was Provincial Administrator.

The officers of the 1790 list include Deputy Master Joseph von Metz (a member of the Dutch Section in the government). *Erster Aufseher* (first warden) was Bro. Joseph Bauernjöpl, a clerk in the Joint Court Chancelleries; *Zweiter Aufseher* (second warden) was Franz Eugen, Count von Traun und Abensperg, Imperial Royal Chancellor; Secretary was Karl Fischer von Ehrenbach, Councillor of the Legation of the Sachsen-Coburgs; the Speaker was Anton Niering von Löwenfels, *Konzepist* (clerk) in the Ecclesiastical Court Commission; treasurer was Johann Nepomuk von Török from the Imperial Royal War Ministry's bookkeeping department.

It was a colourful Lodge with some 200 members and a dozen 'Serving Brothers' (two from Johann Esterházy's household). There was an Abbot of the Augustinian Canons at Huy (Huey) near Liège (Lüttich); the publisher Ignaz

Alberti, who would later issue the libretto of *The Magic Flute*; Karl Ludwig Gieseke, a member of the Schikaneder troupe; Vittorino Colombazzo, an excellent oboist who had served in Haydn's orchestra in Eszterháza; a very grand officer, Feld-Marschall-Leutnant Ferdinand, Count von Harrach, on whose estates in Rohrau Haydn had been born; the engraver Joseph Zaharadnitschek, trumpeter in the Hungarian Bodyguard; and the reigning Prince Anton of Hohenzollern-Siegmaringen. It was a distinguished company, whom Mozart loved individually and collectively. In the commonplace book of one Brother, Johann Georg Kronauer, a teacher of languages, Mozart signed himself (in English): 'Patience and tranquillity of mind contribute more to cure our distempers [than] the whole of medicine' (30 March 1787).[3]

But by 1791 it was nearly midnight for the Freemasons in Austria. If they had been left in relative peace by Joseph II, no one knew for certain what the attitude of Leopold II was going to be. For the moment he did nothing, and it was into this vacuum that Mozart and Schikaneder risked a long shot – to save the Craft by an allegorical opera, *The Magic Flute*.

It has never been clear if, and to what extent, the Lodge or its individual members helped Mozart in his financial crisis at the end of the 1780s. Certainly the treasurer of Haydn's Lodge *Zur wahren Eintracht*, Michael Puchberg, proved to be a devoted friend and supporter of the Mozart family. We do not know for sure whether Puchberg was ever repaid the debt, but according to Nissen he waited until Constanze had recovered her financial stability and then requested repayment.[4] It would have been consistent with Puchberg's character to show such consideration. We do know of two concrete things that the Masons did after Mozart's death; one was to print the new *Kleine Freymaurer-Kantate* in score for the widow's benefit; the other (a matter of Lodge honour) was to publish a speech held at a Lodge of Sorrows in Wolfgang's memory.

Let us for a moment examine Mozart's financial situation in the year 1791. His salary – as we have seen – was 800 Gulden a year, on which he paid 5 per cent tax, making a total of 886 fl. 40 kr. for fourteen months' salary in 1791.[5] Apart from this income, Mozart had arranged to borrow or in some other way to organize no less than 2000 Gulden. In a letter to Puchberg of 25 June 1791 he told his friend that Constanze in Baden needed some money unexpectedly and asked him to send some, as he himself could not. 'In a few days, it can't be more than that, you shall receive in my name 2000f., from which you can subtract the sum at once.'[6] Puchberg sent 25 Gulden. Mozart actually seems to have caused the sum of 2000 fl. to materialize; was it used to pay off Puchberg's debts? Continuing with Mozart's income in 1791, *La clemenza di Tito* brought in 200 ducats (900 Gulden) and 50 ducats (225 Gulden) expenses.[7] I find it impossible to believe that Mozart, who remained good friends with Schikaneder until the end, took less than 200 ducats for *The Magic Flute*, especially since by early December it had been playing to full houses for some thirty-five nights. It may well be, as Constanze later told Rochlitz, that Schikaneder took in all the money for 'foreign' rights (*i.e.*, scores sold abroad), for Mozart became ill before foreign business with the opera started to become financially rewarding.

We have seen earlier that Mozart can have earned 739 Gulden in 1791 from publication and performance rights, though the figure was undoubtedly much higher. (We know little about this side of Mozart's life; he may have sold other manuscript and publication rights abroad which remain unknown and about which no new discoveries may be expected.) And if we assume that the fee for the Requiem amounted to 50 ducats (not 100 ducats), and that Mozart received half upon commission, that would make 25 ducats (112 fl. 30 kr.). If we add these sums together, the result is as follows:

Salary (thirteen months)[8]	886 fl. 40 kr.
Monies received end of June 1791 [loan?]	2000 fl.
La clemenza di Tito	900 fl.
(and expenses)	225 fl.
The Magic Flute	900 fl.
Publication and other rights	739 fl.
Requiem advance payment	112 fl. 30 kr.
Total	5763 fl. 10 kr.

And this is surely a conservative estimate: it omits many imponderables, and rightly so. But in essence it must represent the approximate income of the Mozarts in the dread year of 1791. If we wish to compare other people's income in the same field, the most obvious example is Haydn. It was in this same year, during the summer of 1791, that Mozart appears to have turned against Haydn. We shall never know what it was all about, but here is the relevant passage in Haydn's letter of 13 October from London to Maria Anna von Genzinger:

> *Inter alia* Herr von Keess writes to me that he would like to know my circumstances here in London, because there are various rumours about me in Vienna. From my youth on, I have been exposed to envy, and so I am not surprised that people attempt wholly to crush my modest talents; but the Almighty is my support. My wife writes to me, but I don't believe it, that Mozart speaks very ill of me. I forgive him. There is no doubt that many people in London are also envious of me, and I know almost all of them. Most of them are Italians. But they cannot harm me, for my credit with the common people has been firmly established for a long time. Apart from the professors, I am respected and loved by everyone. As for my remuneration, Mozart can enquire of Count Fries for information, with whom I deposited £500, and of my Prince, who has 1000 Gulden, that

makes nearly 6000 fl. in all. I thank my Creator daily for this boon, and I flatter myself that I can take home a few thousand more, notwithstanding the fact that I have many expenses, and notwithstanding the costs of the journey. Now I won't bother Your Grace any more. Isn't this handwriting appalling? How is Pater–? My compliments to him.[9]

Haydn's trips to London have always been cited as the fabulous, rags-to-riches end of a modest career. Haydn reckoned that he made, in four seasons in London (1791, 1792, 1794 and 1795) 24,000 Gulden (£2400, today perhaps £50,000 or $85,000). To help clarify Haydn's earnings during the 1791 season we happen to have the exact amount he deposited in both his accounts: 5883 Gulden[10] – which is only some 120 Gulden more than Mozart's presumed earnings for that year. (Haydn's earnings in London were geared to the season, which started in February or March and ran until June; hence his earnings would not begin again on a large scale until 1792.) Of course Haydn retained some money to live on in England; and both Haydn's and Mozart's expenses will have been heavy, Haydn's because he had to rent living quarters and eat in restaurants, Mozart's because he had to provide for a household of four adults (counting the servant-girls) and two children, and did a great deal of entertaining. And yet something is radically wrong! How could the Mozarts be in such precarious – not dire, but surely precarious – straits with even an approximate income like that? Granted that it was expensive to have Herr Joseph 'Primus' bring in Mozart's meals from outside, and that Constanze's cures at Baden were costly; yet the sum total of Wolfgang's finances in December 1791 was 60 Gulden in cash, and 133 fl. 20 kr. from the court's salary still outstanding, with immediate debts of 918 fl. 16 kr. Later Constanze thought that 3000 Gulden would clear her debts (Emperor Leopold had been told that Mozart was 30,000 Gulden in debt!);[11] but how did their finances arrive at this chaotic state?

We must look back to 1789, when Mozart's financial situation seemed bleakest, and when only one name (Baron van Swieten's) was put down for a projected subscription series being hawked about town in the hope of clearing his debts. Mozart certainly borrowed money, and large sums too (*e.g.*, the 1000 Gulden Constanze raised when Mozart was in Frankfurt), but we have no complete record. I think we must assume that these sums were larger and more frequent than hitherto realized, and that it was not until 1791 that his income was beginning to be large enough to enable them to live comfortably and to pay off by degrees all their old debts. If Constanze's figure is correct, the 2000 Gulden listed above as 'Monies received' was in fact a loan (from Goldhahn, perhaps?), which, taken with the figure of 918 fl. 16 kr., would make nearly 3000 Gulden.

The Masons have always made a speciality of helping their needy Brethren, especially widows and orphans of those members of the Craft 'who have gone to the eternal east'. No one has ever explained satisfactorily how Constanze was able to get on her feet so quickly after Mozart's death: by 1797 she was able to lend the Duscheks in Prague 3500 Gulden! All the evidence suggests she was an extraordinary and resolute woman who faced the future with courage and firmness, and who set about raising whatever money she could from her late husband's music – whether by performing or selling it (see Chapter XIII). Her trip to Germany in 1796, touring with *La clemenza di Tito* and other music which she thought would be unknown, was a much greater success financially than her late husband's two tours of 1789 and 1790 had been. Two years before (1794) she had put on a concert performance of the opera in Vienna, and had followed it with one in Graz.[12] But, apart from Constanze's admirable determination and fortitude, it seems clear that the Lodge *Zur gekrönten Hoffnung*, as long as it existed (until 1794), must have helped Constanze;

and of course before and after that, individual members would have performed all sorts of services. They would, for instance, have been faithful subscribers to the first serious attempt on the part of the Lodge to raise money for Constanze – a round-robin letter of 5 June 1792 which was sent to the other Lodges.[13] By 1792 the scene in Vienna had changed again: Leopold II died in March and the new Emperor was Francis II. The Masons still entertained hopes that the Lodges might be saved, and in *Zur gekrönten Hoffnung* on 8 September they mounted a performance of the *Kleine Freymaurer-Kantate* in honour of the Emperor, with a new text by Bro. Karl Ludwig Gieseke.[14] (It is always stated, without any foundation, that Schikaneder wrote the original text; when the Lodge published it they clearly stated that the words were by a member of the Lodge; and I suggest that Gieseke was also the author of the original text. It is the obvious choice.)

On 25 January 1792, the *Wiener Zeitung* carried an announcement by Joseph Hraschansky, Imperial Royal Court book publisher (he printed in German and Hebrew): 'Cantata by Mozart: for the benefit of his widow and orphans . . . A swan-song, the performance of which he conducted in a circle of his best friends two days before his final illness. It is a cantata for the opening of a Freemasons' Lodge in Vienna, the words by a member . . .'[15] Subscriptions (2 Gulden) opened on 15 January and continued until 15 July. The score appeared on 14 November 1792 (*Wiener Zeitung*) and the cost to non-subscribers was 3 Gulden (9 on Dutch paper).

The Masons had been loyal to Mozart's memory and magnanimous towards his widow.

VII
Requiem for a Country House

In July 1791 Mozart had just finished composing most of *The Magic Flute*. In the chronicle of Niemetschek, the earliest of them all (1798), Constanze relates an extraordinary tale concerning the mysterious commission to compose a requiem mass. (This text was taken over by Nissen, Constanze's second husband, mostly verbatim, so that we may be assured it is the approved, 'official' version.)

> Shortly before the coronation of Emperor Leopold, even before Mozart had received the order to travel to Prague, a letter without signature was brought to him by an unknown messenger, which with many flattering remarks contained an enquiry as to whether he would be willing to undertake to write a Requiem Mass. What would be the cost, and how long would it take to complete?
>
> Mozart, who never made the least move without his wife's knowledge, told her of this remarkable request, and at the same time expressed a wish to try his hand at this type of composition, the more so as the higher forms of church music had always appealed to his genius. She advised him to accept the offer. He therefore replied to his anonymous patron that he would write a Requiem for a given sum; he could not state exactly how long it would take. He wished, however, to know where the work was to be delivered when ready. In a short while the same messenger appeared again, bringing back not

> only the sum stipulated but also the promise, as Mozart had been so modest in his price, that he would receive another payment on receipt of the composition. He should, moreover, write according to his own ideas and mood, but he should not trouble to find out who had given the order, as it would assuredly be in vain.
>
> In the meantime he received a very flattering and advantageous offer to write the opera seria for the Coronation of Emperor Leopold in Prague. It was too much of a temptation for him to refuse to go to Prague to write for his beloved Bohemians.[1]

In that same year (1798), Friedrich Rochlitz, who had met Constanze when she was travelling through Germany in 1796, published Mozart anecdotes, based largely – though not exclusively – on information she had provided. Since some of Rochlitz's numbered anecdotes were taken over more or less verbatim into the Nissen biography, they lay claim to the same authenticity as Niemetschek. But in the case of the Requiem, Rochlitz's version is longer and raises problems of chronology above and beyond the time sequence as clearly outlined in Niemetschek.

> One day, when he was sitting there . . . a carriage drew up and a stranger had himself announced. He [Mozart] received him. A middle-aged, serious, impressive man, of a very earnest countenance, not known to him or his wife, entered.
>
> The man began:
>
> 'I come to you as the messenger of a very distinguished gentleman.'
>
> 'From whom do you come?' asked Mozart.
>
> 'The gentleman does not wish to be known.'
>
> 'Very well – what does he wish of me?'
>
> 'Someone very near and dear to his person has died; he wishes to remember the day of her death, quietly but in a worthy fashion, and asks you to compose a Requiem for this purpose.'

Mozart – in view of his state of mind at that time – was already much moved inwardly by this conversation; by the mystery in which the whole affair was shrouded; by the man's solemn tone. He [Mozart] promised to do so. The man continued:

'Proceed with all possible diligence: the gentleman is a connoisseur.'

'So much the better.'

'You will not be bound to any period of delivery.'

'Excellent.'

'How much time will you require approximately?'

'About four weeks.'

'Then I shall come again and collect the score. What fee do you require?'

Mozart answered recklessly – 'one hundred ducats.'

'Here they are,' said the man, put the roll of coins on the table and departed. Mozart once again sank into deep reverie, did not heed his wife's entreaties, and finally requested pen, ink and paper. He started at once to compose the commission. His interest in the affair grew with every bar; he wrote day and night. His body could not stand the strain: he fainted several times over the work. Every exhortation to moderation was in vain. Some days thereafter his wife persuaded him to drive with her to the Prater. He always sat quietly and lost in his thoughts. Finally he no longer denied it – he thought for certain that he was writing this piece for his own funeral. He could not be dissuaded from this idea; he worked, therefore, like Raphael on his 'Transfiguration', with the omnipresent feeling of his approaching death and delivered, like the latter, his own transfiguration. He even spoke of very strange thoughts in connection with the curious appearance and commission of this unknown man. If one wanted to persuade him otherwise, he was silent but unconvinced.

Meanwhile, the departure of Leopold to Prague for the coronation approached . . .[2]

In this version, the commission occurs some time before Emperor Leopold leaves for Prague (perhaps July?), and Mozart sets to work on the Requiem at once, working himself into a state of exhaustion. But notice that Constanze is in the picture and that she takes him now for a carriage ride. Constanze was in Baden all during June and until the middle of July; *The Magic Flute* was completed, except for the Overture and March of the Priests, by the middle of July, as the entry in Mozart's thematic catalogue informs us. We shall see that *La clemenza di Tito* must have been commissioned by the middle of July, though as yet without precise knowledge of some of the leading singers. There was simply no time for Mozart to start the Requiem on a large scale. The chronology of Rochlitz's report is wrong: several episodes concerning the Requiem seem to be conflated. In the version I have chosen as the primary source, it is clearly stated that the stranger arrived 'shortly before the coronation'. The fact that in the Nissen biography it is the Niemetschek version (1798) which is used suggests that it is nearer to the truth (as Constanze remembered it).

We may overlook the thousands of pages published between 1792 and 1963 on the subject of the Requiem, for it was not until 1964 that Otto Erich Deutsch astonished the scholarly world with a long and sensational manuscript report on the origins of the Requiem, written by someone with first-hand knowledge. Finally, 172 years after the first printed notices about the work in 1792, the truth came out. Here is the precious document, preserved in the town archives of Wiener Neustadt, thirty miles south of Vienna.

> True and Detailed History of the *Requiem* by W. A. Mozart. From its inception in the year 1791 to the present period of 1839. [By Anton Herzog, Director of the Information Centre, the Region, the Main School, and *Regens chori*]
>
> Herr Franz, Count von Walsegg, owner of the estates Schottwien, Klam, Stuppach, Pottschach and Zieg-

ersberg, in Austria below the [River] Enns . . . lived since his marriage with Anna, *née noble* von Flammberg, in his castle at Stuppach, as a tender husband and true father to his vassals. He was a passionate lover of music and the theatre; hence every week, on Tuesdays and Thursdays, each time fully three hours' long, quartets were played and on Sundays theatre, in which latter Herr Count himself, and Madame Countess and her unmarried Madame Sister, took part, as did all the officials and the entire, numerous household, all of whom had to play roles, each according to his or her capacities. To help with the quartet-playing Herr Count engaged two excellent artists, Herr Johann Benaro as violinist and Herr Louis Prevost as violoncellist; Herr Count played the violoncello in string quartets, and in flute quartets he played the flute, and usually I played the second violin or the viola. In those days I was engaged as teacher in the Patronat-School of the Herr Count, at Klam.

So that we would not lack for new quartets, in view of so frequent productions of them, Herr Count not only procured all those publicly announced but was in touch with many composers, yet without ever revealing his identity; and they delivered to him works of which he retained the sole ownership, and for which he paid well. To name one man, Herr [Franz Anton] Hoffmeister delivered many flute quartets, in which the flute part was quite easily negotiable, but the other three parts extremely difficult, which caused the players to work very hard; and that made the Herr Count laugh.

Since Herr Count never wanted to play from engraved parts, he had them beautifully copied out on ten-stave paper; but the author was never noted. The secretly organized scores he generally copied out in his own hand, and presented them for the parts to be copied out. We never saw an original score. The quartets were then played, and we had to guess who the composer was. Usually we suggested it was the Count himself, because from time to time he actually composed some small things; he smiled and was pleased that we (as he thought) had been mystified; but we were amused that he took us for such simpletons.

We were all young, and thought this an innocent pleasure which we gave to our lord. And in such fashion the mystifications continued among us for some years.

I have thought it necessary to furnish these particulars so that the origin of the *Requiem*, which has been termed mysterious, can be better judged.

On 14 February 1791, death snatched from Herr Count von Walsegg his beloved wife, in the flower of her life [she was not yet twenty-one]. He wanted to erect a double memorial to her, and he had an excellent idea. He arranged through his business representative, Herr Dr Johann Sortschan, Court and Judicial Lawyer, in Vienna, that one of the very best sculptors in Vienna [Johann Martin Fischer, 1740–1820] should model an epitaph; and Mozart should compose a *Requiem*, for which he [the Count] as usual reserved the sole right of possession.

The first item, which cost over 3000 Gulden, was after a time erected in the valley with the spring near Stuppach Castle; and the remains of the lady were taken from the family vault in Schottwien and placed there.

But the *Requiem*, which was supposed to be played every year on the anniversary of Madame Countess's death, took longer than expected; for death surprised Mozart in the midst of this worthy task. What to do now? Who was going to dare to imitate a Mozart? And yet the work had to be finished; for Mozart's widow, who (as was well known) was not in the best circumstances, was to have received one hundred ducats. Whether prepayments had been effected was not precisely known to us, although there are reasons for thinking so.

Finally Süssmayr was persuaded to complete the unfinished great work, and he admits in letters to the music publishers [Breitkopf & Härtel] in Leipzig that during Mozart's lifetime he often played and sang through with him the pieces that had already been composed, namely 'Requiem', 'Kyrie', 'Dies irae', 'Domine', and so forth, and that he [Mozart] very often discussed the completion of this work and communicated [to Süssmayr] the way and the reasons of his orchestration.

[Herzog relates how Süssmayr completed the work and how Mozart's unfinished autograph looked, with the blank sections, etc.] In such fashion the work was completed. Of this score there were at once made two copies. Süssmayr's manuscript was sent to the commissioner. One copy was sent to the music publisher in Leipzig for publication, the second one was retained and the parts copied from it; whereupon this marvellous work was first performed for the benefit of the widow in the Jahn rooms.[3] [Herzog has taken this information from Stadler's published accounts. He now continues:] Therefore Herr Count von Walsegg never received a single note of the whole *Requiem* written by Mozart's own hand [in fact the Walsegg copy consisted of Mozart's autograph of the 'Requiem aeternam' signed by Süssmayr 'dime W: A: Mozart mpria $\overline{792}$' and the autograph of the Kyrie with additions by Freystädtler and Süssmayr; the rest of the manuscript is in Süssmayr's hand, and the other Mozartian originals, as far as they went, were retained by Constanze]. I leave it to be decided whether one dealt in an upright – I won't go so far as to say honest – fashion with Herr Count von Walsegg. He wasn't even told how far Mozart's composition went, he thought up to the 'Agnus Dei'.

That would explain the following circumstance: later when I had the parts copied from the published Leipzig score, for my own use, I asked Herr Count for the Organo of his *Requiem*, because it is not figured in the score, as is known, and I wanted to save myself the trouble of copying the figured bass; but he said I

FIG. 1 *A page from the autograph manuscript of Mozart's Requiem (Kyrie) written in three hands. The vocal parts (staves 8–11) and the basso continuo (bottom line, with figured bass for the organ) are in Mozart's hand, the string and woodwind parts (violins I and II, viola, basset horns I and II, and bassoons, staves 1–5) are in F. J. Freystädtler's hand, and the trumpets and kettledrum parts (staves 6–7) are in F. X. Süssmayr's hand.*

wouldn't be able to use his organ part for the whole piece because it had a different 'Agnus Dei'. I persuaded the Herr Count of the opposite, however, because every note of his *Requiem* copy was known to me; and because the 'Agnus Dei', with its clever connection to the following two Mozart compositions. 'Requiem' and 'Cum sanctis', especially impressed me.

Herr Count sought to prove that he had a different 'Agnus Dei' in his score from that of the Leipzig score in that he always said he had been a pupil of Mozart's, and had sent the score section by section to Vienna to be examined. Shortly before Mozart's death he had just sent to him the completed 'Benedictus' for this purpose.

After Mozart's death they found the score for the *Requiem* from the beginning up to the 'Agnus Dei'; and they thought it was Mozart's composition, because their two handwritings [Walsegg's and Mozart's] were supposed to be extremely similar to each other.

Herr Count then finished the *Requiem* by adding the 'Agnus Dei' and the rest; but Süssmayr had later added his own composition to fill in this part. That is how it happened that Herr Count had a different 'Agnus Dei' from that in the Leipzig score. – From all this one can see the extent to which the commissioner deluded himself. . . .

I myself am convinced that Mozart would not have composed the 'Sanctus' in D major and in that style; for although the text is the same as in the Mass, the circumstances of a Requiem are quite different; this is a Mass of Mourning, the church is draped in black, and the priests wear mourning robes. Dazzling music is not what is wanted. One can cry 'Holy, holy' without having to add kettledrum rolls . . .

Madame Widow Mozart and her circle may not have known about the contract which her late husband made with Herr Doctor Sortschan, according to which Herr Count von Walsegg was to have been the sole owner of the commissioned *Requiem*; otherwise at the time when they delivered the score to the commissioner they would not have sent, without his knowledge and permission, a copy to be sold to the music publisher in Leipzig. One can imagine what an impression it made on the Herr Count, when he learned that the score of his property had appeared publicly in print in Leipzig. [Constanze had, when she delivered the score to Walsegg, made it a condition that she 'could sell the score to princes who of course would not publish it';[4] but this Breitkopf & Härtel operation was obviously not in that class.]

Herr Count actually intended at first to take serious

action against the Widow Mozart, but the matter was settled in good faith, thanks to his kind heart.

After Herr Count Walsegg had received the score of the *Requiem*, he copied the whole at once, in his usual fashion, note for note in his own very fair hand; and gave it movement by movement to his violinist Benaro, so he could copy the parts.

During this work I sat for hours at Benaro's side and followed the course of this excellent work with increasing interest; for the whole previous history of the *Requiem* was well known to me through our Senior Official [Franz Anton] Leitgeb [1744–1812], who had been ordered to pay out the honorarium through the gypsum office in Vienna [the Walsegg family owned gypsum works in Schottwien].

When all the individual parts were written out, preparations for performing the *Requiem* were at once set in motion. But because in the region of Stuppach not all the necessary musicians could be brought together, it was arranged that the first performance take place in Wiener Neustadt. Among the musicians, the choice of the instrumental and vocal soloists was made from among the best available; and so it happened that the soprano was sung by Ferenz [a choirboy?] from [Wiener] Neustadt, the contralto by Kernbeiß from Schottwien, the tenor by Klein of [Wiener] Neustadt, and the bass by Thurner of Gloggnitz – these were the soloists. On 12 December 1793 the general rehearsal was held in the evening, in the choir-loft of the Cistercian Abbey and Parish Church of Neustadt; and on 14 December at 10 o'clock in the morning a requiem memorial service was held in that same church, during which this famous *Requiem* was given for the first time in the fashion for which it was intended.

Herr Count von Walsegg conducted the whole. Of all the musicians who participated in it, as far as I know, and at the moment of writing, none is alive except for myself and Herr Anton Plaimschauer, at present *Thurnermeister* [leader of the city band] here in Wiener-Neustadt.

On 14 February 1794, on the anniversary of Mad. Countess's death, the *Requiem* was performed in the Patronat Church of Herr Count, at Maria-Schutz on Semmering; and from this time on Herr Count made no use of it, except that he arranged it as a quintet for strings, the score of which I kept for many years. [He relates that the full score – supposedly, but as we have seen wrongly, written in Süssmayr's hand – had never been seen by him or anyone else in the entourage, but] the score which the Herr Count gave me to use for rehearsing the singers was in his own hand, and I would have recognized it at once.

That Herr Count wanted to mystify with the *Requiem*, as he had done with the quartets, was well known to all of us; in our presence he always said it was his composition, but when he said that he smiled.

. . . Following the death of Herr Count von Walsegg [11 November 1827] his sister and residuary legatee, Madame Countess von Sternberg, sold the whole musical archives to her steward, Herr Leitner. Among these items there must have been many valuable pieces of music.

In the summer of 1838 the manorial secretary Hagg died in Stuppach Castle and left his effects to the Stuppach court clerk, his residuary legatee. There was a small collection of music included. And, O miracle! They discovered the manuscript score of the *Mozart* Requiem, and they thought they saw at once that it was the original score in Mozart's own handwriting. [This was true of the first two movements, and the rest looked very like his handwriting, although it was actually Süssmayr's.]

The affair came to the notice of Herr Count Moritz von Dietrichstein, Excellency, and also to that of Herr Court Councillor von Mosel, and arrangements were made for the score to be sent to Vienna, so that it could be purchased by the I.[mperial] R.[oyal] Court Library, where it is to be found at present . . .

Peace be on the ashes of the great master, and also on his revered patron [Walsegg], to whose liberality we are indebted for this so valuable work of art.[5]

For some reason this document came to the attention of the Viennese authorities. Perhaps Herzog wanted to publish it. The authorities, however, took a severe view of the whole situation. At the bottom of the document we read:

Not allowed
by I.[mperial] R.[oyal] Ministry
Vienna, 8 Feb. 1839
Freyberger mpria.

There is something infinitely touching and innocent about the whole Walsegg operation; like Nelson, when he died, Walsegg could have whispered, 'I have not been a *great* sinner, doctor.'[6] He was not; but he was surely slightly demented, living like some caricature of a grand eighteenth-century *seigneur* in his beautiful and rather remote castle, with its magnificent view towards the austere Semmering mountains, pretending (but only slightly) that he was a great composer *manqué*. One can see that he was much loved by his subjects: and, after all, we do owe the Requiem – its forbidding majesty coupled with deep consolation – to him and to the death of his beautiful young wife. It was a tale worthy of E. T. A. Hoffmann.

Recently the brilliant young Austrian scholar Otto Biba has discovered remnants of the Walsegg papers,[7] in which the Viennese music manuscripts (prepared by local scribes) have had their attributions changed from, respectively, François Devienne and Franz [Anton] Hoffmeister to 'Fr. C.[omte] de Wallsegg'.

So the grand mystery of the Requiem, the commissioning

FIGS. 2, 3 *Count Walsegg, the mysterious nobleman who commissioned Mozart's Requiem, performed this and other pieces by Austrian composers under his own name. Shown here is a contemporary manuscript of a work by Franz Anton Hoffmeister, in which the composer's name has been substituted by that of Walsegg.*

of which so terrified the weak and ailing Mozart, has ended in farce.

Its history, as far as the composer was concerned in 1791, was divided in two parts: the period when he received the commission; and the period during which he began to work on it with complete concentration. Between these two parts, interrupting the commission, came the trip to Prague and the first performance of *The Magic Flute*.

VIII
A Journey to Prague

La clemenza di Tito, Mozart's last opera (K.621), languished in almost complete obscurity throughout most of the nineteenth century and the first half of the twentieth. Only in the last twenty-five years has it come to be recognized as one of the composer's major achievements. Opera houses in Europe and America have mounted important productions of the work, and it has even been filmed for television in a memorable adaptation by Jean-Pierre Ponnelle, using the Baths of Caracalla in Rome as its *mise-en-scène*. There were several reasons for the opera's long neglect, one being that the major role of Sextus was written for a castrato (male soprano or alto), a breed of singer that was to disappear from the opera houses of Europe not long after the work was composed. Today, however, we have come to appreciate it as a work of considerable psychological insight, containing at least an hour of the greatest music Mozart was capable of writing. Surely that is enough to give it immortality.

The story of how Mozart came to write *La clemenza di Tito* for the coronation festivities at Prague starts in an unlikely fashion: with Haydn in England. As we have already seen, Haydn had been invited there by J. P. Salomon, and had enjoyed a spectacularly successful season in the first half of 1791. We have also seen that he was able to save 5883 Gulden by the middle of July. On 20 July the composer wrote to Prince Esterházy, saying that Salomon had asked him to stay another season and requesting the

Prince for a further leave of absence. Haydn must have been deeply distressed to read the answer, sent on 21 August from Eisenstadt:

> It is with much pleasure that I learn from your letter of 20 July how much your talents are prized in London and I genuinely rejoice thereat; but at the same time I cannot conceal from you that your present, already extended absence has turned out to be not only very vexatious for me but also very expensive since I was compelled to have recourse to outsiders for the festivities held at Eszterháza this month. You will not think ill of me therefore that I cannot grant you the requested extension for a further year of your leave of absence; but instead expect to hear from you by the next post the exact time when you will arrive back here again.

In the event, Haydn did stay on until the end of June 1792 and Prince Esterházy did not dismiss his faithful *Kapellmeister*; the Prince is reported to have said, when he met the composer at the coronation festivities for the new Emperor Francis II at Frankfurt, 'You could have saved me 40,000 Gulden, Haydn.'

It was specifically the festivities held at Eszterháza that set in motion the whole train of events that landed Mozart in Prague. Between 3 and 6 August 1791, Prince Anton Esterházy celebrated his installation as lord-lieutenant of the county of Oedenburg (now Sopron, Hungary), to which Eszterháza belonged, at the famous castle where Haydn had directed the music from 1766 to September 1790.[1] It is reported that Esterházy spent 300,000 Gulden, including 40,000 for a new cantata entitled *Venere ed Adone*, the text by Abbate G. B. Casti and the music composed by Haydn's godchild Joseph Weigl, now a star pupil of Antonio Salieri and an unofficial conductor of the Imperial Court Theatre of Vienna. In order to mount this new production, Weigl brought with him several of the Vienna Opera's leading singers, including Cecilia Giuliani, Dorothea Bussani, Vincenzo Calvesi and Joseph Valentin Adamberger, of whom the last three had sung in Mozart's operas under his direction. Apart from the cantata, there was a grand ball, fireworks and hunts; the palace and park were illuminated by 80,000 oil containers with floating wicks.[2] The Emperor had, of course, been invited but was prevented from coming by the many duties and affairs of state which required his urgent attention;[3] but Archduke Francis, the heir to the crown, Archdukes Charles and Alexander Leopold (the Palatine and Prince-primate of Hungary) were in attendance.

As a result of Weigl's absence from the Vienna theatre, Salieri was forced to take over his duties; and this increased amount of work meant, in turn, that Salieri was forced to turn down a very interesting offer. We learn of all this from an autograph letter written about the end of August 1791 from the composer to Prince Anton Esterházy, recently discovered in the Esterházy archives in Budapest.

FIG. 4 *Antonio Salieri. Silhouette by Hieronymus Löschenkohl, 1786.*

Your Highness, immediately upon the return of the Italian opera company, which had the honour to serve Your Highness in the last magnificent fête in Eszterháza, I was informed that someone had written to Your Highness that I had refused the Imperial Court Prompter permission to leave for Eszterháza which caused some discomfort at the rehearsals for this fête and also casts the most humiliating suspicions on me.

The person who suggested such a thing must have surely been unaware that for the last seven years I have been the teacher of the young Weigl for whose talent and habits I can take credit, in that I myself gave him, and got him to compose, a poem by a famous poet for the opera [*i.e.*, the cantata *Venere ed Adone*] for Eszterháza which I myself had started to put into music. Moreover, in order to allow my pupil more free time to finish his music in the allotted time and to do himself credit on such a wonderful occasion for him and for his master, I myself for more than two months took over his duties at the Court Theatre, to the point of attending the minor rehearsals of the *opera buffe* myself whenever the other work of my own situation did not prevent me. And furthermore, without regretting it, however, I had to decline to write the opera which is being prepared for the coronation in Bohemia, for which opera the impresario came five times from Prague to Vienna to press the commission on me to the point of showing me 200 zecchini [ducats], a commission which I could not accept since I alone was attending to the affairs of the Court Theatre.

Such sacrifices stand singularly opposed to the accusations brought against me. That similar details were disregarded or intended to be disregarded by the person who cast me as the author of the possible or actual upheaval would not upset me much or even at all, but it is my duty to explain my actions in this instance to Your Highness, because an honest man, an artist, and head of the family who spends the few free hours which his occupation leave him doing good to his neighbour, without any ulterior motives, the same good which he has unreservedly received from others, cannot and must not remain indifferent in the face of this kind of judgment passed on him.

I know through the troupe that the real author of this intrigue was finally discovered, but I am in doubt if that fact is known to Your Highness and that is the reason that I have taken the decision to write to you respectfully this justification which I beg Your Highness to receive as a mark of my profound respect with which I beg to subscribe myself as Your Highness's most humble and obedient Servant

Antonio Salieri.
Principal Kapellmeister at the
Imperial Court of Vienna.[4]

From this hitherto unknown source, then, we see that Antonio Salieri was the Prague impresario's first choice as the composer of the new coronation opera. The impresario in question was Domenico Guardasoni, an Italian theatrical manager who had been in charge of the National Theatre at Prague intermittently since 1788. Some time after 10 June 1791, when Guardasoni had returned to Prague from Warsaw, the Bohemian Estates[5] approached him regarding a new opera to be performed for the coronation of Leopold II as King of Bohemia on 6 September. Evidently the Prague authorities had left everything until the very last moment. Their contract with Guardasoni is dated 8 July 1791, less than two months before the new opera was due to be given. The document (in Italian) reads:

Specification of the points which I the undersigned agree to maintain in respect of the High Estates of Bohemia . . . concerning a grand opera seria to be put on in this National Theatre for the occasion of the coronation of T[heir] I[mperial] R[oyal] M[ajesties], to take place within the first days of September next; for which purpose I shall be given and assigned six thousand florins, or six thousand five hundred if the castrato, Marchesi be engaged.

1mo I obligate myself to engage a first castrato, of leading quality, such as for example Marchesini [Marchesi], or Rubinelli, or Crescentini, or Violani, or another, but always of leading quality.

And equally I obligate myself to engage a prima donna, also of leading quality, and certainly the best of that level who is free, and I agree that my company shall provide the remaining singers.

2do I agree to have the libretto caused to be written, either on the two subjects given to me by H.E. the Count of the Castle, and to cause it to be set to music by a celebrated master; but in case it will prove to be impossible to do this because the time is so short, I obligate myself to procure an opera newly composed on the subject of *Tito* by Metastasio.

3^{zio} I obligate myself to cause to be made for this opera two new changes of scenery.

And equally I obligate myself to have new costumes made, and specifically for the leading parts of this opera.

4to I obligate myself to illuminate and to provide the theatre with garlands, to mount in every detail the said opera and to perform it gratis for one evening, at the disposition of said High Estates, within the time specified.

Urgent requirements:–

1mo That I shall be advanced the sum of six hundred florins for my trip to Vienna, and to Italy, on an order payable by a banker in Vienna and in Italy, and that I shall be given a draft for some two thousand florins in case the singers require some monies in advance.

2do That the remaining honorarium be paid to me on the day that the opera is executed.

3^{zio} That if, within the space of 14 days after the day

I shall leave for Italy, the opera is cancelled, then only the expenses of the trip shall be paid.

4to Guardasoni will announce at once the day on which he engages a singer; from that day, in case the opera is not given, said singer will be reimbursed if he or she has already left Italy.

5to In case said opera is not given, those items purchased for the money which has been advanced shall be retained, whereas those for which no contract has been issued shall be returned; and a remuneration shall be made to Guardasoni if he can show that the expenses of the trip prove to be greater than the sum advanced. Prague, 8 July 1791.

Henrico Conte di Rottenhan [Bohemian Count of the Castle][6]

Casparo Ermanno Conte Kinigl [Künigl]
Giuseppe Conte di Sweerth
Giovanni Conte Unwerth
Giovanni Baron d'Hennet

Domenico Guardasoni
Impresario[7]

It is clear from this document that even in July it was not entirely certain whether there was going to be any coronation opera in Prague at all. The Estates showed no particular preference for any composer, only that if the (unknown) subjects provided by Count Heinrich Rottenhan could not be made into a libretto, then the old and successful book, *La clemenza di Tito*, by Pietro Metastasio should be chosen. There is no mention of any other writer or adapter.

Guardasoni had in fact made an appearance in Mozart's life two years earlier, in connection with what was almost certainly a different work altogether. On Good Friday (10 April) 1789 Mozart had written to his wife from Prague: 'I went on to Guardasoni who has almost arranged for me to write the opera for next autumn with him for 200 [ducats] and 50 travel expenses . . .'[8] This project never materialized because Guardasoni was called to Warsaw that same year and did not return to Prague until 10 June 1791.

The company, which the *Prager Oberpostamtszeitung* on 14 June 1791 reports as living in the *Blauer Stern* (Blue Star) inn, consisted of 'Mr Guardasoni, Director of the Italian Opera Company, Mr Bassi, Mr Balleoni [Baglioni], Mad. Perini with three daughters, Mad. Katharina Mitschelli, Mad. Michalowicz, Mr Bonziani, Mr Campi, Mr Lolli, opera virtuosi from Warsaw . . .'[9] Many of these singers were to take part in the first performances of *La clemenza di Tito*.

On 9 July 1791, the day after signature of the contract, Guardasoni received his advance payment of 600 Gulden and left for Vienna and then for Bologna, where the Bohemian Estates had sent him 2000 Gulden to engage the singers.[10]

Now if Guardasoni made five different trips from Prague to Vienna to persuade Salieri to compose the coronation opera – as Salieri maintains, though it is hard to believe – he was evidently under the misapprehension that Salieri was the court's preferred composer. In fact, contrary to what is generally believed, Salieri was not much in favour with Leopold II. In his memoirs, Lorenzo da Ponte describes a meeting with the Emperor in which Leopold is purported to have said:

> Oh! never mind Salieri, I know all about him. I know all his intrigues, and I know the intrigues of the Cavalieri woman [Salieri's mistress]. Salieri is an insufferable egoist. He wants successes in my theatre only for his own operas and his own woman. He is not only your enemy. He is an enemy of all composers, all singers, all Italians; and above all, my enemy, because he knows that I know him. I don't want either him or his German woman in my theatre any more . . .

If Da Ponte's account contains even a modicum of truth –

and there is outside corroboration for Salieri's unease over his position[11] – Salieri was hardly the court's favourite composer.

Leopold's choice – if indeed he could have found time to interest himself in the subject – would probably have been Domenico Cimarosa. The Emperor had a plan to recall Cimarosa from Russia (where he was composing operas for Catherine the Great) to Vienna and to send Salieri for three years to Naples, where Cimarosa was supposed to return. As matters turned out, Cimarosa did come to Vienna and wrote for the court theatre his masterpiece. *Il matrimonio segreto*, in February 1792.[12] This work so pleased the Emperor that he personally caused it to be repeated the very same evening it was first performed, paid Cimarosa 1350 Gulden, and gave him the box-office receipts of the entire third performance (sold out, like the previous two), as well as a golden snuff-box with diamonds.

So how did Mozart come into the picture? And how was it that the Estates had already suggested to Guardasoni that *La clemenza di Tito* be the first choice if an original libretto was not forthcoming? The answers to these questions come from authentic contemporary documents. The first concerns a benefit concert given by Mozart's friend, Josepha Duschek, in Prague, the announcement of which read as follows:

With high and gracious permission,
Upon this day, Tuesday, 26 April 1791,
Madame Duschek
will have the honour
to present a musical academy in the
Royal National Theatre

Programme
First: A Symphony by Mr Girovetz [Adalbert Gyrowetz]
Secondly: an Allegro Aria by Mr Cimarosa
Thirdly: a movement from a Symphony

Fourthly: a brand new Grand Scene by Mr Mozart
Fifthly: a Concerto for the Forte piano by Mr Mozart, played by Mr Witassek
Sixthly: a Rondo by Mr Mozart with obbligato basset-horn
Seventhly: the Conclusion is a movement from a Symphony[13]

Now if the identification of the fourth number presents considerable difficulty, the sixth is a distinct sensation, for the only candidate for a Mozart rondo (in this context an aria consisting of a slow section followed by a fast one) with basset-horn is *Non più di fiori*, sung by Vitellia in Act II of *La clemenza di Tito*. But how is this possible? The commission for the opera cannot possibly have been given to Mozart before 14 July 1791, and here we have Mozart's friend, Madame Duschek, ostensibly singing an aria from it in April. (The fourth item might also be from the opera, if we could identify it.) That Madame Duschek actually had the Rondo in her repertoire is seen from her inclusion of it in a Vienna concert of 29 March 1798 as 'Rondo with obbligato basset-horn by Mozart, accompanied by Mr Stadler'. The basset-horn part, then, was evidently composed for Mozart's friend Anton Stadler, who also played in the first performance of the opera in Prague.

To take this matter further, we are lucky that the autograph manuscript of most of *La clemenza di Tito* has survived; it certainly helps us to establish which parts of the opera were written in Prague, because one of the paper types involved is a kind that Mozart had used for the Overture to *Don Giovanni* (notoriously written at the last minute) as well as the concert aria *Bella mia fiamma* (K.528), composed for Madame Duschek when Mozart was in Prague in November 1787. These hints as to the order of composition of the opera will be discussed below, but there is one astonishing fact which directly concerns our Rondo with basset-horn. Before I reveal it, we must examine the structure of the piece, No. 23 in the numerical order of the opera. It is as follows:

Scene 15 of Act II reveals Vitellia alone; she first sings an accompanied recitative (No. 22), *Ecco il punto, o Vitellia*, which ends with a cadence in the key of B flat. The next scene, No. 23, is entitled *Rondo*, and is worked out as follows:

Part one: *Larghetto*, 3/8 time, F major. Scoring: one basset-horn, with flute, two oboes, two bassoons and two horns. Text begins *Non più di fiori*. Bars 1–43 incl.

Part two: *Allegro*, 4/4 time, same scoring. Text begins *Infelice! qual orrore!* Bars 44–180.
Bar 180: modulation from F major to next number, the lead-in to No. 24 (Scene 16) Chorus (the March, *Che del ciel*).

Part two is written on paper which appears nowhere else in the whole of the autograph of *La clemenza di Tito*, and indeed it is very rare in Mozart's oeuvre altogether. It is found in some scores by Haydn (*e.g.*, an authentic copy of the 'Aria di Rosina', *Signor, voi sapete*,[14] an insertion in Anfossi's *Il matrimonio per inganno*, performed at Eszterháza Castle in the summer of 1785). The watermarks suggest north Italian paper: three crescents of declining size, crown over letters G/FA. Part one, on the other hand, is written on paper used in many other numbers of the opera, and the last bar of music written on it is in fact the first of the ensuing Allegro. Not only that: there is an earlier, discarded version of Part one, and it too is written on the same paper. The implications are obvious: the Allegro section, Part two, originally formed part of an earlier score. And not only that: in its very last bar (180) Mozart originally wrote on the autograph three fermatas or pauses 𝄐 to show that the music ended at the first note. He then tacked on, in the same bar, the modulation and began on a fresh sheet at bar 181. Surely, then, at least the Allegro section of the Rondo was in all probability part of the Rondo with basset-horn that Madame Duschek sang earlier in 1791. (She cannot have sung the present Part one because it was not yet composed; perhaps there was an earlier introduction which has not survived.)[15]

The Czech scholar Tomislav Volek has revolutionized our knowledge of this curious chapter in Mozart's life with his discovery of the relevant Prague documents concerning *La clemenza di Tito*.[16] Once he had established the priority of (at least part of) *Non più di fiori* over the rest of the opera, the next step was to suggest that Mozart had already begun to occupy himself with the music of *La clemenza di Tito* long before there was any firm commitment to write a coronation opera; and that the discussion of an opera with Guardasoni in 1789, to which reference was made above, must have been for this pre-version of *Tito*. This is, however, speculation. It presupposes that Mozart had already been in contact with the man who ultimately adapted Metastasio's libretto and brought it 'up to date', as it were: Caterino Mazzolà, an Italian who was poet at the court of Dresden. And there is no evidence that Mozart met Mazzolà before the summer of 1791.

But the text of our famous No. 23 is not that of Metastasio's original, written in Vienna for the court composer Antonio Caldara in 1734. In that original. Vitellia's aria occurs in Act III (rather than in Mozart's Act II). The recitative *Ecco il punto, o Vitellia* is the same as Mozart's No. 22; with the exception of a small cut at the end, the texts are identical. But in Metastasio's original of 1734 the text of the aria is as follows:

Getta il nocchier talora
  Pur que' tesori all'onde,
  Che da remote sponde
  Per tanto mar portò.

E, giunto al lido amico,
Gli Dei ringrazia ancora,
Che ritornò mendíco,
Ma salvo ritorno.
Parte

In Mozart's continuation, the Rondo has the words:

Non più di fiori vaghe catene
discenda Imene ad intrecciar.
Stretta fra barbare aspre ritorte
veggo la morte ver me avanzar.

Non più di fiori, ecc.

Infelice! qual orrore!
Ah di me che si dirà?
Chi vedesse il mio dolore,
pur avria de me pietà,

Non più di fiori, ecc.

Infelice! qual orrore! ecc.[17]

These words never formed part of Metastasio's original, nor do they figure in any other opera by the famous poet. So there is no evidence whatever that Mozart thought he was composing a part of *La clemenza di Tito* when he started to write the bravura aria for Madame Duschek. Then who wrote the words for his aria? Do they come from some hitherto untraced opera? And if, as seems likely from present evidence, this music was originally a grand concert aria for Madame Duschek, why was it not entered in Mozart's meticulously kept thematic catalogue? But supposing this scene was *not* a concert piece but part of a plan for *La clemenza di Tito*; how does all this fit in with Caterino Mazzolà? When did Mozart meet him?

To answer that question we must return to Guardasoni. When he, obviously in a state of some harassment, left

Prague for Vienna, he had as a fall-back the idea of getting someone to rewrite Metastasio's *Tito*; but before he could even think of engaging a composer, he had to find a poet with whom he could discuss the two subjects for an opera suggested by Count Rottenhan. If there were not time to write a new libretto using one of the proposals, then that poet would have to adapt *La clemenza di Tito* of 1734 for 1791. Guardasoni must have arrived in Vienna on or about 14 July – having left Prague on the 10th or 11th – and once there, the most natural thing would have been for him to get in touch immediately with the official court poet.

Lorenzo da Ponte had been dismissed in the spring of 1791, and to fill his place, the court had appointed Mazzolà, who had been working in Dresden. Mazzolà travelled via Prague, where he had arrived on 6 May.[18] The general administration lists for the court theatres in Vienna carry Mazzolà's name from May to the end of July, when he in turn was dismissed to make way for the much more famous poet and librettist, Giovanni Bertati.[19]

In the middle of July, however, Mazzolà was still the official Caesarian[20] poet in Vienna, and it was obviously to him that Guardasoni turned for a libretto. As regards the music, it is uncertain whether he had a last try to persuade Salieri to take it on; but in the end he went to Mozart and the Mazzola–Mozart–Guardasoni collaboration began.[21]

As for the potential cast of *La clemenza di Tito*, all Guardasoni knew was that the two principal singers had to be engaged in Italy. Before Mozart knew who they were going to be, and what their vocal ranges were, he could hardly write anything for them except ensemble numbers where he could apply a range suitable (let us say) to any soprano or tenor. (Speaking of ranges, the Allegro portion of Madame Duschek's Rondo extends from g below middle c to a′′ with some concentration on her middle and lower chest-notes – her speciality; whereas the singer finally hired to perform the part of Vitellia, Maria Marchetti-Fantozzi, had a range from middle c to c′′; but Mozart obviously saw when she arrived that she could navigate the lower notes of Duschek's original as well as reach high d′ ′.)

The one voice well known to Mozart was that of the future Titus – Antonio Baglioni, tenor, who had created Don Ottavio in *Don Giovanni* in Prague 1787. Apart from music for this one singer, Mozart thought he could only risk writing some ensemble numbers without knowing the voices which would perform them. Accordingly, he was able to start with some sketches and drafts for numbers involving Vitellia, Sextus, Servilia, and Annius; it was, after all, known from the contract that Sextus was going to be a castrato.

The compositional process and sequence can be elucidated by an examination of the various types of paper used by Mozart. The English scholar Alan Tyson, in a major study of the paper types and watermarks of the sketches for *La clemenza di Tito*,[22] has identified five types. Of these, type I had been used by Mozart in works such as *Così fan tutte* (1789) and others completed in 1790. Type II was that used by Mozart at a time when he was still unwilling to tackle any more than two new solo arias. Type III must have been used for numbers written after Guardasoni had been to Italy and returned to Vienna with detailed information about the cast – mostly the crucial arias which Mozart hardly wished to approach before that information was to hand.[23] Only the last eight leaves of a single aria belong to type IV, while type V was used for the music composed at the last minute in Prague.

Thus, with the help of the evidence of paper types, a possible chronology of events from the middle of July 1791 can be established as follows.

Guardasoni arrives in Vienna on or about 14 July 1791. On 15 or 16 July he meets the poet Mazzolà and they agree on *La clemenza di Tito* as the subject; Mazzolà decides to revise, but mainly to shorten, the libretto. Guardasoni makes a last-minute attempt to engage Antonio Salieri, but after a fifth refusal (if we are to believe the composer) hastens to Mozart with the same offer (in financial terms the same as was offered to Mozart at Prague in 1789: a fee of 200 ducats and 50 ducats travelling expenses, 250 ducats or 1150 Gulden in total). Mozart accepts and Guardasoni continues his trip to Bologna and back. Meanwhile Mozart begins his collaboration with Mazzolà and suggests among other things that the scene (Rondo) already written for Madame Duschek be worked into Act II of the opera; this revision has always been accounted particularly successful, improving the original dramatic situation. How much Mozart influenced Mazzolà, given the pressing schedule under which both were obliged to work, is an open question. But, as we shall see, Mozart described Mazzolà's efforts as having turned *La clemenza di Tito* 'into a real opera'. Otherwise, between mid-July and mid-August, Mozart can hardly have done more than write the numbers listed in Appendix D (pp. 227–29) on paper types I and II. Let us assume that Guardasoni arrived back in Vienna by the middle of August: he can hardly have reached the Austrian capital before that date. Between 15 and 25 August Mozart would now be able to start work on the numbers listed under paper type III; if he arrived in Prague on 28 August, as we know he did from the *Prager Oberpostamtszeitung* of 30 August, he must have left on the 25th because the journey in the fast mail-coach took three nights and four days.[24] Probably he had some of paper type III with him. No doubt he used the time on the stagecoach to compose the missing numbers in his head (that was his usual procedure: the actual writing down of the piece was a purely mechanical operation for him).

Mozart had found yet another way to make this whole rather hair-raising operation possible: to give his pupil Süssmayr the task of composing all the secco recitatives (those accompanied only by harpsichord with a cello and double bass). Süssmayr accompanied Mozart and his wife on the journey to Prague, and although it is always said that the pupil composed these recitatives, we have no actual proof. The autographs of the secco recitatives have not survived, but Nissen says that they were 'composed by his pupil Süssmayr'. Hence, since Süssmayr was actually with the Mozarts during all the rehearsals in Prague, there is no reason to doubt the story; and Mozart would certainly have overseen his pupil's work.

It is extraordinary that Constanze managed to come too. She had given birth to their sixth child, Franz Xaver Wolfgang, on 26 July (the christening had taken place in St Stephen's Cathedral, which also functioned as the Mozarts' parish church), and was prepared a month later to farm out the infant (to one of her sisters, perhaps?) and embark on what would have been potentially a dangerous voyage for a woman in her condition. Wolfgang must have been particularly anxious to have her accompany him, and she in turn may have started to worry about his health. Certainly Mozart was now dangerously overworked.

As they were boarding the coach, the messenger of the Requiem suddenly materialized 'like a ghost' (wrote Niemetschek and Nissen) and plucked the hem of Constanze's travelling cloak. 'And what is going to happen with the Requiem?' he asked. Both writers then continue:

> Mozart apologized, saying that the trip was necessary and explaining that it was impossible to acquaint his unknown master with the news; but that as soon as he returned it would be the first thing he would undertake; it was entirely up to the unknown patron if he wanted to wait that long; but the messenger was quite satisfied with the answer.[25]

The last stagecoach ride to the city that had always particularly loved his music and encouraged him took place during the final week in August, when the Austrian countryside always looks its most beautiful: the harvest is being taken by men and women on high-wheeled carts, the fields are slowly beginning to turn brown, and the first touches of red and gold are beginning to appear on the leaves of the vineyards north of Vienna. But as the carriage climbs towards Znaim on the post-road, the fields are too windswept for vines; and barley, oats and hay fill the huge fields, sloping in slow curves upwards towards Bohemia. The mail-coach with four horses left Vienna at eight o'clock in the morning and took three days, with twenty-one post stations, to arrive at Prague in the morning. It passed the huge country seats of the nobility along the Danube Valley; after the busy market-town of Stockerau, the traveller passed Sierndorf, the castle of the Princes Colloredo-Mansfeld, and then near Göllersdorf the ancestral seat of the Counts of Schönborn. As the coach climbed to 785 feet, Mozart looked out on the vineyards of Retz, which produced a tart white wine much appreciated by the Viennese; then on to Znaim, 'picturesquely situated on the left bank of the Thaya' with the old castle of the Margraves of Moravia. After leaving Znaim (950 feet), the sixth post station, the carriage toiled past four more post stations before arriving at Iglau, the border town between Moravia and Bohemia, at an altitude of 1695 feet. From there the road descended slightly through woods and fields to Deutsch-Brod and the ancient market-town of Caslau (Czaslau) near the dread battlefield of Chotusitz, where Frederick the Great had defeated the Austrians in 1742. By this time the principal language would have gradually changed from German to Czech (Bohemian). Seventeen post stations away from Vienna was Kolin (Neu-Kollin or Collin), where important roads branched away towards Zittau in Germany and, in the other direction, towards Neisse in Silesia. Near Kolin there was a more comforting reminder of the war against Frederick the Great: the Friedrichsberg, where Frederick surveyed the great battle during which he was defeated on 18 June 1757 by the Austrian Marshal Daun, and Prince Nicolaus Esterházy, then a colonel in the Austrian Cavalry, led his wavering troops to victory (he would never have imagined that 200 years later his name would be associated more with Joseph

Haydn than with the battle of Kolin).[26] The Mozarts would have reached Prague by the New Gate (Neuthor) on the fourth morning, twenty-one post stations and 150 miles away from Vienna.[27]

In Nissen's biography we read the following description of the trip: 'Work on this opera [*Tito*] began in his travelling coach *en route* from Vienna to Prague, and he finished it in eighteen days in Prague . . .'[28] This statement is taken, more or less verbatim, from the Niemetschek biography where the information is given twice in slightly different form (both times specifically mentioning eighteen days). Even allowing for Mozart's exceptional genius, this statement has generally been regarded as rather reckless poetic licence. But if we reckon eighteen days backwards from the day of the first performance of the opera in Prague on 6 September, we arrive at 19 or 20 August 1791. We have seen above that Guardasoni must have arrived in Italy from Vienna with details of the cast about the middle of August; but perhaps he only arrived on the 18th, and Mozart did not hear all the details he required to know until the afternoon of the 19th. Hence this figure of eighteen days would seem to suggest that, apart from the music written before that date (on paper types I and II), the bulk of *Tito* really was composed (using type III and Prague type V) in those eighteen days. It is near enough the truth to cause astonishment even now. (The Prague paper (type V) was noticeably smaller in size; hence it has been long recognized that it must have contained the music for the opera (including the soon celebrated Overture) composed at the last minute in the Bohemian capital; see Appendix D, pp. 227–29.)

As we arrive, with the Mozarts and Süssmayr, in the golden city of Prague, we might ask ourselves, as no doubt those three had been doing for some weeks now: why *La clemenza di Tito*?[29] Perhaps the obvious reason was that it had proved to be one of Metastasio's most successful and long-lived libretti, having enjoyed settings – after Caldara's of 1734 – by leading composers throughout Europe, including J. A. Hasse (three times), Wagenseil, Gluck (1752 in Naples), Holzbauer, Galuppi, Anfossi, Naumann, Traetta, Sarti, Mysliveček, Guglielmi and Haydn's impresario J. P. Salomon.

The second reason was that the Emperor and, to an even greater degree, the Empress, were devoted to *opera seria* as a genre and it would not, in any case, have been considered suitable to mount a comic opera for the solemnities of a coronation.

Thirdly, the subject-matter – an Emperor forgiving his potential assassins, and showing mildness and goodness – was considered suitable not only for the character of Leopold II (who had abolished torture in Tuscany) but for the Age of Enlightenment in general. *La clemenza di Tito* in Prague was to represent the ideal, the Enlightenment, which should be in stark contrast to the alarming events in France. Paul Nettl also suggests an intriguing reason why the Bohemian Estates had a special reason to choose the Titus material:

> It should also not be forgotten that Mozart was already near to the ideas of *The Magic Flute* and saw in the figure of Titus, the all-forgiving, the principles of Masonic tolerance.
>
> Those who had the last word concerning the choice of the subject might also have been motivated by these same thoughts: the Counts Thun, Canal, Pachta, Lazansky, Clary, Hartig, Sporck, Kinigl (Künigl), all members of the [Prague] Lodge 'Truth and Unity at the Three Crowned Pillars' (*Wahrheit und Einigkeit zu den drei gekrönten Säulen*) or at any rate Freemasons, who through their vows were obliged to propagate humanitarian ideals whenever they could.[30]

Although it was considered appropriate to perform Metastasio's old and famous opera for the coronation, it was also, as we have seen, considered necessary to bring it up to date; and Mazzolà did this very adroitly, cutting out a long-winded section in the middle and reducing the whole drama from three to two acts. Whether Mozart was responsible for some of these changes or not, the results were certainly in line with his ideas. A case in point is the insertion of a quintet with chorus at the end of the first act (No. 12, *Deh conservate, Oh Dei, a Roma il suo splendor*), certainly the greatest single number of the opera; this necessitated cancelling scenes 8–13 of the second act and fusing the former scene 7 with Act II, scenes 14–16, and the former Act III, so that there would be only two acts. In this way the contents of this great quintet and chorus No. 12 are dictated by what then follows in Mazzolà's hands, and we end up with a uniquely grand finale to Act I. The German scholar Helga Lühning believes that this procedure may be traced back to a similar operation in *The Abduction from the Seraglio* where, after having completed the whole of the first act, Mozart caused his librettist Stephanie to rewrite the second – 'at the beginning of the third act is a charming quintet or rather finale – but I would prefer to have this as the end of the second act. In order to arrange that, there has to be a big change, even a whole new intrigue must be planned . . .' (letter from Mozart to his father, 26 September 1781).[31]

Mozart and Mazzolà (who, by the way, came to Prague for the event, though we only know the date he departed for Dresden, 13 September 1791[32]) did wonders in the short time they had at their disposal, but when all is said and done *La clemenza di Tito* remains an *opera seria* with castrato part, entirely outside the line of development of Mozart's other operas from 1782. However, the deliberate simplicity of its language is misleading. It is nowadays taken seriously again after a long eclipse, and indeed much of it is up to Mozart's very highest standards – from the magnificent Overture to the conclusion of Act II, with the gripping March and Chorus in G (No. 24) which succeeds *Non più di fiori*. And it was composed along the lines of the latest, Paisiello-like Italian *opera seria* which, far from being moribund, was actually flourishing in Italy.[33]

IX
Coronation Diary

Prague is, by any standards, one of the most beautiful cities in Europe: the dominating position of the old fortress (Vyšehrad), where the semi-mythical Prince Kiok and his daughter Libussa with her peasant husband Premysl are believed to have lived, is one of the city's wonders. The visitor of today is fascinated by the Old Town (Stare Mesto, Alstadt) with its medieval streets and partly Gothic monuments. Mozart, who was no great friend of the Gothic style, would have been more admiring of the handsome Baroque palaces of the nobility in the Little Town (Mala Strana, Kleinseite) – where the Waldsteins, Rosenbergs, Thuns and Lobkowitzes lived – and of Strahov Abbey, where the view over the city is unsurpassed. With his many Jewish friends and connections, Mozart would have known the Jewish Quarter (Josephstadt) with the oldest synagogue in Prague, the Altneuschule (Staronová Škola), and its Jewish burial ground (Beth-Khayim, House of Life), disused since 1787 (the year of *Don Giovanni*), the moss-covered burial stones of which must bring tears to anyone's eyes.

Crowning the Old Town is the Hradčany (Hradschin), a quadrangle bounded by the Archiepiscopal Palace and what was at that time the palace of Prince Schwarzenberg. On the east side was the Royal Palace (Hofburg), where Leopold II and his entourage resided.[1]

Mozart's friends the Duscheks (Josepha's husband was the composer Franz Xaver, whose early string quartets were written almost simultaneously with Haydn's) lived in the Villa Bertramka, a vineyard in the suburb of Koschirsch, fifteen minutes from the Palacky Bridge. Mozart sometimes spent the night there and was a frequent guest of the hospitable family.[2]

The following 'diary' is a day-by-day account of the coronation festivities in Prague, with particular reference to Mozart's participation.

Sunday, 28 August 1791.
Wolfgang and Constanze Mozart arrive, with Süssmayr; it is not known where they stayed; since Prague was exceedingly full, perhaps they lived as guests of the Duscheks, at least until quarters could be organized. Two days before, on the 26th, Court *Kapellmeister* Antonio Salieri passed through the New Gate with five carriages carrying twenty court musicians, who were lodged in various places. Actually the number of musicians imported from Vienna seems to have been greatly increased at the last minute. On 1 May the court had ordered Salieri 'to make a list of those members of the court chapel orchestra who are required for the Royal Bohemian coronation and to deliver it at once.' Salieri thought that 'one Maestro di Capella [himself], an organist, a bass singer, a tenor, two contralti, two sopranos are necessary for Prague', adding that 'hence two violas, a violoncello and a double bass are unnecessary', by which he meant that such string players could easily be found among local Prague orchestras. On 8 June 1791, the *Obersthofmeisteramt* (Master of the Royal Household) had issued the following orders to Wenzel von Ugarte, *Hofmusikgraf* (Count in charge of the court music): 'His Majesty is graciously minded to leave here on 27th Aug. for Prague, to hold his official arrival in Prague on 31st Aug., to open the Landtag [Parliament] on 3rd Sept., to hold the service of allegiance on the 4th and the Coronation on the 6th. – Since H.M. has at the same time issued permission for the Court Kapellmeister to receive a per diem allowance of 4 f. and seven court musicians with a per diem of 2 f. to leave

for Prague . . . , Count v. Ugarte . . . is to request the necessary transport from the court Equerry Office . . .' On 10 June Ugarte had asked Salieri to name the musicians, who turned out to include Johann Georg Albrechtsberger, the court organist and Mozart's friend.[3]

Among the works that Salieri brought with him – the reader will be astonished to learn – were no fewer than three Mozart masses in manuscript score and parts: K.258 (known as the 'Piccolomini' Mass not because of the famous Tuscan family but because the court musicians referred to it as a *piccolo missa*, a little or short mass, a term which was corrupted into its present name), K.317 ('Coronation') and the magnificent and nowadays hardly known K.337. These were all Salzburg masses, the latter two dating from 1779 and 1780 respectively. The late Karl Pfannhauser has shown that both K.317 and K.337 were referred to as *Krönungsmesse* (Coronation Mass) in court music circles,[4] though the latter was also occasionally called *Missa Aulica* (Court Mass). The Hofburg score of K.317 has not survived, but the original parts, dating from around 1790, have; and in the score of K.337 are various remarks and performance guides actually in the hand of Antonio Salieri. Pfannhauser was able to show that in I.F.E. von Mosel's biography of Salieri of 1827 it is stated that Salieri conducted 'almost the exact same music' in all three coronation ceremonies:[5] Frankfurt 1790 (Leopold II), Prague 1791 (Leopold II), Frankfurt 1792 (Francis II), and that apart from the three masses, Salieri also conducted one of the most splendid choruses from Mozart's earlier *Thamos* (K.345), arranged as a Latin motet, as well as the austerely magnificent D minor Offertorium *Misericordias Domini* (K.222), of which a copy in the Imperial Chapel is signed 'Authore W. Amad: Mozart Vienae/Aulicae Capellae Magistro/Francoforti Anno 1792. producta'. I shall follow Pfannhauser's suggestions as to the position occupied by these Mozart compositions in the liturgical routine.

What is more difficult to explain is how it was possible

for seven musicians to turn into twenty. One suggestion is that some special instrumentalists, such as Mozart's friend Anton Stadler, were at the last minute given free transportation. Stadler was to play the clarinet and basset horn solos in *Tito* and there is no record when he entered Prague (as there would have been if he had arrived alone in the usual stagecoach).

On Sunday evening, in Count Thun's theatre in the Little Town, the Sekonda Troupe gave *Menzikof, or the Conspiracy against Peter the Great*, a tragedy in five acts by Herr Kratter.

Apart from a theatrical troupe and the Guardasoni company, Prague was host to many other groups and individuals, all anxious to siphon off money from the crowds. There was a 'Persian Fair' organized by Herr Massieri and Company, with a two-storey building and some hundred little boutiques. For the performances Massieri needed 120 pairs of children, many adults and over a hundred horses, some disguised as camels. In the room at the 'Iron Door' in the Michaelergasse, Messieurs Pierre and Degabriel offered a kind of magic theatre: one saw 'strange lands, landscapes and towns . . . and various effects of nature, such as the rising sun, sundry mechanical works of art, automats which move as the onlooker commands and answer all questions.' There were also fireworks, chemical experiments, and so on. The shows took place daily, at 4 and 7 p.m.

There was also a circus, the master of which was Monsieur Balp, 'Royal French and Sardinian trainer'; he set up in the riding school in the Tummelplatz in the Old Town. Herr Franz Koch offered himself to groups between a dozen and twenty strong, playing the double Jew's harp. Three musicians from Transylvania, two hunting horns and a clarinet, offered their services 'to a high nobility for morning, evening and Tafelmusik' (music performed at table). Blanchard, the famous balloon experimenter, who had been in Prague the year before, now proposed to float off for the forty-second time on 14 September in a field at Bubenecz.

The aristocracy held banquets, garden parties, masked balls and musical soirées. On Coronation Day, fireworks went off all over the ancient city.

Monday, 29 August 1791.
Emperor Leopold II arrives with his entourage to take up residence in the court castle on the hill. That evening Guardasoni's troupe gives Paisiello's *Pirro* and the play is *Das Galeriengemälde* (The Gallery Painting) by Karl Friedrich Hensler.

Tuesday, 30 August 1791.
Empress Maria Luisa arrives with her entourage and takes up residence in the town castle known as 'Lieben', where the Emperor and the Imperial Court greet her arrival officially. The play is *Das Portrait der Mutter* (The Mother's Portrait) by Schröder, in the Thun Theatre.

Count von Zinzendorf also arrives in Prague.

Wednesday, 31 August 1791.
Festive procession, to mark the royal couple's official arrival, from the Invalidenhaus to St Vitus Cathedral, the Metropolitan Church of Prague, with military and city officials in full dress. As the couple enters the Cathedral, choirs of trumpets and kettledrums sound from the organ loft. The Court Chapel musicians then perform the antiphon *Ecce mitto angelum* and a Te Deum, conducted by Salieri. In the evening the Thun Theatre offers *Er mengt sich in alles* (He Mixes into Everything); followed by *Der weibliche Jakobiner-Chlubb* (The Ladies' Jacobine club).

Thursday, 1 September 1791.
From Zinzendorf's Diary we have the first account of a piece by Mozart:

> We gathered in the Empress's antechamber, we were

> 100 persons dining in the coronation room . . . I found myself almost at the foot of the table between the Charwunschers, Lisette Schoenborn and Auguste Sternberg. The dinner good . . . Innumerable spectators . . . Music from Don Juan. After table we stayed a long time in the salon despite the bad smell from the audience.[6]

Zinzendorf refers here to Mozart's *Don Giovanni* arranged as *Tafelmusik* and probably played by a wind band: the usual scoring for such arrangements was two oboes, two clarinets, two bassoons and two horns. Were these perhaps the extra musicians put into Salieri's five coaches? And what was Mozart himself doing, apart from rehearsing the singers and frantically finishing off the rest of *La clemenza di Tito?* Fortunately there is a passage in Nissen's biography which can only have come from Constanze, and which gives us a delightful anecdote about Mozart during his last sojourn in Prague.

> While Mozart was composing his coronation opera *La clemenza di Tito* in 1791, he went with his friends to visit a coffee house which was not far from his apartment, to distract himself by playing billiards. For some days it was noticed that as he played he sang a motif very softly to himself, *hm, hm, hm*; and several times when the other was playing his shot, [Mozart] took a book out of his pocket, glanced quickly at it, and then went on playing. How astonished one was when Mozart sat down at the piano at Duschek's house and played to his friends the beautiful quintet from *The Magic Flute* between Tamino, Papageno and the Three Ladies ('Wie, wie, wie?'), which begins with just that same motif that occupied Mozart while he was playing billiards. Not only a demonstration of the continual exercise of his creative imagination, which, even in the middle of amusements and distractions, was uninterrupted, but also of the giant strength of his genius, capable of undertaking two such different activities at one and the same time. As is well

known, Mozart was well ahead with *The Magic Flute* before he travelled to Prague to compose and perform *La clemenza di Tito*.[7]

The play that evening is August von Kotzebue's *Bruder Moritz der Sonderling* (Brother Moritz, the Outsider) in the Thun Theatre.[8]

Friday, 2 September 1791.
The official Coronation *Tagebuch* contains the important announcement:

> Today in the National Theatre in the Old Town will be performed: *Il dissoluto Punito ossia: Il D. Giovanni*, The Punished Dissolute or Don Juan. A comic opera in two acts. The music is by Mozart.[9]

A hitherto unpublished account of this performance is in the *Pressburger Zeitung* No. 73 (10 September):

> Prague, 5 September . . . in the evening [of 2 September] Their I.[mperial] R.[oyal] Majesties with Their More Serene Princes and Princesses, I.[mperial] R.[oyal] Highnesses, honoured the National Theatre in the Old Town with Their Highest Presences where, by highest request, the Italian Opera *Il dissoluto puniro [sic]* or Don Jiovanni [*sic*] was given. The theatre was beautifully lighted with chandeliers and the Imperial Box decorated.[10]

Christopher Raeburn, who has done so much in uncovering authentic documents concerning the first performances and the casts of Mozart's operas, also found the following notice in the *Prager Oberpostamtszeitung* of 6 September:

> Prague, 4 September.
> The day before yesterday . . . Their All-Highest Majesties honoured our National Theatre in the Old Town with Their Presences, where the Italian opera *Il dissoluto punito* was performed. The spacious theatre, which is

quite capable of holding some thousand persons, was full to the rafters, and the route which the All-Highest took was entirely crowded with onlookers.

It has always been asserted that Mozart himself conducted this performance, but this is most unlikely. Mozart's name is not mentioned in the newspaper reports or the announcement, and it would have been just one more exhausting thing to do in the middle of last-minute rehearsals for *Tito*. Moreover, an eye-witness account mentions Mozart's presence, but apparently among the audience; this was written by the German author, Franz Alexander von Kleist, who had arrived in Prague on the same day as the Mozarts, 28 August ('10:45 o'clock a.m. Mr Kleist, Saxon nobleman, from Karlsbad'). He published his reminiscences the next year (*Phantasien auf einer Reise nach Prag von* K., Dresden and Leipzig, 1792):

> Never did I leave an opera house so rewarded as I did today, where I saw in a single room so many remarkable persons of such different positions. The Emperor together with his family were supposed to attend the opera today, and the whole way from the castle to the opera house was mobbed with persons who were curious to see how an Emperor looked when he was driving to a play. In the theatre all the boxes and the pit were filled with people, and when the Emperor finally arrived, they received him with threefold applause and *vivat*! . . . The Emperor seemed to be satisfied with his welcome and bowed several times to the audience . . . [There follow some remarks about the public, including some distinguished French émigrés such as General Bouille, the Duke of Polignac, etc.] . . . Away with these people, I am drawn to better ideas by the sight of a little man in a green coat, whose eye reveals what his modest condition hides. It is Mozart, whose opera *Don Juan* will be given today, who has the pleasure of seeing with what delight his beautiful harmonies fill the hearts of the audience.

Who can be prouder and happier than he? Who could be more satisfied with himself? In vain would monarchs lavish their fortunes, in vain the ancestor-worshipper his riches; he cannot purchase a tiny spark of the feeling with which Art rewards her darlings! . . . Everyone must fear death, only the artist fears it not. His immortality is his hope, his certainty . . . It reaches to unborn generations when the bodies of kings have long rotted. And with all these persuasions Mozart could witness how a thousand ears followed every string's vibration, every lisp of the flute, and how throbbing bosoms and quickly beating hearts revealed the holy impressions that his harmonies awoke . . . Whether it be *Schwärmerei* [passionate, but possibly transitory enthusiasm] or a real feeling among people, enough, at this moment I would have preferred to be Mozart rather than Leopold . . . [11]

As for the cast of the performance, we know that the protagonist was Luigi Bassi, who had been twenty-one when he created the part in 1787.[12] As hardly any serious descriptions of his voice exist, one is glad to find a report of December 1794 by Niemetschek, entitled *Some news concerning the condition of the theatre in Prague*, published in a journal entitled *Allgemeines europäisches Journal* (Brünn, now Brno, Czechoslovakia):

Mr Bassi is quite a good actor but no singer, for he has not the primary requisite to be one – a voice! I would wish he had this in addition to his other advantages, for then we could hardly wish for a better Don Giovanni, Almaviva [in *The Marriage of Figaro*] and Axur [the title role in Salieri's opera of that name], which roles he plays incomparably. He possesses the best taste of all his fellow singers and is prepared to admit the advantages of German artists. During all the years of his engagements in Prague, he has retained the public's favour.

Concerning the part of Don Ottavio, here too Guardasoni

could count on a tenor who had studied the part with Mozart and sung at the première of 1787 – Antonio Baglioni (whom we have already encountered in connection with *La clemenza di Tito*). In the same article Niemetschek wrote:

> This artist left the company a year ago and spent some time in Italy; here he diligently acquired all the bad habits of Italian artists and non-artists, and thus favoured he returned to Signor Guardasoni. He sings not one note as the composer wrote it and expected it, he drowns the most beautiful thoughts with his Italian runs and trills and allows his uniform method of gesticulating with his hands to serve for action, so that one is hard pressed to recognize the aria he is singing. Of course he is in need of such fripperies to disguise his defective voice, which is more of a mezzo basso; but because Signor Baglioni cannot cope with his arias in Mozart's *Così fan tutte*, he should not give out that for this reason the arias are badly written: for the great Mozart, whose spirit is too incomprehensible for flighty Italians, did not take Signor Baglioni as his standard when composing.

The revealing fact about this article is that, even by 1794, Italian singers (especially, no doubt, tenors) were ornamenting Mozart's music far more assiduously than the composer intended. Niemetschek castigates Madame Campi for not singing simply enough, and adds, 'by omitting the unnecessary fripperies in Mozart's simple melodies, she would give them more dignity.'[13]

In Kleist's interesting comments, we gather that the Prague audience was, as always, fascinated by *Don Giovanni* and its many novel effects, dramatic and musical. It is also instructive to have the following report from a sixteen-year-old Bohemian lad who would grow up to be a respectable composer: Wenzel Johann Tomaschek, who in his autobiography describes his impressions – and especially the first dramatic appearance of terror on the operatic stage – upon hearing the opera in Prague in 1790.

> Wrapped in our coats, we [Tomaschek and his brother] sat next to each other, awaiting the beginning. The Overture begins; its grand ideas and its quicker continuation, with its rich orchestration, altogether the noble life of that organic work of art, moved me to such an extent that I sat there like a dreamer, hardly breathing; and in my heavenly joy I saw a sun rising, felt as something darkly imagined my whole soul warmed with a magical force. My interest in the whole grew with each moment, and during the scene where the ghost of the Governor [Commendatore] appears, my hair stood on end with fright. On the way back home I thanked my brother with tears in my eyes, pressed his hand, and left him without being able to get a word out. This evening had without any question the most decisive influence on my musical career. [He continues by saying that the Guardasoni company was considered excellent, names many of the singers and then adds:] Nothing but the finest could be expected, especially when the singers were electrified by such a perfect orchestra as was then the case. Mozart, who had precise knowledge of all the orchestras in Germany, used always to say: my orchestra is in Prague.[14]

There is one point that needs to be stressed: even though the royal couple apparently entertained a 'strongly preconceived aversion to Mozart's composition', there was an extraordinary amount of his music being played, some in fact almost every day. *Don Giovanni* for wind instruments on 1 September, the opera itself the next day 'by highest request' (does that mean that Leopold and Maria Luisa especially asked for a performance of an opera by a composer whose music they disliked?), and church music on the 6th, 8th and 12th as well as *Tito* on the 6th and, if we surmise correctly, much Mozart dance music on the 12th. It is a very odd situation. If they really disapproved of

Mozart's music to that extent, were the Emperor and his wife in fact powerless to prevent its being performed?

Saturday, 3 September 1791.
The Sekonda Company gives in the evening *Die Sonnen-Jungfrau* (The Sun-Virgin), a German play in five acts, in the National Theatre.

Sunday, 4 September 1791.[15]
The first of the coronation ceremonies proper, the *Erbhuldigung* (Oath of Allegiance to the Crown), takes place in the Cathedral of St Vitus. The court musicians under Antonio Salieri perform a newly composed Coronation Mass by the Prague Cathedral *Kapellmeister*, Johann Anton Koželuch (1738–1814), a cousin of the better-known Leopold who lived in Vienna, and who would also contribute a cantata to the events. In addition, Salieri conducts the *Veni, Sancte Spiritus*, the Gradual and the Offertory; it is not known by whom these pieces were composed, but it is entirely possible that Salieri chose Mozart's Offertorium *Misericordias Domini* in D minor (K.222), whose severe and solemn style might have been considered more appropriate to the solemn Oath of Allegiance than to the gayer coronation services proper. At any rate, it seems certain that the Offertorium was one of the Mozart works Salieri conducted in Prague during the coronation festivities.[16]

Monday, 5 September 1791.
In his thematic catalogue, Mozart lists the new opera as follows:

> the 5th September. – performed in *Prague on 6th September*. La clemenza di Tito. Opera seria in two acts for the coronation of His Majesty Emperor Leopold II. – reduced to a true opera by Sig[no]re Mazzolà, poet of his Serene Highness the Elector of Saxony. *Actresses:*

Sig[no]ra Marchetti Fantozi. Sig[no]ra Antonini. – Actors: Sig[no]re. Bedini. Sig[no]ra Carolina Perini (as a man) *Sig[no]re, Baglioni. Sig[no]re Campi.* – and Choruses. – 24 *numbers*[17]

It was clear that everything connected with the opera was executed under considerable stress, and we shall see that the official Coronation Diary reports Mozart as being ill when composing the final sections. In the Nissen biography we read that 'the time for preparing [the opera] was so short that Mozart could not write the unaccompanied recitatives himself; and each number of the work, as soon as it was ready, had to be put directly into [orchestral and choral] parts so that the whole thing could be ready in time . . .'[18]

Once again it is Christopher Raeburn who has been able to establish the cast of the première:[19]

Titus	– Antonia Baglioni
Vitellia	– Maria Marchetti-Fantozzi (*recte*)
Servilia	– Signora Antonini
Sextus	– Domenico Bedini
Annius	– Carolina Perini (trouser role)
Publius	– Gaetano Campi

One supposes that the dress rehearsal took place in the afternoon, because the theatre was occupied in the evening with a performance of Iffland's *Der Herbsttag* (Autumn Day), a play in five acts given by the Sekonda Company.[20]

Coronation Day, Tuesday, 6th September 1791.
The coronation service was held in the Cathedral of St Vitus. Leopold was crowned King of Bohemia, and the church music conducted by Antonio Salieri included:

Antiphon *Ecce mitto angelum*
Mass – probably Mozart's 'Coronation' in C (K.317), possibly the other 'Coronation' Mass in C (K.337)
Offertory – probably the motet *Splendete te, Deus* (K.

ATTO PRIMO.

SCENA PRIMA.

Logge a viſta del Tevere negli appartamenti di VITELLIA.

VITELLIA, E SESTO.

VITELLIA.

MA che! Sempre l' isteſſo,
Seſto, a dir mi verrai? So che ſedotto
Fu Lentulo da te; che i ſuoi ſeguaci
Son pronti già, che il Campidoglio acceſo
Darà moto a un tumulto, e ſarà il ſegno,
Onde poſſiate uniti
K 2 Tito

ATTO II.

SCENA PRIMA.

Portici.

SESTO *ſolo col diſtintivo de' Congiurati ſul manto.*

OH Dei, che ſmania è queſta!
Che tumulto ho nel cor! Palpito, agghiaccio,
M'incammino, m'arreſto: ogn'aura, ogn'ombra
Mi fa tremare. Io non credea che foſſe
Sì difficile impreſa eſſer malvagio.
Ma compirla convien. Già per mio cenno
Lentulo corre al Campidoglio. Io deggio
Tito aſſalir. Nel precipizio orrendo
E' ſcor-

4

INTERLOCUTORI.

TITO VESPASIANO,	*Imperator di Roma.*
VITELLIA,	*Figlia dell' Imperator Vitellio.*
SERVILIA,	*Sorella di Seſto, amante d' Annio.*
SESTO,	*Amico di Tito, amante di Vitellia.*
ANNIO,	*Amico di Seſto, amante di Servilia.*
PUBLIO,	*Prefetto del Pretorio.*

La Scena è in Roma.

112 *ASSOCIATI.*

valiere di Camera di S. E. Reverendiſs. Monſig. Veſcovo di Padova.
Mainetti, Illuſt. Sig. Girolamo.
Malaguti, Illuſt. Sig. Ab. Dot. Franceſco
Manetti, Reverendiſs. Sig. D. Giuſeppe, Pievano alle Gambarare.
Mancorti, Illuſt. Sig. Camillo.
Manzini, Sig. Giovanni.
Maraſca, Rev. Sig. D. Giacomo.
* *Marini*, Rev. Sig. D. Anſelmo Bibliotecario dell' Eccellentiſs. Caſa Albani.
Marinucci, Illuſtriſs. Sig. Giovanni Franceſco, Chirurgo ſoſtituto nell'Arcioſpedale di S. Spirito.
Marſilj Illuſt. Sig. Pietro.
Martelli, Sig. Giovanni Luigi.
Martipelli, Illuſt. Sig. Dottore ...
Maſetti, Illuſt. Sig. Dottore Antonio.
Maſini, Signora Veronica.
* *de Matha*, Illuſt. Sig. March. Giovanna.
Mattei, Illuſt. Sig. Ab. Domenico Maria.
Mattei, Sig. Giacomo.
Mazzarini, Illuſt. Sig. Domenico Giampaolo, Luogotenente.
Mazzolà, Sig. Caterino, Poeta all'attual ſervizio di S. A. S. E. di Saſſonia.
Merli, Sig. Giovanni.
Migliori, Sig. Michele, Studente in S. Spirito di Roma.
Miotti, Reverendiſs. Sig. D. Bartolommeo, Parroco di Creſpignago.
Miſ-

FIGS. 5–8 *Four pages from Metastasio's libretto for* La clemenza di Tito. *This edition, by A. Zatta in Venice, is the one Mozart owned. Fig. 7 shows the* dramatis personae, *and fig. 8 a section of the list of subscribers to the edition, including the Dresden court poet Caterino Mazzolà, who condensed and adapted the lengthy libretto for Mozart.*

Anh. 121) *i.e.*, the arrangement of the first chorus *Schon weichet dir, Sonne* from *Thamos, King of Egypt* (K.345)

Te Deum[21]

As for the actual ceremony, the Archbishop of Prague bared the left shoulder of the Emperor and anointed it with holy oil; after the blessing, the oil was removed by rubbing it with bread and salt. The Emperor then received the crown of St Wenceslaus, which was placed on his head; he was given the sceptre and the golden apple of the Empire in his hand and a ceremonial sword was girded round his waist. Trumpets and kettledrums sounded when he took the solemn oath and cannon were fired.[22]

The performance of *Tito* took place that evening in the National (now known as the Tyl) Theatre. When the audience streamed into the theatre (entry was gratis that night, though front seats were reserved for distinguished foreigners), they were confronted with a simple libretto. The *Argomento* sums up the plot very briefly: how the Emperor Titus Vespasius was universally loved and called the Delight of Humanity. Nevertheless, two young patricians, one of them the Imperial favourite, conspire against him. The plot is discovered and the Senate condemns them both to death. 'But the most clement Caesar, content to warn them in paternal fashion, forgives them and all their accomplices in a general pardon . . .'[23] The libretto was obviously prepared before the exact cast was known, for none of the singers is listed, nor is there any mention, for some extraordinary reason, of either the poet Caterino Mazzolà or, for that matter, of Pietro Metastasio (most of the audience would have known the latter's primary participation, but few would have known of Mazzolà's role). 'The music is all new, composed by the famous Mr Wolfgang Amadeus Mozart, *Kapellmeister* presently in the service of His Imperial Majesty. The first three changes of scene are the invention of Sig. Pietro Travaglia, presently in the service of H[is] H[ighness] Prince Esterhazi [*sic*]. The fourth change of scene is by Mr Preisig of Coblenz. The costumes, all new and of rich and charming invention, by Sig. Cherubino Babbini of Mantua.'

It is not known how Pietro Travaglia, who had worked for years with Haydn in the theatre at Eszterháza, and was afterwards engaged in the Vienna Court Theatre, managed to secure this honourable appointment. We know practically nothing about Preisig or Babbini, except that the former was Johann Breysig (1766–1831).[24]

The most complete report of the event is in Zinzendorf's Diary:

> At 5 o'clock to the theatre in the Old Town, to the opera which is given by the Estates. I was put into a box in the first tier; there were Mr de Braun, his niece Melle Destary, Melle de Klebersberg and Mr Tourinette, Melle [Maréchal] Wallis and the Amb[assador] of Venice . . . The court did not arrive until after 7:30. They gave us the most boring opera *La clemenza di Tito*. Rotenhan was in the box of the Emperor . . . Marchetti sang quite well, the Emperor was enthusiastic about her. It was extremely difficult getting out of the theatre . . . Very fine day . . . [25]

There follow several contemporary reports:

> *Tagebuch der böhmischen Königskrönung* (Diary of the Bohemian Royal Coronation): In the evening was gratis opera, which His Majesty with His Most Serene family and the court attended in boxes prepared for Their High Selves, arriving after 8 o'clock. They were greeted with general expressions of joy and *vivat* calls along the whole route which Their High Selves passed on their way to the theatre.
>
> *Krönungsjournal für Prag* (Coronation Journal for Prague):

Festivities of the Noble Estates

On the 6th, Coronation Day, the Noble Estates, in order to glorify his Majesty on this day, gave an opera newly composed but on an Italian text by Metastasio, changed however by Mr Mazzola [*sic*], theatrical poet in Dresden. The composition is by the famous Mozart, and is an honour to him, although he had not much time for writing it, and moreover fell ill as he was in the process of finishing the last part.

On the performance the Noble Estates lavished everything; they had sent the entrepreneur to Italy in order to bring back a *prima donna* and a leading male singer. The entrance was gratis, and many tickets distributed. The house is capable of holding a large number of persons, but one can imagine that on such an occasion, the request for tickets was so great that finally there were none, so that some local citizens and foreigners, even members of the nobility, had to leave because there were no tickets for them.

His majesty appeared at 7:30 and was greeted with loud cries by the audience. Members of the Noble Estates themselves took in the tickets and saw that proper order was kept, so that no one with a ticket was refused and no one without a ticket could enter.

About the Plays

The court paid a visit to the National Theatre and saw a performance of the opera *Don Juan or the Dissolute Punished*, of which the text is by *da Ponte* and the music by Mozart. One must admit that the company of Mr Guardasoni performs this piece excellently, and that many of the individual singers especially excelled themselves . . .

Meanwhile the plays are not very full. Either the other amusements are the reason, or it is the high price of the tickets which drives the enthusiasts away. Neither the second performance of the opera given by the Noble Estates, nor the house in the Little Town [where Haydn's opera *Orlando Paladino* was being prepared by a German-Bohemian company in German translation] had many listeners.[26]

After the run of performances was over, Guardasoni petitioned the Bohemian Estates for various sums of money which he considered were owed to him.[27] One of his claims concerned the two new pieces of scenery which, as Count Rottenham notes in his comments on the document, were certainly prepared because the old scenery was 'too worn to be able to be used in the new opera'. Another claim was Guardasoni's attempt to be reimbursed for the box-office failure of the new opera. That would be only an act of grace, Rottenhan comments, because the whole matter had been settled in the contract. 'But it is generally known that on account of the many court festivities, the balls and the parties which were given in private houses, both theatrical companies [there was a second company giving spoken plays as well as Guardasoni's opera troupe] had very poor houses, and also at court there was a preconceived aversion to Mozart's composition, so that the opera after the first ceremonious performance was hardly attended any more; hence the whole speculation of the entrepreneur, that apart from the fee given by the Estates the succeeding box-office income would be considerable, proved to be totally mistaken.' (One of the commission's members thought that Guardasoni was right and ought to be given an *ex gratia* payment of 150 ducats. In this second protocol appeared the additional note that there had been 'a *strongly* preconceived aversion to Mozart's composition'. Guardasoni was actually given a recompense of 150 ducats, which made 675 Gulden.)

Count Hartmann, when weighing Guardasoni's petition to be recompensed for the poor box-office receipts, thought the impresario must have recouped his money because 'decorations and costumes did not correspond to the brilliance expected of such a festive occasion', and adds: 'I call to witness, as far as these matters are concerned, the general and in this regard wholly unanimous opinion of the public.'[28] Was there something slightly shoddy about the performance?

The most interesting report is again from Niemetschek, writing in 1794:

> *Tito* was given at the time of the coronation as a gratis opera, and then given several more times; but as fate willed it, a miserable castrato and a *prima donna* who sang more with her hands than in her throat, and whom one had to consider a lunatic, sang the principal parts; since the subject is too simple to be able to interest the mass of people busy with coronation festivities, balls and illuminations; and since it is – shame on our age – a serious opera, it pleased less in general than its really heavenly music deserved. There is a certain Grecian simplicity, a still sublimity, which strike a sensitive heart gently but none the less profoundly – which fit admirably to the character of *Titus*, the times and the entire subject, and also reflect honour on Mozart's delicate taste and his sense of characterization. The vocal parts, let it be said, are throughout, but especially in the andantes, of a heavenly sweetness, full of emotion and expression; the choruses are full of pomp and dignity; in short, Gluck's dignity is united to Mozart's original art, his flowing sense of emotion and his wholly magnificent harmonies. Unexcelled, and perhaps a *non plus ultra* of music, is the last trio and finale of the first act. Connoisseurs are in no doubt whether *Tito* does not in fact surpass *Don Giovanni*. This heavenly work of an immortal spirit [*i.e.*, *Don Giovanni*] was given to us on 3 December inst. [*i.e.*, 1794] by Mr Guardasoni, to a house full to overflowing and to the most complete approval of the public . . . [29]

In the Mozart literature, it has been repeatedly stated that Empress Maria Luisa described *La clemenza di Tito* as *una porcheria tedesca* (a German swinishness): there is no contemporary verification of this remark, but if it is true – and the circumstances mentioned above (see pp. 111 and 117) make it a distinct possibility – she has left her imprint on the work for all time. And the court's disapproval certainly manifested itself in the empty houses to which the opera played except, as we shall see, for the last performance, which took place on the same day (30 September) as the première of *The Magic Flute* in Vienna. (Mozart was informed of the reception of these later performances of *Tito* in Prague by Anton Stadler, who had stayed on to give a benefit concert on 16 October, at which Mozart's last completed instrumental piece, the Clarinet Concerto in A, K.622, was first performed.)

Thursday, 8 September 1791.

The Archduchess Maria Anna is installed as Abbess of the Royal Convent for Gentlewomen. There, in the Convent Church, Antonio Salieri and the court musicians were responsible for the musical part of the celebration, which included:

A short Mass – probably Mozart's in C (K.258), the wrongly titled 'Piccolomini' Mass, of which a score by the same Viennese copyist as that of K.337 exists in the archives of the Imperial Royal Chapel; this work is the shortest of the three Mozart masses performed at the 1791 coronation ceremonies

Offertory

Te Deum[30]

Friday, 9 September 1791.

In a book by Alfred Meissner entitled *Rococo–Bilder*, there is an interesting report of Mozart attending a Prague Masonic Lodge about this time. Meissner, whose grandfather August Gottlieb took over the Prague publishing house of Schönfeld, under which *impressum* the libretto of *La clemenza di Tito* was printed in 1791, is not a particularly reliable witness; but this is information which he may have had from his grandfather at second hand, and it is appended here with due scholarly reservations (Deutsch also accepts the report in his *Dokumente*):[31]

> [Mozart visited the Prague Lodge *Wahrheit und Einigkeit zu den drei gekrönten Säulen* (Truth and Unity at the Three Crowned Pillars) several times during his last visit to Prague in 1791.] When he attended the last time, the Brothers were standing in two rows and when he entered he was greeted with the cantata *Die Maurerfreude* [K.471] which he had composed in 1785 in honour of [Ignaz von] Born [the Master of Haydn's Lodge *Zur wahren Eintracht* in Vienna, who had entered the Craft in Prague and preserved friendly associations with the Prague Brethren]. Mozart was deeply touched by this attention and when he thanked them, he said that soon he would offer Freemasonry a better act of allegiance. By that he meant *The Magic Flute*, which was already ripening in his mind.

In the evening, 'at the highest request' – *i.e.*, by Leopold II and/or his entourage – the Sekonda Company again performed, in the National Theatre, *Der Herbsttag* and *Der weibliche Jakobiner Chlubb*.[32]

Saturday, 10 September 1791.
No one seems to have established the date of the second performance of *La clemenza di Tito*. Possibly it took place today, when no play is listed as being given in the National Theatre.

Sunday, 11 September 1791.
The identity of the mass performed at St Vitus' Cathedral is not known, but it is entirely likely that a mass by Mozart was given, considering the composer's presence in the city.

Monday, 12 September 1791.
Coronation of Maria Luisa as Queen of Bohemia in the Metropolitan Church of Prague (*i.e.*, St Vitus' Cathedral). Antonio Salieri and the Imperial Royal Chapel provided the appropriate music:

Antiphon *Ecce mitto angelum*
Mass – probably Mozart's other 'Coronation' Mass in C (K.337), possibly the first 'Coronation' Mass, also in C (K.317)
Offertory
Te Deum

In the National Theatre that evening another celebration took place in the form of a gala supper and ball. During the supper, Josepha Duschek sang a new cantata, *Huldigungskantate* (Allegiance cantata), by August Gottlieb Meissner, music by Leopold Koželuch, in the presence of Their Majesties.[33] About the ball we have an interesting notice in the *Pressburger Zeitung* No. 77 of 24 September:

> Prague, the 12th . . . in the evening was a gratis ball given by the Estates in a newly constructed building next to the National Theatre. Three orchestras in the new room and two in that which connects to the National Theatre were manned with some 300 musicians, and only the best of them were chosen.

It is certain that much of the music of this gala event was from Mozart's pen, including some of those minuets and German dances which the Prague public so dearly loved.

We have shown that it was Haydn's presence in England that set in motion a complicated chain of events which resulted in Mozart's composing *La clemenza di Tito*. We have also shown that many reports – including those describing the opera on 6 September – simply omitted Mozart's name, even though he was surely the composer best represented in the coronation festivities, with two operas, three masses, an offertory, a motet and probably many minuets and German dances. What must Haydn have thought, when he opened the *Morning Chronicle* in London on 21 November 1791, and read a report on the coronation festivities, where Koželuch's name is given twice, once as the composer of the cantata listed under 12 September and once as director of the large orchestral concert, but where Mozart and *La clemenza di Tito* are not even mentioned?[34] Haydn did not think much of Koželuch, and Beethoven had the perfect description for him: *miserabilis*![35]

Mozart's biographer Niemetschek now makes a personal appearance: he told Breitkopf & Härtel that it was during the coronation festivities that he became Mozart's friend. He wrote to the Leipzig firm in 1799: 'Leopold Koželuch . . . continually followed Mozart in Prague with the most petty jealousy. At coronation time he slandered him villainously and even attacked his moral character. Koželuch lost all his credit: *I got to know this small man and small composer* since he lived at a friend's and did not compose the cantata on Meißner's text within four weeks but with the sweat of his brow he patched it together and with a curse gave birth to – a changeling.'[36]

The cantata was a great success. It was repeated. Leopold Koželuch, *miserabilis*, became court composer in Vienna on 12 June 1792, at double Mozart's salary. He was expected to compose operas or oratorios; his was the kind of music the man in the street and the privy councillors really liked and understood.

X
The Magic Flute

The inception

It is significant that after Emperor Joseph II's death, Mozart received no further commissions to write operas for the Viennese Court, where Antonio Salieri was *Kapellmeister*. Mozart's isolation from the official court theatre was made even more apparent to him in the spring of 1791 when his collaborator in three Italian operas, Lorenzo da Ponte, having become involved in one scandal after another, was finally dismissed from his post as librettist by royal command. One of the greatest collaborations in operatic history was at an end. It is difficult to know whether Mozart and Da Ponte were intimate friends. It does not appear likely; but Da Ponte's dismissal must have been a great shock for Mozart. Whatever else Da Ponte was to the composer, the wily Italian had been Mozart's principal link with the official court opera and perhaps even a kind of buffer between him and Salieri.

Da Ponte, who was in deep trouble not only with Emperor Leopold II, but also with his consort, Empress Maria Luisa ('already not well disposed toward me'), now received an offer to go to St Petersburg, where his friend Martini (Martin y Soler) was resident composer; but Leopold refused at first to cancel Da Ponte's contract, which 'had still almost six months to run.' Thirty days later, however, around the beginning of March 1791, the Viennese court changed its mind. They paid for an unfinished libretto with which Da Ponte was occupied and also his back salary; but by then he had already written to St Petersburg

> that . . . I would not be able to go to [Russia] for many months. Suspecting that they had probably written to Italy already for another poet, I had a talk with Mozart and strove to persuade him to go with me to London. But a short time previous he had received a life pension [actually a normal contract which a succeeding sovereign could renew or cancel at will] from the Emperor Joseph in recognition of his divine operas; and he was then setting to music a German opera, *The Magic Flute*, from which he was hoping for new glories. He asked for six months' time to make up his mind, and I, meanwhile, fell victim to circumstances that forced me almost willy-nilly along wholly different paths.[1]

Shortly before, one of Mozart's old friends had returned from abroad and had taken over the directorship of the Theater auf der Wieden, known as the Freyhaustheater (because it stood in a complex of buildings known as the Freyhaus, or the Free House).[2] This friend was Emanuel Schikaneder, actor, impresario, writer of plays and operas and destined to replace Da Ponte as the first of the two new operatic collaborators with whom Mozart worked in 1791 (the other being Caterino Mazzolà). Schikaneder opened the theatre on 12 July 1789 with a German comic opera entitled *Der dumme Gärtner aus dem Gebirge, oder die zween Anton* (The Foolish Gardener from the Mountains, or The Two Antons); the text was by Schikaneder himself and the music by two members of his company, the tenor Benedikt Schack and the bass singer Franz Xaver Gerl (who was to be Mozart's Sarastro). The opera was an instant success and was performed thirty-two times in 1789. Its 'arias' became the rage of the town, especially one with the title *Ein Weib ist das herrlichste Ding auf der Welt* (A girl is the most marvellous thing in the world), which, as we have seen, Mozart used earlier in the year as the theme for a set of piano variations. The troupe which Schikaneder put together included some excellent singers, such as Mozart's sister-in-law, the brilliant coloratura soprano Josepha Hofer (Queen of the Night in *The Magic Flute*). The orchestra consisted of thirty-five players and included five first violins, four second violins, four violas, three cellos, three double basses, pairs of flutes, oboes, clarinets, bassoons, horns and trumpets, three trombones and a kettle-drummer.[3] This was a 'provincial' (*i.e.*, suburban) band, but much larger than usual. Even the court theatres in town hardly included trombones except for very special occasions, such as performances of *Don Giovanni*. Mozart's orchestra for the Frankfurt concert in 1790 had been substantially smaller in size (only five or six violins; see pp. 4–5).

How did *The Magic Flute* come into being? So many myths have been generated about this operatic collaboration that it is now very difficult to separate fact from fiction. The following account comes from Nissen's biography, which, as always, assumes Constanze's knowledge and collaboration.[4] Commenting on the list of works that Mozart wrote during the last four months of his life, Nissen

FIG. 9 *Josepha Hofer, later Mayer, Mozart's sister-in-law, the first Queen of the Night in* The Magic Flute. *Anonymous silhouette.*

notes that 'he was already sickly and made two trips'. (Apart from trips to Baden, however, Mozart undertook only one major trip in these four months, to Prague for the coronation opera.)

> Even when composing the first of these operas [*The Magic Flute*; the second was *La clemenza di Tito*] he, to whom, when genius gripped him, day and night were interchangeable, often exhausted himself so much that he fainted and was unconscious for minutes on end.
>
> He composed *The Magic Flute* for the theatre of Schikaneder, who was an old acquaintance, and at his request, to help him out of his straitened circumstances. The book is by Schikaneder himself, who in this fashion was dragged into immortality.
>
> Schikaneder was, in fact, partly through his own fault, partly through the lack of support from the public, in greatly reduced circumstances. Half desperate, he came to Mozart, explained the situation and concluded that only he could save him.
>
> *I? – How?*
>
> Write an opera for me, entirely in the taste of the present Viennese public; you can surely satisfy not only the connoisseurs but also your own reputation, but see to it that you cater primarily to the lowest common denominator of all classes. I will care for the text and see to the decorations, and so forth. Everything that they look for nowadays –
>
> *Good – I'll take it on!*
>
> What honorarium do you ask for?
>
> *You don't have anything! Well, let's arrange matters so that you are helped and yet I won't be deprived of every advantage. I shall give the score to you and you only; give me whatever you think right but on the condition that you promise not to let it be copied. If the opera is a success, I shall sell it to other theatres, and that shall be my payment.–*

The theatre director drew up the contract with delight and full of solemn promises. Mozart wrote diligently, and entirely according to the man's will. The opera was put on, the success was great, its reputation flew round the whole of Germany, and after some weeks it was given in several foreign theatres, without one of the scores having been received from Mozart! When Mozart heard of this person's deceit, all he said was: The rascal! – and all was forgotten. Mozart was not bothered by unthankfulness; it upset him hardly longer than a few minutes.

It is not certain from where (with or without Constanze's active participation) this rather curious description of the opera's beginnings was derived. Are we really to understand that Mozart took no fee (he can hardly have had time to sell the score abroad)? That Schikaneder paid him nothing for the score of *The Magic Flute*? With all brotherly love, it seems a very unlikely story. In the spring of 1791, Mozart was hardly in a position to take several months off to write a huge opera 'on speculation': I suggest that he took 200 ducats.

The trouble with this version, moreover, is that it too seems to be partly a myth. Schikaneder was certainly in no deep financial trouble by 1791; on the contrary, his new operas were great successes and he had, by March 1791, established a whole repertoire of German-language plays and *Singspiele* (plays with music) which took into account the Viennese delight in low comedy and local dialect as well. (Viennese dialect is almost as colourful as Cockney English and both have the same kind of wry humour). Of course, Mozart was delighted to try his hand at another German opera, for the phenomenal success of *The Abduction from the Seraglio* all over Germany was well known to him (he had even seen a performance when he was in Berlin in 1789).

The question of Mozart's share in the libretto of *The*

Magic Flute has been hotly disputed for nearly two hundred years, without any concrete evidence coming to light except for the relatively minor changes between the printed libretto of 1791 and Mozart's autograph manuscript. These are mere details and do not answer the principal question at all. Even more widely discussed have been the origins of the libretto and the supposed participation of hands other than Schikaneder's in it.[5] One of the principal sources has always been recognized: the opera *Oberon* by the Court *Kapellmeister* Paul Wranizky (or Wranitzky), which Schikaneder put on in 1789 and which was well known to Mozart (he attended the first performance and owned a printed textbook). A plagiarized version for Schikaneder was made by Mozart's fellow-Mason and member of the Freyhaus company, Karl Ludwig Gieseke, who later claimed that he had written a substantial part of *The Magic Flute*. Another contributing factor to the *Flute*'s libretto was the play *Thamos, King of Egypt* by Tobias Phillip von Gebler, a Freemason and a leading member of the Austrian government, for which Mozart had composed incidental music on an unprecedented scale (K.345). In this play, the principal theme is the victory of faithfulness despite all adversity; and the music, which the composer wrote partly in Vienna in 1773 and partly in Salzburg in 1775 and 1779, is full of hints of the future Mozart and especially the Mozart of *The Magic Flute*. Another source is the German playwright Christopher Martin Wieland's three-volume collection of fairy-tales entitled *Dschinnistan*, in the final volume of which (1789) was a story entitled *Lulu, oder die Zauberflöte* (Lulu or The Magic Flute), from which the new opera's title was taken.

The question of Gieseke's authorship, and also that of another, one Pater Cantes, a 'Co-operator' of the Paulines,[6] does not require further elucidation in view of the limited aspect of our investigations. The libretto was surely organized, and in large part actually written, by Schikaneder, for whom the part of Papageno was also conceived. Mozart obviously found the amazing diversity of the subject immensely attractive. In the final score, this ranges from the Haydnesque folk-tunes of the music for the 'simple' beings, Papageno and Papagena, to the mystical and ritualistic music for Sarastro and his court, and from the mad coloratura of the Queen of the Night (and the raging *Sturm und Drang* of the second aria, in D minor, *Der Hölle Rache* (The revenge of Hell), which recalls so many other Mozartian works in that key), to the inclusion of an antique-sounding north German Lutheran chorale tune, sung by the two men in armour. It was this same diversity that so impressed Beethoven[7] (who in any case disapproved of Da Ponte's texts for the Italian operas as being too frivolous) and which impresses us, too.

The message

When the first printed libretto of *The Magic Flute* appeared, to coincide with the première, readers who opened it saw an engraved frontispiece by the printer himself, Ignaz Alberti, a member of Mozart's Masonic Lodge *Zur gekrönten Hoffnung*. To the uninitiated this sheet would have looked like a then current reproduction of an archaeological excavation in Egypt: on the left, the bottom of a pyramid with symbols (including the Ibis); in the middle, a series of arches leading to a wall with niches and a round portal, all bathed in light. From the middle arch hangs a chain with a five-pointed star. To the right is an elaborate rococo vase with curious squatting figures on the base; in the foreground is a trowel, a pair of compasses, an hourglass and ruined fragments. Many people will have thought they were seeing some abstruse Oriental vision; some middle-class ladies and gentlemen no doubt thought of the cult of Isis and Osiris. But some of the audience knew that the symbolism referred in a whole series of unmistakable hints to the Ancient and Venerable Order of Free Masons. Those men – women's Lodges existed only in France – who still belonged to the Craft, tottering in 1791 and no longer the brilliant élite society of the mid-1780s which it had been in Vienna when Mozart and Haydn joined it, might well have wondered if their secrets were betrayed. And if, as people looking at a libretto for the first time often do, they turned idly to the last page (107), they could read, with considerable shock, the words

Heil sey euch Geweihten! Ihr drängt durch die Nacht!
Dank sey dir, Osiris und Isis, gebracht!
Es siegte die Stärke, und krönet zum Lohn
Die Schönheit und Weisheit mit ewiger Kron.
(Hail to you, sacred ones, who press through the night!
Thanks to you, Osiris and Isis, be proffered!
Strength has conquered and as reward
Presents the eternal crown to beauty and wisdom.)

In the St John Masonic ritual, towards the conclusion of the Lodge meeting, these very words (in the German version Mozart would have heard) occurred: 'Weisheit . . . Schönheit . . . Stärke'; they also form the central triangle of the Thirty-third Degree of the so-called Scottish Ritual of the Masons – what might be called a parallel or extension of the St John ceremony.

Having been uneasily prepared for something vaguely connected with the Masonic ritual, many Brothers in the audience of 1791 would have had even more of a shock when, in the middle of the Overture, they heard the music come to a stop and, after a pause, continue in very slow tempo (*Adagio*) with three-times-three chords in the following rhythm:

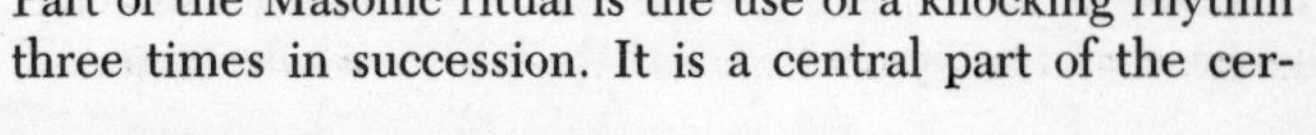

Part of the Masonic ritual is the use of a knocking rhythm three times in succession. It is a central part of the ceremony and appears many times – as indeed the motif does in *The Magic Flute*. My colleague Philippe A. Autexier, who is at present preparing a book on Mozart and *The Magic Flute*, was kind enough to inform me of some important research which he has conducted with regard to the 'knocks' in eighteenth-century Viennese lodges. It seems, according to M. Autexier, that the ritual used in Mozart's time contained characteristic rhythms for each degree:

– U – for the Entered Apprentice;
U – – for the Fellow Craft;
U U – for the Master Mason.

Hence the oft-repeated three-times-three chords refer to the second, or Fellow Craft, degree.

As the opera unfolded, Masons in the audience would have been stupefied: one symbol after the other derived from the Craft. The symbolic figure three dominates the entire work: there are three flats in the signature of the principal key (E flat major), three boys, three ladies. Tamino is clearly shown to be, initially, a 'profane' (*i.e.*, non-Mason), then a 'seeker' (note his conversation with the speaker, Act I, Scene 15: the speaker asks him: 'Wo willst du kühner Fremdling, hin? Was suchst du hier im Heiligthum?' – Where do you wish to go, bold stranger? What do you seek here in this holy place?), then a young Mason with the degree of Fellow Craft (with its ceremony of travelling and vow of silence), then the second degree, an entered apprentice (with its vow of fasting), and finally the third degree, Master Mason (Act II, Scene 21). The symbolic passage from darkness to light, an integral part of the St John ceremony, occurs with brilliant effect in *The Magic Flute* and is clearly indicated on the illustration in the 1791 libretto.

But Mozart and Schikaneder intended to show more than the Masonry of the St John ceremony; they also represented that of the higher degrees (the so-called 'Scots Degree'). In Scene 28 of Act II the curtain opens to reveal

1 *Plaster cast of Mozart by or after L. Posch, 1788–9.*

2 *The large Redoutensaal (court ballroom) in Vienna. Coloured engraving by Joseph Schütz,* c. *1800. Note the orchestra on the left-hand balcony.*

3 *The suburb of St Marx, Vienna, in the cemetery of which Mozart was buried in December 1791. Coloured engraving by Carl Schütz, 1792.*

4 Antonio Salieri, court Kapellmeister *and opera composer. Although Salieri was intensely jealous of Mozart, the theory that he poisoned him is untenable – despite Salieri's alleged deathbed confession.*

5 Johann Peter Salomon, the German-born violinist, portrayed by Thomas Hardy, 1791. Salomon's Viennese trip of 1790 was undertaken to engage Mozart, as well as Haydn, for London. Haydn was engaged, but the plan to import Mozart was thwarted by the younger composer's death the following year.

6 *Anonymous oil painting showing a meeting of a Viennese Lodge, c. 1790. It has now been demonstrated that the Master of Ceremonies* (CENTRE) *is Haydn's patron, Prince Nicolaus Esterházy. A document listing the Prince together with Mozart further confirms that the figure on the far right is Mozart.*

7 *Programme bill for the first performance of* The Magic Flute, *on 30 September 1791 at the Freyhaus Theatre in the Viennese suburb of Wieden.*

9 (OPPOSITE) *Frontispiece from the original libretto of* The Magic Flute, *printed by Mozart's Lodge brother, Ignaz Alberti, Vienna, 1791. The frontispiece, suppressed in later editions, is rich in Masonic symbols.*

8 (BELOW) *Frontispiece portrait of the impresario (and first Papageno) Emanuel Schikaneder and title-page showing the Freyhaus Theatre, from the* Almanach für Theaterfreunde, *1791.*

10 *Portrait of Constanze Mozart, painted* c. *1782 in Vienna by Joseph Lange, her brother-in-law.*

11 *Unfinished portrait of Mozart, also by Lange, dating from 1789–90; considered by Constanze to be the best likeness of her husband.*

two men in black armour and then Tamino and Pamina. This is the beginning of the famous fire and water trials and brings us into another Masonic world, that of the Sovereign Rose-Croix Degree, the eighteenth in the 'Ancient and Accepted Scottish Rite 33°'. The original libretto of 1791 rather discreetly notes that 'they [the armed men] read to him [Tamino] the transparent writing which is graven on a pyramid.' At the words 'fire, water, air and earth' the holy tetragammaton *JHVH* was presumably shown, the central part of this Sovereign Rose-Croix Degree. The Thirtieth Scene in Act II, where Monostatos, the blackamoor, together with the Queen of the Night and her retinue, attempt to storm and destroy Sarastro's temple, is symbolic of the 30° in the Scottish Rite, the 'Degree of Revenge', while the very end of the opera, Act II, Scene 33, when darkness (The Queen of the Night) has been vanquished and light (Sarastro, Tamino/Pamina, Papageno/Papagena) triumphs, is represented by the final degree (33°) of the Scottish rite – in the triangle of which the meaning is 'wisdom, beauty, strength' (*Weisheit, Schönheit, Stärke*) as in the libretto. The motto of 33° is *Ordo ab Chao*, order out of chaos, or darkness into light.[9]

In order to underline the musical part of this central Sovereign Cross scene with the armed men, Mozart chose a kind of chorale prelude using the ancient Lutheran melody of 1524 *Ach Gott, vom Himmel sieh' darein*[10] (he had written it down in a very different context as a contrapuntal study in his pupil Barbara Ployer's or some other person's MS book in 1784[11]). The solemnity of this part of the opera is thus remotely different from anything in the Austrian and Catholic experience. It is of a Biblical solemnity – and by Biblical I mean literally derived from the Bible. See Isaiah 43/2:

> When thou passest through the waters, I will be with thee; and through the rivers, they shall not overflow

thee; when thou walkest through the fire, thou shalt not be burned; neither shall the flame kindle upon thee.

In case the reader is beginning to look on all this numerology with scepticism, I might add that the orchestral introduction of this scene contains precisely eighteen groups of notes. Sarastro, the High Priest (*i.e.*, Worshipful Master in the Lodge), first appears in Act I, Scene 18. At the beginning of Act II, Sarastro and his Priests enter: there are (as the libretto of 1791 makes sure to mention) precisely eighteen priests and eighteen chairs, and the first section of the chorus they sing, *O Isis und Osiris*, is eighteen bars long. When Papageno asks the hideous old woman, who will turn out to be Papagena, how old she is, she answers 'eighteen' (whereupon the audience always laughs). And when the three boys appear suspended above the stage in a machine, it (notes the libretto of 1791) 'is covered with roses'. But leaving this almost hypnotic fascination with the 18° (Rose-Croix), we must remember that eighteen is made up of six times three – and three is indeed the crucial and basic symbolic number of the opera. (While the Scottish Rite has always been a rather élite organization, the more usual St John ritual is the one to which most of the Viennese Masons who attended the first performance of *The Magic Flute* would have belonged.)

In a booklet printed in London in 1725 entitled *The Grand Mystery of the Free Masons discovered*, we read in the 'Examination Upon Entrance into the Lodge':

Q. How many precious Jewels?
A. Three; a square Asher [Ashet? *i.e.*, dish or platter], a Diamond, and a Square.
Q. How many Lights?
A. Three; a Right East, South and West.
Q. What do they represent?
A. The Three Persons, Father, Son and Holy Ghost.
. . .
Q. How many steps belong to a right Mason?

A. Three.

. . .

Q. How many particular Points pertain to a Free-Mason?

A. Three: Fraternity, Fidelity, and Taciturnity.

Q. What do they represent?

A. Brotherly Love, Relief, and Truth, among all Right Masons; for which all Masons were ordain'd at the Building of the Tower of *Babel*, and at the Temple of *Jerusalem*.

In 1723, another print revealed

If a Master-Mason you would be,
Observe you well the *Rule of Three* . . .[12]

By the time our Mason in the Freyhaustheater auf der Wieden had finished listening to *The Magic Flute*, he realized that he had heard the first Masonic opera. Naturally, the exact ritual was not presented on stage, but there was enough of it, shown obliquely and heavily illustrated by numerology, for there to be no doubt of the work's Masonic content. But how was this possible? In the 1725 publication referred to above, we read:

Q. In the name of, &c., are you a Mason?
What is a Mason?

A. A Man begot of a Man, born of a Woman, Brother to a King.

Q. What is a Fellow?

A. A Companion of a Prince.

Q. How shall I know you are a Free Mason?

A. By Signs, Tokens, and Points of my Entry.

Q. Which is the Point of your Entry?

A. I Hear and Conceal, under the Penalty of having my Throat cut, or my Tongue pull'd out of my Head.

Now there must have been very urgent reasons for Mozart and Schikaneder to break this rule of silence. (The same formula, more or less, existed in the German-language St John Ritual.) And while on this subject, it was suggested long ago (and this suggestion has been put forward even more strongly by three German doctors in a book entitled *Mozarts Tod*, published in 1971, where they actually use the words 'ritual murder') that the Masons killed Mozart. There are, very simply, two facts which render this theory – which is considered very attractive in some quarters even today – not only unlikely but impossible. The first is that no one killed Schikaneder, who was just as responsible for 'betraying Masonic secrets' as Mozart. (Schikaneder had entered the Craft in Regensburg but had never joined a St John Lodge in Vienna.) For Schikaneder went on to live to what was then a ripe old age of 61 and died in 1812 (mad, it is true, but the Masons cannot have been responsible for that since they officially ceased to exist in 1795 and Schikaneder's death occurred seventeen years later). And the second reason is equally, if not more, convincing: Mozart's own Lodge *Zur gekrönten Hoffnung* held a Lodge of Sorrows for their composer, printed the main speech, and also printed the Masonic cantata (K.623), Mozart had composed just before he died.

No, there must have been another reason why Mozart and Schikaneder were permitted to choose an opera subject glorifying Masonry. It is a point which many scholars have either neglected or misunderstood, but one which can be solved by examining the Masonic files that were kept by Austrian police at this period. The fact of the matter is that Freemasonry in Austria was in acute danger of extinction – just how acute may be judged by the fact that the Masons voluntarily closed their Lodges in 1794, while in 1795 a young and new Emperor forbade all secret societies, including of course the Masons. The reason for this sudden danger in which the Masons found themselves was their supposed involvement with the French Revolution and Jacobinism, and with a similar movement in Austria which the secret police – rightly, as it turned out – suspected of existing.

This meddling in revolutionary ideas went further back than 1789, the beginning of the French Revolution: in the previous decade, most of the leading Americans who broke away from England and declared their independence had been Masons, including Franklin, Washington, Jefferson (who formulated the extremely Masonic-sounding *Declaration of Independence*), and so on. This fact was known not only to members of the Craft in Europe but also to the sovereigns and their police. In 1789, many of the leading members of those groups in favour of a republican government in France had been Masons. But in the event, the Craft collapsed during the Terror: the Grand Orient in Paris closed its doors in 1791, and by 1794 Freemasonry in France had practically ceased to exist. Many of the French Masons had wanted a republican kind of government, but in 1789 they certainly had no ideas of regicide in the back of their minds. On the contrary, many leading Masons were aristocrats and/or members of the royal government. Hence when one courageous Mason managed to reconstitute the Grand Orient in 1795, he found most of its members dead. A nineteenth-century historian of Freemasonry argues: 'If we consider that the members of Grand Orient had in great part consisted of personages attached in one way or another to the court of Louis XVI, we shall not be surprised to find that even on June 24, 1797, the number which assembled was only forty . . . The first new constitution was issued to a Geneva Lodge, June 17, 1796; and the report of June 24 only includes eighteen Lodges, of which three met at Paris.'[13]

In Vienna, when *The Magic Flute* was being staged, Leopold II was watching with increasing apprehension the events in France, and this same apprehension was growing to a fear, almost paranoid in its intensity, in the minds of the secret police and other members of the Austrian government. At the outset of his reign, Leopold II was by no means inimical to the Craft, and Count Zinzendorf actually heard that Leopold had been a member of the Sovereign Prince Rose-Croix in Italy[14] – a report which, of course, cannot be confirmed or denied. In any case, organizations like the *Illuminati*, the Strict Observance, the Asiatic Brethren, the St John Masons and even (if it is true he belonged to it) his former Rose-Croix all now seemed much more dangerous to the Emperor and his advisers.

Johann Anton, Count von Pergen, was President of the Lower Austrian government from 1782 to 1789 and Minister of Police from 1789 until he resigned from the position in March 1791. (In 1793 he was persuaded by the new Emperor, Francis II, to reassume the post.) In a memorandum dated 4 January 1791,[15] Pergen stated that the Freemasons in Austria and, more particularly, in France, had been instrumental in spreading revolutionary ideas.

> In every age there have been secret societies, whose members were banded together in brotherhoods and worked together in some common cause, and who drew a veil of deepest secrecy over their intentions as well as over the methods by which these intentions might be realized. But never was the mania to establish such secret and ambiguous societies greater than in our age; and one knows for certain that many of these secret societies, known under various names, are not – as they pretend – simply there for the purpose of sensible enlightenment and active philanthropy, but that their intention is none other than slowly to undermine the reputation and power of the monarchs, to excite the sense of freedom among the nations, to change the processes of thought among the people, and to guide them according to their principles by means of a secret ruling élite. The defection of the English colonies in America was the first operation of this secret ruling élite; from there it sought to spread out, and there can be no doubt that the overthrow of the French monarch is the work

of such a secret society. That it does not intend to rest satisfied with matters as they are, may be seen from the emissaries they sent out to all countries, and by the challenging missives they are able to circulate in other countries; the French Masonic Lodges especially seek to awaken similar sentiments in the breasts of their brothers in other countries. A passage in such a letter from a Bordeaux Lodge is remarkable, wherein it is stated that the wise principles of the new French constitution are in such close proximity to the basic Masonic precepts of freedom, equality, justice, tolerance, philosophy, charity and order – that actually every good French citizen in the future is worthy of being a Mason, because he is free . . .

There were numerous attempts to persuade Leopold II to reform the Craft – but not to abolish it. One suggested how 'the danger of the French system within the Freemason Lodges might be combatted' and wanted to create a citizen's *Bund* (federation) using three men from Pest (Budapest) under the name of 'Leopold Order'.[16] Its purpose was to educate the citizens to be proud of their status and to fight against the excessive power wielded by the nobility. A retired gubernatorial secretary by the name of Anton Feldhofer wrote a memorandum concerning Freemasonry on 15 August 1790, in which he stated flatly that 'the wheel of the present mistakes and revolutions in Europe is driven by the Brotherhood of Freemasons.'[17] Feldhofer wanted not to abolish but to reform the Craft. 'Not, then, to dissolve this society entirely but to set upon it limitations so that as far as possible it will be rendered innocuous to Your Majesty, the State and all its subjects.' Feldhofer thought that the 'Masonic Patent' which Joseph II had instituted in 1785 did not go far enough in its aim to bring the Masons under strict control.

In the face of such suspicion and hostility, how was Masonry to be protected? How were its greatness and universality to be presented to the general public? The two Masons, Mozart and Schikaneder, decided to write the first Masonic opera – *The Magic Flute*. Wisely, they treated the whole subject in two ways: with dignity, love and respect – as true Brothers – but also not without humour, with even a hint of malicious satire. It was always said that the figure of Sarastro was based on the great scientist, Ignaz von Born, Master of Haydn's Lodge *Zur wahren Eintracht*. But Born had his human failings, too – he was vain and hardly tolerated other views than his own (which were, admittedly, wise and far-reaching). When he took over the new Lodge, which was founded on 12 March 1781, he intended to make of it a kind of society of the sciences, and within a few years he turned it into the élite Lodge of Vienna, filling it with writers, scientists, Catholic and Protestant clerics, government officials – and Joseph Haydn, who joined in February 1785. This was about six months before Joseph II issued his famous and devastating decree on the Masons (11 December 1785), wherein he sought to centralize them and limit their powers. It was, in fact, as noted earlier, the beginning of the end of the great period of Masonry in Austria (and the beginning of the downfall of Born's Lodge and ultimately of Born as a leading Master-Mason; he resigned from the Craft in 1786, his Lodge having been disbanded on Christmas Eve 1785). Born lived until July 1791, just when Mozart entered his new opera in his thematic catalogue (except for the Overture and the March of the Priests, which were only completed before the first performance in September).[18]

Whether, as the romantic legend has it, Born was consulted about the details of the opera, and whether he even knew that Sarastro was to symbolize himself as the essence of tolerance, wisdom and justice, no one will ever be able to tell. But there are some details of Sarastro's character that are not wholly sympathetic and certainly not Masonic: he owns slaves; he describes his slave, the blackamoor Monostatos, as having a soul as black as his skin (racial discrimination, we would say nowadays); he condemns him to be beaten seventy-seven times on the soles of his feet. And to appoint Monostatos as Pamina's guardian, almost enabling him to rape her as she sleeps, is not exactly the act of a wise Master.

Mozart and Schikaneder did not overplay their hand. The basic tenets of Freemasonry are presented with great sympathy, and Mozart was clearly at his best in the scenes which glorify the Enlightenment (*In diesen heil'gen Hallen*, *O Isis und Osiris*, the March of the Priests, and especially the immense horizons of the final chorus, *Heil sey euch Geweihten!*). But Sarastro, like Born, is not a perfect man and there is no attempt to conceal the anti-feminist side of the Masons (an aspect which Leopold II, incidentally, also considered ridiculous). Masonry had its informers and traitors, especially after the Josephinian 'Patent' of 1785; Sarastro has Monostatos. But the audience in September 1791 went home with the feeling that the Masons were the embodiment of the Josephinian Enlightenment – and besides, much of the opera was genuine good fun. There was something in it for everybody; connoisseur and shopkeeper left deeply satisfied. The Masons might have hoped that the Craft had been, perhaps, even saved from downfall. But this was not to be; by 1794 Masonry in Austria ceased to exist.

The great Mozart scholar, Otto Erich Deutsch, wrote in 1937 about *The Magic Flute*'s libretto, warning us not to judge it exclusively as a Masonic opera.

> More mysterious than the actual connections with Freemasonry is the real history of the work's origin, which has a clearly felt hiatus [between the carefree first section and the solemn second Act], probably the result of external circumstances, such as the rivalry of the Leopoldstadt Theatre; but despite everything, the libretto is also a masterpiece, having its desired effect on young and old,

on rich and poor, then as now and surely for all ages. Even the ungainliness of some of Schikaneder's verses has not stopped some of them from becoming part of the language.[19]

The première

The Freyhaus (in modern German with 'i' instead of 'y', Freihaus) was a large plot of land, once situated on an island in the middle of the river Wien. In Egon Komorzynski's classic description, by the time Mozart was frequenting the theatre (and the inn which was in one of the courtyards near the theatre) the Freihaus

> consisted of a monstrous complex of houses connected to each other with six large courtyards, thirty-two stairways and 325 apartments; it had its own church, dedicated to Saint Rosalia, workshops for almost every kind of handicraft, an oil press belonging to the Marsano family, an apothecary and a mill, the wheel of which was driven by a stream diverted from the river Wien. It was called 'Freihaus' because – thanks to the owners – it was freed of all taxes. In the great courtyard there was a garden with allées, flowerbeds and a wooden pavilion: that was where Schikaneder's people gathered after the rehearsals and after performances, making a great racket well into the night, under the leadership of the jovial director, who called the actors and actresses 'his children' and who presided with good humour. The one, lengthwise side of the courtyard was taken up by the theatre, an impressive building of stone with a tile roof, which Schikaneder enlarged and raised. It accommodated 1000 people, was thirty metres long and fifteen metres wide, the stage was twelve metres deep and was equipped with all the necessary requisites – safety, comfort and

stage machinery; it had a double row of boxes, an orchestra [*parterre*] of two parts and, in Mozart's time, two galleries (Schikaneder later added a third).

Since, in this enormous place, there was no lack of apartments, the director and most of the members of the company lived in the Freihaus . . .[20]

Haydn's mistress, Luigia Polzelli, lived there (in apartment no. 161) during this period when Haydn was in England, but she left for Italy about August 1791.[21] (Some of the Freyhaus survived until the 1950s, when sadly, the last part of this historic building gave way to the bulldozers.)

The wooden pavilion referred to above is now in the garden of the Mozarteum in Salzburg, while the furniture is in the family castle of the Counts (later Princes) von Starhemberg, the owners of the land on which the Freyhaus stood, in Eferding in Upper Austria. Mozart is supposed to have written parts of *The Magic Flute* in this little pavilion, and also to have used it for rehearsal purposes (a more likely operation if one imagines a clavichord, or spinet, as the small instrument used to accompany the singers).

The poet Ignaz Franz Castelli, who grew up in the Viennese district of Mariahilf, used to attend the theatre in its final days. He was there for the first time in 1798 and paid 7 Kreuzer. He described the theatre as a large, rectangular building of box-like structure. The interior was simply decorated; on the side of the door where one entered was the stage, in front of which were two life-size statues, on the right a knight with a poniard, on the left a half-nude woman. Tickets in the pit cost 17 Kreuzer and in the top gallery a 7 Kreuzer coin.

In order to secure a cheap seat, Castelli had to arrive there at three in the afternoon.

After the theatre opened . . . I had to sit for three hours, bathed in heat and sweat and impregnated by the gar-

> licky fumes of the smoked meats being consumed . . . Finally the lamps were dimmed and my sun started to rise. The musicians came into the pit one by one, those lucky ones, who can sit there every day . . .[22]

Castelli once played an ape in *The Magic Flute*.

Schikaneder came by the theatre in the following way. It had been rebuilt and re-opened in 1786 under the direction of Christian Rohrbach, principal of a group of strolling players. Two years later it was taken over by Johann Friedl, and with success; but he soon died and in his will he left the direction of the theatre to his residuary legatee, the 25-year-old Madame Schikaneder, who at once called for her husband, who was then in Regensburg (Ratisbon), to come and help her set up the theatre. Schikaneder received the official privilege to do so from Emperor Joseph II and soon began to win a large and faithful public with his 'machine comedies' (in which ingenious stage machines performed acts of prestidigitation, sometimes with actors and actresses), fairy tales and magic operas – all in German or Viennese dialect.

Schikaneder was a full-blooded man of the theatre, but he was also a clever impresario and careful not to hoodwink his public. In the preface to his libretto *Der Spiegel von Arkadien* (The Mirror of Arcadia), Vienna 1795 (first performance at the Theater auf der Wieden, 14 November 1794, music by Süssmayr), he had this to say:

> I write to amuse the public and do not wish to appear learned. I am an actor – a director – and work for the box-office: but not to cheat the public of its money, because the intelligent man only lets himself be cheated once.

Mozart returned to Vienna shortly after 15 September 1791, less than two weeks before the final rehearsals of *The Magic Flute*. On 28 September he entered into his catalogue the two last pieces to be composed, the March of the Priests and the Overture;[23] the first performance took place at the Freyhaustheater only two days later.

The playbill,[24] which has by some miracle survived, reads as follows:

Imperial Royal Priv. Wieden Theatre
Today, Friday, the 30th September 1791.
The Actors and Actresses of the Imp. Roy. Priv. Theatre
on the Wieden have the honour to perform
for the first time
THE
MAGIC FLUTE
A Grand Opera in Two Acts by Emanuel Schikaneder

Persons

Sarastro		Hr. Gerl.
Tamino		Hr. Schack.
Speaker		Hr. Winter.
First		Hr. Schikaneder, Senior.
Second	Priest	Hr. Kistler.
Third		Hr. Moll.
Queen of the Night		Mad. Hofer.
Pramina [*sic*]		Mlle. Gottlieb.
First		Mlle. Klöpfler
Second	Lady	Mlle. Hofman.
Third		Mad. Schack.
Papageno		Hr. Schikaneder, Junior.
An old Woman [= Papagena]		Mad. Gerl.
Monostatos, a Blackamoor		Hr. Nouseul.
First		Hr. Gieseke.
Second	Slave	Hr. Frasel.
Third		Hr. Starke.

Priests, Slaves, Followers.

The Music is by Herr Wolfgang Amade Mozart, Kapellmeister, and present Imp. Roy. Chamber Composer. Herr Mozard [*sic*] will, out of respect for a gracious and respected public, and out of friendship for the writer of the piece, himself conduct the orchestra today.

The word-books of the opera, which include two engravings, where Herr Schikaneder has been engraved in the role of Papageno with the actual costume, will be sold at the box office for 30 kr.

Herr Gayl, theatrical designer, and Herr Nesslthaler as decorator, flatter themselves to have worked with all possible artistic diligence according to the preconceived plan of the piece.

The entrance prices are as usual.
The beginning is at 7 o'clock

In the order in which they appear on the plan, the singers (and players) who took part in this historic event were; Franz Xaver Gerl (bass); Benedikt Schack (tenor), a good friend of Mozart's; Winter (the Speaker) was an apprentice. The First Priest was played by Schikaneder's elder brother, Urban; Johann Michael Kistler was the Second Priest (tenor) and a bass singer Moll the Third. Josepha Hofer, Constanze Mozart's sister, was Queen of the Night. Anna Gottlieb had sung Barbarina in *Le nozze di Figaro* at the first performance in 1786 (Burgtheater, Vienna); she was then a child of twelve and was now seventeen. It is reported that she was Mozart's pupil, that she was in love with him, and that she retired from the stage after *The Magic Flute*, none of which is supported by any contemporary sources. The first Three Ladies were sung by a soubrette (Miss Klöpfler), a Miss Hofman (who otherwise interpreted 'young ladies in love') and Benedikt Schack's wife, née Weinhold. Schikaneder was, of course, Papageno. The old woman was played by Gerl's wife Barbara, née Reisinger. Johann Joseph Nouseul, an actor – they could all sing a little in those days and were engaged to do both

– had been with the Burgtheater. The First Slave was the notorious Karl Ludwig Gieseke (whose real name was Metzler), who later went to Dublin as Professor of Mineralogy and stated that he wrote large parts of the libretto. Second Slave was Wilhelm Frasel and the Third was a *super* or 'extra' named Starke. The three Boys are not named. The painter was Joseph Gayl and O. E. Deutsch has identified the decorator as the uncle of the painter Andreas Nesslthaler, who had lived in Salzburg since 1789.

Mozart evidently conducted from the fortepiano. As to the public's reaction, the reports we have seem to stem mainly from the nineteenth century. Most of them are unverifiable, and those that can be verified can be proved to be inventions. (The young composer Johann Schenk is said to have secured a seat in the orchestra pit at the last moment and after the dead silence that followed the Overture crawled up to the rostrum and kissed Mozart's hand. This delightful fairy-tale is supposed to be from Schenk's manuscript autobiography in Göttweig Abbey; but no such tale exists in it at all.)[25]

After returning from Prague, Constanze stayed in Vienna until the première of *The Magic Flute*, but in the first week of October she returned to Baden to continue her cure. At the end of the first week of October, on the 7th and 8th, Mozart wrote to his wife:

> Friday, 10:30 p.m. [7 October]
>
> Dearest, best little wife! –
>
> I have just come from the opera; – it was just as full as usual. – The duetto 'Mann und Weib etc.' and the Glockenspiel in the 1st Act were repeated as usual – also in the 2nd Act the trio with the boys – but what pleases me the most is the *silent applause* – one can readily see how much this opera continues to grow. Now my biography: – right after you sailed off I played 2 games of billiards with Hr. von Mozart (who wrote the opera

at Schikaneder's). – Then I sold my nag [the riding-horse] for 14 ducats. – then I had Joseph the First [his manservant] bring a black coffee, and enjoyed a marvellous pipe of tobacco; then I orchestrated almost the whole Rondò [of the Clarinet Concerto in A (K.622)] for Stadler, in the meantime there arrived a letter from Stadler in Prague: – all in the Dusseks [*sic*] are fine; – it seems she [Josepha Duschek] hasn't received any letter from you – and yet I can hardly believe it! – enough – they all know about the magnificent reception of my German opera. –

The most curious thing is, that on the evening when my new opera was being received with so much success for the first time, on the same evening in Prague *Tito* was being given the last time, also with extraordinary success . . . He also writes (*Stodla* ['Stadler' in a Bohemian–German accent]) that [words later crossed out by Nissen; probably 'I must admit that I realize now that I was wrong and that'] it's true that [Süssmayr] is an ass, well we know that – Stodla is only a bit of an ass, not much; – but that [Süssmayr] – well, yes, he's a real ass.

At 5:30 I went out to the Stubenthor and took my favourite walk along the Glacis to the theatre [Theater auf der Wieden] – what do I see? – what do I smell? Don Primus [the servant] with the Carbonadeln [pork cutlets] – che gusto! – I eat to your health – it's just striking 11 o'clock; – perhaps you're asleep already? – St! St! St! – I don't want to wake you! –

Saturday the 8th! – You should have seen me yesterday at dinner! – I couldn't find the old dinner service, so I took the white one with the snowdrops and used my candlestick with the two arms . . . You'll be having a good swim just as I write these lines. – The hairdresser came promptly at 6 o'clock – and Primus came to light the fire at 5:30 and to wake me at 5:45. – Why does it have to rain just now? – I had hoped you would have nice weather! – Keep yourself well bundled up so you don't catch a cold; I hope the baths will give you a good winter – for it was only the wish to keep you healthy that made me send you to Baaden [*sic*] – It's already too long that you've been away, but I saw all that coming. – If I had nothing to do, I would have gone along with you for the 8 days; – but out *there* I don't have any *decent place* to work; – and I want to avoid, as much as possible, all the *difficulties*; there's nothing more pleasant than being able to live nicely and quietly, therefore I have to work hard and I do it gladly. - . . .

You can box . . . [name erased: probably 'Süssmayr']'s ears several times from me, and I send [name erased: probably Constanze's sister Sophie] 1000 kisses, and she can give him a few, too – for God's sake don't let him lack for anything! –

[There follow some more rude suggestions what to do with Süssmayr.] . . . adieu, dear little wife! – the [mail] coach wants to leave. – I hope to read something from your hand, and in that sweet hope I kiss you 1000 times and am always your

Loving Husband
W. A. Mozart

Later the same day Wolfgang reports to Constanze again about *The Magic Flute*:

With the greatest pleasure and delight I found your letter when I returned from the opera; – the opera, although Saturday is always a bad day because it's mail day, was given to a very full house with the usual applause and encores; – they will give it tomorrow, but not on Monday – therefore Siessmayer [*sic*: Mozart is writing the name as it would sound in Viennese dialect] should bring [Anton] Stoll here on *Tuesday* [to see *The Magic Flute*.].

. . . Right after lunch I went home again and wrote until it was time to go to the opera. [The horn-player]

> Leitgeb [Leutgeb] asked me to take him again, and I did so, too. – Tomorrow I shall take Mama [Mozart's mother-in-law]; – Hofer has already given her the libretto to read. – In Mama's case it will mean that she *sees* the opera, but doesn't *hear* the opera. [The following names were rendered illegible by Nissen] . . . had a box today. – . . . were ready to applaud *everything* heartily, but he, the all-knowing, behaved so much the *Bavarian* that I couldn't stay or I would have had to call him an ass; – unfortunately I was just in his box when the 2nd Act began, thus with the solemn scene. – He laughed at everything; at the beginning I summoned up enough patience to draw his attention to some speeches, but – he laughed at everything; – that was too much for me – I called him *Papageno*, and left – but I think the idiot didn't understand. – I went into another box, where *Flamm* [Franz Karl Flamm, employed in the Vienna Magistracy and a good amateur musician] and his wife were; I was very pleased and stayed there right to the end. – Only I went behind the stage for Papageno's aria with the Glockenspiel, because I had an urge today to play it myself. – I then made a joke, and when Schikaneder had a speech, I played an arpeggio – he jumped – looked behind the scenery and saw me – when it happened the 2nd time – I didn't play – now he stopped and didn't want to go on – I read his thoughts and played a chord again – then he struck his Glockenspiel and said, '*Shut up*' – whereupon everybody laughed – as a result of the joke, many people I think realized for the first time that he didn't play the instrument himself. – By the way, you can't imagine how charming the music sounds in a box near the orchestra – much better than in the gallery; – as soon as you get back you must try it. –

On Friday, 14 October, Mozart again wrote about the opera:

Dearest, best little wife,

Yesterday, Thursday the 13th, Hofer went out with me to see Carl [Mozart's seven-year-old son, boarding in the country outside Vienna at Perchtoldsdorf], we ate out there and then drove in, at 6 o'clock I fetched Salieri and [his mistress, the singer Caterina] Cavalieri with the carriage, and then I took them to the box – then I hastened to fetch Mama and Carl, whom I had meanwhile left at the Hofers. You can't believe how nice both of them [Salieri and Cavalieri] were, – how much they liked not only my music but the book and everything together. – They both said it was a grand opera, – worthy of being performed at the greatest festival for the greatest monarchs, – and they will certainly see it often, for they have never seen a more beautiful or pleasant production. – He listened and looked with the greatest attention and from the Overture to the last chorus there wasn't a piece which didn't call forth a 'bravo' or 'bello' from him, and they couldn't thank me enough for this courtesy. They had intended to go to the opera yesterday, but they would have had to seek their places by 4 o'clock – this way they could hear and see it in peace and quiet. – After the theatre I had them taken home, and then had supper at Hofer's with Carl. – Then I drove home with him and we both slept exceedingly well. I did Carl no small favour by fetching him to hear the opera. – He looks wonderful – as far as his health is concerned, he could not have found a better place, but the rest is alas terrible! – They [the country-folk with whom Carl was boarding] are probably capable of raising up a good farmer! – but enough. Because his big studies don't start until Monday (God help him!), I asked them to let me have Carl until Sunday after lunch; I said that you would like to see him. – Tomorrow Sunday [Saturday, unless there was a day's interruption in the letter which was started on a Friday] I shall come out to you with him –

you can keep him or I shall drive him back to Hecker [Wenzel Bernhard Heeger in Perchtoldsdorf]; – think it over, on account of one month he can't really be ruined, I think! – meanwhile that business with the Piarists [the religious order with which Mozart was trying to place Carl] can come to pass, which we are really working hard at. – Otherwise he's not any worse, but certainly not a whit better, than he always was. He still has the same uniform, he's as vexing as ever, and *studies even less* willingly than before, he does nothing but spend 5 hours in the morning walking round the garden and after lunch another 5 hours, as he himself admitted to me, in a word the children don't do anything except eat, drink, sleep and walk. . . . Yesterday the trip to Bernstorf [Mozart means Perchtoldsdorf, which the local population calls 'Petersdorf'] robbed me of a whole day, that's why I couldn't write – but that you haven't written for 2 days is unforgivable, but today I surely expect news from you, and to speak to you myself tomorrow and to kiss you from the heart.

Farewell, always your

14 Oct. 791. Mozart[26]. . . .

This is the last letter by Mozart to have survived. It shows him – as usual – working desperately hard, first on the Clarinet Concerto, which was written not for the clarinet but for a basset-horn-like instrument in A with an extended downward compass – the original version has not survived – and was first performed by Anton Stadler (for whom it was composed) at his benefit concert in the Prague Theatre on 16 October 1791.[27] After the Concerto was finished and dispatched to Bohemia, he was working on the Requiem. It must be stressed that, although chronically overworked, Mozart writes in his usual, normally affectionate way to Constanze; he appears to be serene, confident and deeply satisfied with the reception of *The Magic Flute*. It is interesting to observe in these letters that he took special pains to quote Salieri's praise of the libretto (hence implying Mozart's tacit approval as well); and that one person missed the serious, Masonic implications. Did Mozart try to explain, perhaps to a 'profane' listener, the content and message of Act II? ('I summoned up enough patience to draw his attention to some speeches . . .') And in all these letters, Mozart gives the impression of a young man, full of fun and gaiety, in the prime of his life, joking with Schikaneder from the wings of the theatre and happily married to a wife who evidently returned his affection with interest.

In view of the current myths concerning Salieri, it is refreshing to read Mozart's careful description of the Italian *maestro*'s praise – which no doubt occurred exactly as reported. Salieri may have been as jealous of Mozart as before – he would have been superhuman not to be a little jealous of such overwhelming genius – but both men were being very careful to observe the amenities; and it was courteous of Mozart to fetch Salieri and the bewitching Cavalieri in a carriage.

Some three weeks later, on 6 November, Count Carl von Zinzendorf went to see the new production. He wrote:

> At 6:30 to the Starhemberg Theatre in the suburb of Wieden in the box of M. and Mme Auersperg to hear the 24th performance of *The Magic Flute*. The music and the decorations are pretty, the rest an unbelievable farce. A huge crowd. M. de Seilern and de Kinsky in our box . . .[28]

There can be no doubt that *The Magic Flute* was already the greatest operatic success of Mozart's life. It should have been the beginning of a new era for its composer; and yet the new era was to be over exactly one month after Zinzendorf attended the twenty-fourth performance.

That last month witnessed what is surely the greatest tragedy in the history of music.

XI
The Final Illness

We join Mozart in the Rauhensteingasse, living as 'grass-widower'. His letters to Constanze during October, when she was in Baden, do not show someone possessed with the idea of death or in a state of total exhaustion. On the contrary, we see a man who, though working too hard and too concentratedly, gives every appearance of normality. If we read, on the other hand, a report of this period by Rochlitz in the *Allgemeine Musikalische Zeitung* of 19 December 1798, Mozart is seen to have returned from Prague already exhausted.

> Now, surfeited by the magnificence and extravagance [of the Prague coronation], as if famished, he began to take up the continuation of the interrupted work on his *Requiem*. The period of four weeks which he himself had set for its completion had now passed, and hardly was he back when the strange man appeared again.
>
> 'I could not keep to my word,' said Mozart.
>
> 'I know that,' was the answer. 'You were right not to force yourself. How long will you require now?'
>
> 'Another four weeks – the work has become more and more interesting to me; I am expanding it more than I at first wished to do.'
>
> 'Good – but you must be paid more, too. Here are another hundred ducats.'
>
> 'Sir – who has sent you?'
>
> 'The man wishes to remain anonymous.'

'Who are you?'

'That is even less to the point – in four weeks I shall come back to you.'

And with that he left. He was put under surveillance, to see where he went, but either those who were sent after him were too careless, or they were cleverly given the slip – in short, they learned nothing. Now Mozart was fully persuaded (I must actually admit this) that the man with the noble aspect was a quite extraordinary person, most closely associated with the Other World, or even sent by It, to announce his [Mozart's] end. Thus he decided, even more seriously, to create a worthy monument to his name. He worked further under these impressions, and it is therefore no surprise that such a perfect work came into being. During this work he often sank into complete exhaustion and fainted. He was even ready before the end of the four weeks, but also – dead.[1]

There are several points that need to be made about this long and interesting report (which was, after all, written only seven years after the event). The first is that it conflates the chronology of the whole Requiem affair. But there is no reason to doubt that the messenger did appear again after Mozart's return from Prague and that Mozart was given a second instalment of money. Almost all the sources mention that fact, though the total sum can hardly have amounted to 200 ducats, the honorarium for a coronation opera. (An account of 1792, quoted on p. 169 below, gives as the figure twice 30 ducats, i.e. a total of 60. When the whole affair became public and Count Walsegg contacted Constanze, he said he had paid the composer 50 ducats.) Constanze collected 100 ducats (450 Gulden) from the Prussian Ambassador for a copy of the Requiem in 1792; as we shall see, she was very interested in maintaining the myth that the Requiem had been finished before Mozart died.

There is no doubt that even after his return from Prague,

it was not the Requiem but the Clarinet Concerto for Stadler that first required Mozart's urgent attention. And even the Concerto could not be attacked until *The Magic Flute* was completed. But now the stage was set for the Requiem.

If my calculation is correct, the entire period in which Mozart composed the Requiem, or what survives of it (some sketches must be lost), spanned only 8 October to 20 November (when he took to his bed); and we must, moreover, subtract the time required for composing and writing down the *Kleine Freymaurer-Kantate* (K.623), which, after all, consists of thirty-six pages in Mozart's autograph. If we allow four or five days for the Cantata (he composed the much longer 'Linz' Symphony (K.425) in five in 1783,[2] but he was writing much more slowly in November 1791) and two days for fetching Constanze from Baden on 16 October and settling down again in the Vienna apartment, there remains little more than a month in which the bulk of the Requiem was written down. It must be reiterated that *only* the Requiem aeternam (Introitus) was fully scored by Mozart: all the other pieces, from the Kyrie fugue to the end of the Hostias, were sketched in Mozart's customary *particella*. The missing instrumentation of the Kyrie (largely doubling) was added by a local *Kapellmeister* and composer named F. J. Freystädtler, except for the trumpet and kettledrum parts, which are clearly in Süssmayr's hand.[3] Mozart composed in *particella* form a total of 99 sheets, an astounding, almost incredible, amount of music to have been composed, even in sketch form, in little over a month. Mozart did not compose the Requiem in its liturgical order, hence the Lachrymosa – which comes before the Offertory – was left incomplete with only eight bars sketched: presumably this is the last music Mozart composed.

There are two distinct types of paper (with corresponding water-marks) in the Requiem's autograph,[4] which is in the Austrian National Library, Vienna:

Type I. Introitus (Requiem aeternam)

Kyrie up to bar 45.
Sequence: Dies irae to bar 10 of Recordare

Type II. Rest of Kyrie (bars 46ff., sheet 9)

Rest of Sequence (Recordare, bars 11 ff., Confutatis)
Fragment of Lachrymosa (8 bars)
Offertory: Hostia, at the end of which were the last words Mozart wrote: 'Quam olim da capo' [*i.e.*, repeat music of 'Quam olim Abrahae' from the previous movement], which were torn out of the autograph by a thief in 1958.[5]

Previous writers have tried to relate these paper types to the following schedule: Mozart begins the Requiem upon receiving the commission in July. He uses paper type I. Then he is obliged to go to Prague, and upon his return begins the Requiem again, having meanwhile run out of type I. He then turns to paper type II. But this division, although it appears entirely plausible, presupposes that Mozart dropped work on *The Magic Flute* as soon as the 'messenger' appeared, and wrote a substantial part of the Requiem in *particella* (the instrumentation of the Requiem aeternam was added by the composer later, in a different ink and possibly with a different quill). But this is surely mere speculation. The use of different papers could also be explained simply by the fact that Mozart exhausted his supply of type I as he was composing; or it might be that Constanze purchased type II when her husband was ill (which would explain why there is much less music included on type II – Mozart was already getting weak).

This is the background, from the point of view of the music he was working on, of this last period of Mozart's life; and we must bear it in mind when reconstructing the biographical part. Given the gravity of the subject and the frequently wrong interpretations of the sources (and even their actual falsification), the best course is to examine all the authentic documents. These are more numerous than some imagine and only by studying them shall we ever come close to the truth of this heart-rending tale.

The first account, chronologically speaking, is Niemetschek's biography of the composer (1798), dedicated to Haydn and prepared with the active collaboration of Constanze; that it was based on her oral evidence can be seen in the fact that it was repeated, partly verbatim, in Nissen's biography. Niemetschek tells us that he wrote it 'as he has often heard it from the lips of Mozart's widow . . .' Rather than reproduce both Niemetschek's and Nissen's versions, which are almost identical, I have chosen Nissen's, which may be regarded as the more authoritative (being the work of Constanze's second husband):

> After Mozart's return from Prague, he began at once to work on the *Requiem* and travailed with exceptional diligence and lively interest; but his illness continued and depressed him. With deep sorrow his wife saw his health gradually deteriorating. When, on a fine autumn day [27 or 28 October],[6] she drove with him to the Prater to distract him, and the two were sitting alone, Mozart began to speak of death; he maintained that he was writing the *Requiem* for himself. As he said this, the tears came to his eyes, and when she attempted to talk him out of those black thoughts, he answered: 'No, no, I feel it too strongly, I won't last much longer: surely I have been poisoned! I can't free myself of these thoughts.'
>
> This talk fell with dread on his wife's heart; she was hardly able to console him and to show that his melancholy imagination was unfounded. She was of the opinion that his illness was worsening and that the work on the *Requiem* was too exhausting for him; she consulted a doctor and took the *Requiem* away from him.

And really his condition improved somewhat, and during this period he was able, on 15 November 1791, to complete a little Cantata [*Eine kleine Freymaurer-Kantate* (K.623)],[7] which had been ordered by a society for a festivity [the opening of new quarters]. The good performance and the great applause with which it was received lent new strength to his spirit. He became more cheerful now and kept asking for his *Requiem*, to continue and complete it. His wife now saw no reason not to give him his score again. But this hopeful condition was of short duration; in a few days he sank into his previous depression, he became fainter and weaker, until he was obliged to take to his bed, from which, alas, he never rose again . . .

Mozart remained fully conscious during his illness, right to the end; he died peacefully, but very reluctantly. Anyone will understand this if one considers that, upon his return from Prague, Mozart received the confirmation of his engagement as *Kapellmeister* of St Stephen's Cathedral with all the emoluments which from time immemorial were associated with the position, and at the same time, apart from works ordered for the Vienna [Schikaneder?] and Prague [Guardasoni?] theatres, he had received impressive offers from Hungary and Amsterdam for regular deliveries [of compositions]: so that he had the happy expectation of a future entirely freed from the necessities of earning his living.

All too late! He already felt his strength ebbing. And this had entirely natural causes, without the need for thinking (as he did) that he was being poisoned. He was a fruit that ripened early, which lasted only for a short while. At the delicate age when nature is still bringing forth and collecting the essence of life, he hindered the process not only by his sedentary way of life but also consumed without pause that very essence of life by continually composing. This appetite for composition also hastened his death, to which his celebrity lent only too much occasion. How was it possible for a frame by nature weak and ruined by illness to survive the exhaustion of the last four months? And not with easy scores such as with Pergolesi and Hasse, but in his manner, with rich, full treatment of the individual parts.

This curious concurrence – a more fortunate harbinger of a better fate, the present sad state of his finances, the sight of his desperate wife, the thought of his two orphaned children – all this was not designed to console an admired artist who was never a stoic, to sweeten the bitterness of death at the age of thirty-five.

'Just now,' he often lamented during his illness, 'I must die, when I could live quietly! Now to leave my Art, when I must no longer be a slave to fashion, no longer chained by speculators, when I could follow the flights of my fantasy, when I could compose freely and independently whatever my heart dictates! I must leave my family, my poor children, in that moment when I would be in a better condition to care for them . . .'

His final illness, when he was bedridden, lasted fifteen days. It began with swelling in his hands and feet and an almost total inability to move: this was followed by sudden vomiting, and this is called acute miliary fever [*hitziges Frieselfieber*]. He was completely conscious until two hours before his death; the sensations of his forthcoming death, his sorrow at having to leave wife and children unprovided for, certainly tripled the martyrdom of his sickness . . .

On the day he died, he had the score of the *Requiem* brought to his bed. 'Didn't I say before that I was writing this *Requiem* for myself?' Thus he spoke and looked over the whole attentively, with tears in his eyes. It was the last painful farewell to his beloved Art . . .

Baron van Swieten came at once after [Mozart's] death, to weep with the widow, who had crawled into the bed of her dead husband, to catch his illness and die with him . . . Mozart's death caused public concern. On the very day he died, many people stood in front of the house and showed their sympathy in various ways. Schikaneder paced up and down and cried out: 'His ghost follows me all the time: he's always right there in front of me.'

Mozart's health, which in the last period visibly failed, was always frail, and as is the case with persons of delicate sensibility, he was very afraid of death.[8]

In 1829 the British composer and publisher, Vincent Novello, and his wife Mary, left London for the Continent. They were heading for Salzburg, in order to present (as the editor of their diaries puts it) 'to Mozart's aged and invalid sister a modest sum of money subscribed by Novello and his brother musicians in London: to collect materials for a projected Life of the composer himself: and to make arrangements, in Paris, for the musical education of their little daughter Clara, soon to become one of the most famous singers of her time.'

Both Novellos recorded in their diaries the conversations with Constanze immediately afterwards, day by day; the information thus gathered is invaluable. In the following transcript, which was not published until 1955, V.N. = Vincent Novello and M.N. = his wife. Constanze's sister, Sophie Haibel, was also present, as was Mozart's younger son, Franz Xaver Wolfgang.

M.N. July 17th. Some six months [weeks?] before his death he was possessed with the idea of his being poisoned – 'I know I must die,' he exclaimed, 'someone has given me acqua toffana and has calculated the precise time of my death – for which they have ordered a Requiem, it is for myself I am writing this.' His wife entreated him to let her put it aside, saying that he was ill, otherwise he would not have such an absurd idea. He agreed she should and wrote a masonic ode which so delighted the company for whom it was written that he returned quite elated; 'Did I not know that I have written better I should think this the best of my work, but I will put it in score. Yes I see I was ill to have had such an absurd idea of having taken poison, give me back the Requiem and I will go on with it.' But in a few days he was as ill as ever and possessed with the same idea . . .

But three days before his death he received the order of his appointment from the Emperor of being music director at St Stephen's which at once relieved him from the cabal and intrigue of Salieri and the singers. He wept bitterly: 'Now that I am appointed to a situation where I could please myself in my writings, and feel I could do something worthy, I must die . . .'

A short time before his death he sang with Madame [Constanze] and Süssmayr the Requiem, several of the movements oppressed him to tears, he wrote the *Recordare* and principal parts first, saying, 'If I do not live these are of most consequence.' When they had finished he called Süssmayr to him and desired that if he died before he had completed the work, the fugue he had written at the commencement might be repeated and pointed out where and how other parts should be filled up that were already sketched. It was in consequence of this, that Süssmayr afterwards wrote to Breitkopf of Leipzig that he had written the principal part of this Requiem, but as Madame just observed, any one could have written what he had done, after the sketching and precise directions of Mozart, and nothing Süssmayr ever did, before or after, proved him to have any talent of a similar kind.

The abuse that has by some persons been heaped upon this last work of Mozart's originated in Weber, the director of the [journal entitled] *Cäcilia* (no relation of C. M. Weber), who has written also a Requiem but not being of the same genre as Mozart's was not liked. Envy made him wish to decry this standard of perfection which he could not reach, but this was a difficult affair, as people would but laugh at him for his pains; his object therefore was to deny that Mozart ever wrote it and this he asserted in one of the numbers of the periodical which he edits. There are always plenty of envious poor souls ready to join in the hue and cry raised against a great genius, whom they can never imitate or appreciate, and on this occasion there were some who lent an ear to this scribbler's assertion. This point gained, he ventured to attack its merits and in short proved his ignorance by denying it to possess any as the work of Süssmayr – yet not perceiving that if it had originated with this latter, how came it that he never before or after wrote anything else like it.

July 15th. Salieri's enmity arose from Mozart's setting the *Così fan tutte* which he had originally commenced and given up as unworthy [of] musical invention. The son denies he poisoned him although his father thought so and Salieri himself confessed the fact in his last moments, but as he was embittered all his life by cabals and intrigues, he may truly be said to have poisoned his [Mozart's] life and this thought, the son thinks, pressed upon the wretched man when dying.

V.N. July 15th. Salieri first tried to set this opera but failed, and the great success of Mozart in accomplishing what he [Salieri] could make nothing of is supposed to have been the first origin of his enmity and malice towards Mozart (Süssmayr a friend of Salieri). It was about six months [weeks?] before he died that he was impressed with the horrid idea that someone had poisoned him with acqua toffana – he came to her one day and complained that he felt great pain in his loins and a general languor spreading over him by degrees – that some one of his enemies had succeeded in administering the deleterious mixture which would cause his death and that they could already calculate at what precise time it would infallibly take place. The engagement for the

Requiem hurt him much as it fed these sad thoughts that naturally resulted from his weak state of health.

The great success of a little Masonic ode which he wrote at this instant cheered his spirits for a time, but his melancholy forebodings again returned in a few days, when he again set to work on the Requiem. On one occasion he himself with Süssmayr and Madame Mozart tried over part of the Requiem together, but some of the passages so excited him that he could not refrain from tears, and was unable to proceed.

I was pleased to find that I had guessed right in supposing that the *Recordare* (one of the most divine and enchanting movements ever written) was one of his own great favourites.

She also confirmed the truth of his having said only three days before he died, 'I am appointed to a situation which will afford me leisure to write in future *just what I like myself*, and I feel capable of doing something worthy of the fame I have acquired, but instead of that I find that I must die.'

What glorious productions have been lost to the world by his unfortunate early death – for incomparable as his works are I have not the least doubt but that he would [have] written still finer things such as Oratorios and other extensive works (of the Epic class) had he lived.[9]

One of the most interesting and enterprising publishers in Germany was the firm of André in Offenbach am Main. They were put in touch with Constanze by Haydn, who passed through Offenbach on the way back from England in 1792 and told the firm's co-director Johann Anton André, that he and his father (who founded the press) should speedily purchase everything they could of Mozart's works from his widow. After some time elapsed, young André went to Vienna and did just that. Constanze had been dealing with the much better known firm of Breitkopf & Härtel in Leipzig, but André was a persuasive young man and he acquired, in the year 1800, a huge body of Mozart autographs which he proceeded to issue during the succeeding decades in editions which were remarkably scholarly and accurate for the time; *e.g.*, the Mass in C minor (K.427), where he left blank those passages in Mozart's *particella* which the composer had not filled in, and the Kyrie in D minor (K.341). In both cases the autographs have since been lost (some of the Mass still exists, but not the Benedictus), making André's edition our primary source.

Johann Anton André was a spirited young man, witty and sarcastic as well as being a composer in his own right. He began to interest himself in Mozart; not only in his works but in his life, and it was obvious that he would become involved in the Requiem. As a result of this, we have a long and fascinating correspondence between André and various friends and acquaintances, with whom he hoped to clarify the Requiem's history.[10]

To put it bluntly, André thought the story of the messenger and the tottering Mozart, believing he had received a commission from the 'Other World', was a lot of nonsense; in a letter of 10 February 1826 to his son-in-law, Johann Baptist Streicher, son of the famous piano-manufacturer in Vienna and a friend of Beethoven's, he wrote:

> I believe the anecdote which has been spread about the *Requiem* to have been a fairy-tale concocted by Mozart's widow. I have *reasons* for my opinion and I shall air them, but I want to protect the widow M. as far as possible; however I should like to receive information about several matters which can be had only in Vienna.
>
> 1. How soon after Mozart's death was the anecdote about the *unknown* person in circulation? Or was something known even during his lifetime, during his last days? . . .
>
> 2. *How early* was Mozart's *Requiem* known in Vienna and under which circumstances? . . .

In another letter, André explained that it was the history of the Requiem as found in Niemetschek's biography, which Constanze had recommended to André, that he wanted to be re-examined. 'Niemtschek [*sic*] can tell it any way he wants, I still think it's a fairy-story.' The answer from Vienna was astonishing. There are two letters on the subject; the first is from Streicher (12 March 1826):

> I can tell you the following, for the authenticity of which Abbé Stadler vouches . . .
> The anecdote about the unknown person [ordering the Requiem] was already known during Mozart's lifetime. This anecdote is *wholly true*, and the man who ordered it was Count Walseck [*sic*], who is still alive; but that is just *between us*.

Abbé Maximilian Stadler, a friend of Haydn and Mozart, and a clever musician, wrote himself to André on 1 October 1826 from Vienna as follows:

> That Count Wallseeg [*sic*] ordered the *Requiem* from Moz. is something I knew right after Mozart's death. I also knew the whole time about the commissioner's plans and everything that was being kept secret. From time to time I received, without asking for it, family news about that Count. But because it is unseemly and forbidden to reveal secrets, I never permitted myself even once to reveal the commissioner's name. But that happened through someone else . . . What is certain is that Moz. himself worked out the first three movements up to the Sanctus with much effort and diligence and love. Respected men have already declared publicly that they ran into Mozart shortly before his death and he was quite enthusiastic about that work, and even three days before he, quite exhausted, had to take to his sickbed, from which he never arose. The original manuscript of Moz. and the masterly movements they contain have been recognized by all true connoisseurs, and these

> movements, and only these, are the true witnesses for this work. Everything else is beside the point. Whoever has examined these manuscripts in detail must admit that Moz. is the sole composer and Süssmayr had no more part in it than any man somewhat trained in figured bass. All the essentials come from Moz. . . .

This amazing confirmation of Constanze's version of the Requiem, as she told it to Rochlitz, Niemetschek and the Novellos, was not known to the scholarly world until Wolfgang Plath, the co-general editor of the new collected edition of Mozart's music, published it in the *Mozart-Jahrbuch 1976/77*. The frightening tale was quite simply true. Mozart had 'beheld a pale horse, and he that sat upon him his name was Death . . .'

In the second half of October 1791 it did not help Mozart's health that the weather was abominable. We are now able to reconstruct its course from contemporary records. The only warm days when Constanze can have taken her husband for the carriage drive in the Prater were 20 and 21 October, when the afternoon temperature rose to about 18°C by 3 o'clock. Otherwise, the period 16 October–15 November was like the end of the world. Between 27 and 28 October, after pouring rain, there was suddenly snow, which fell during the whole of the 28th and only ceased for a few hours at mid-day on the 29th. On the 31st there was another snowstorm which lasted for several hours, and on 1 November there was heavy and frequent snow accompanied by high winds, more typical of January or February. In some parts of the country the grain had not been harvested and had to be abandoned.

This foul weather is without doubt the origin of the 'rain and snow' myth at Mozart's funeral; as we shall see, the weather had become much milder by then, but people had it in their minds that Mozart's death was accompanied by rain, sleet and snow. It was not accompanied by, it was *preceded* by, this devastatingly bad weather – which speeded Mozart to his grave as surely as acqua toffana or Salieri's malice.

An undated memorandum by Carl Thomas Mozart, the elder son, is also valuable. A passage from the middle reads as follows:

> Particularly remarkable is in my opinion the fact that a few days before [my father] died, his whole body became so swollen that the patient was unable to make the smallest movement, moreover there was a stench, which reflected an internal disintegration and after death increased to the extent that an autopsy was rendered impossible.
>
> Another typical circumstance is that the corpse did not become stiff and cold but, as was the case with Pope Ganganelli and those who die from poisoning by plants, remained soft and elastic.

Ganganelli (Pope Clemens XIV) was popularly supposed to have died in this fashion, but the supposition in Mozart's case is medical nonsense; Mozart's body was 'soft and elastic' after death because the 'cells collected water through dropsy, which is characteristic for a terminal collapse of the kidneys.'[11]

The most recent medical views on Mozart's death will be found in the next chapter; here, only the contemporary chronicle has been attempted. In any case, if the freezing wintry weather in October boded ill even for healthy Viennese, the crucial 'incubatory' period, 11–20 November, was wet and unstable, ranging from *brouillard de froid* (icy fog) to *sirocco* and *chaud et grand vent* (warm, high wind):[12] the barometer was falling, and the abnormally warm, wet, oppressive south wind – the *Föhn* so feared in much of central Europe as causing everything from toothache to avalanches – set off Mozart's attack of rheumatism. It is in the light of newly won medical knowledge that we may turn to further documents in this attempt to reconstruct the last month of Mozart's life, using only contemporary sources or reports by eye-witnesses.

A curious account of the Requiem appeared in the *Salzburger Intelligenzblatt* of 7 January 1792:

> About Mozart – Some months before his death he received a letter without signature, asking him to compose a Requiem, and to ask whatever fee he wanted for it. Since this idea did not in the least appeal to him, he thought, I shall ask so much that the amateur [*Liebhaber*] will surely let me go. The next day a servant came to fetch the answer; Mozart wrote to the unknown man that he could not undertake to do the work for less than 60 ducats, and he could not start, moreover, for two or three months. The servant came again, brought 30 ducats instantly and said he would enquire again in three months, and when the Mass is finished, he will bring the other half of the money. Now Mozart had to write, which he did, often with tears in his eyes, always saying 'I am writing a Requiem for myself'; he finished it a few days before his death. When his death was known, the servant came again and brought the remaining 30 ducats, asked for no Requiem, and since that time there was no further enquiry. It will actually be performed, when it is copied, in his memory in St Michael's Church [at Salzburg].[13]

The explanation for this account is extremely simple: by about that time (early January) Constanze and her advisers had decided to finish the Requiem so that she could collect the rest of the money owed to her late husband; hence she was eager to give the impression that he had actually finished it. Meanwhile the team of Süssmayr, Freystädtler and another young man were working (perhaps not simultaneously) to complete it, using Süssmayr as the main copyist *because his handwriting was most like Mozart's* (which is why he was chosen to falsify Mozart's signature on the top right-hand corner of the first page: 'di me W: A: Mozart mpria. /792.'). The third member of the Requiem team was a friend of Haydn's and a protégé of Mozart's – Jospeh Eybler. Mozart obviously considered him more talented than Süssmayr.

As presented to Walsegg, then, the score of the Requiem included the Introitus's beginning (Requiem aeternam) in Mozart's completed autograph, with Süssmayr's fake signature;[14] the Kyrie in Mozart's autograph sketch filled in by Freystädtler *and* Süssmayr; and the rest of the work copied or composed by Süssmayr.

In an autobiographical note for the *Allgemeine Musikalische Zeitung*, Eybler wrote as follows: 'I had the luck to retain his [Mozart's] friendship undamaged up to his death, so that I could help him during his painful last illness, lifting him, laying him down and waiting on him . . .'[15] It is entirely possible that Eybler actually filled in those parts from the Dies irae to the Hostias (which Mozart had only written in *particella*) directly under Mozart's own supervision: they are entered right on Mozart's manuscript, and they are incomparably better than Süssmayr's additions, particularly the trumpet and kettledrum parts of the Dies irae. Some real clarification into this incredibly complex affair is introduced by the following little-known letter from Constanze, dated Salzburg, 31 May 1827, to Abbé Maximilian Stadler, an old family friend, who had just earned Constanze's loving gratitude by defending the Requiem against some slander in a German periodical:

> Now I can't do differently than to relate to you and all Mozart's friends the history of the Requiem, which consists of this: that Mozart never thought of beginning a Requiem [at any other time], and often said to me that he undertook this work (*i.e.*, the one commissioned by Anonymous) with the greatest pleasure, since that was his favourite genre [*i.e.*, church music] and he was going to do it and compose it with such fervour that his friends and enemies would study it after his death; 'if I can only

stay alive that long; for this must be my masterpiece and my swan-song.' And he did compose it with great fervour; when he felt weak, however, Süssmayr often had to sing, with me and him [Mozart], what he had written, and thus Süssmayr received a real lesson from Mozart. And I can hear Mozart, when he often said to Süssmayr: 'Ey – there you stand like a duck in a thunderstorm; you won't understand that for a long time,' took the quill and wrote down principal parts which, I suppose, were too much for Süssmayr. – What Mozart can be blamed for is that he wasn't very orderly with his papers and sometimes mislaid what he'd started to compose; and so as not to search for it endlessly he simply wrote it again; that is how it could happen that some things turned up twice, but the second wasn't any different from the first; for once he had made up his mind from the mass of thoughts, that idea was as solid as a rock, and was never changed; that is something you can see in his scores, too, so beautiful, so efficient, so cleanly written, and certainly not a note altered. – Let us assume the case that Süssmayr finds some remains by Mozart (for the Sanctus, etc.), that would mean the Requiem is after all Mozart's work. – That I gave it to Eybler to finish occurred because I was then (I don't remember why) annoyed at Süssmayr, and Mozart himself thought highly of Eybler. I thought myself that anyone can do it, since all the principal sections are written out. And so I had Eybler sent to me, and told him of my wish; since he at once turned me down with beautiful excuses, he wasn't given it . . . [16]

The last point is wrong: Constanze forgot that on 21 December 1791 she had actually given the score to, and received a receipt from, Eybler.[17] But Eybler may already have made the additions and hence Süssmayr was offended at them and at Mozart's scathing remarks; perhaps Eybler had another good look at the whole score again, and after

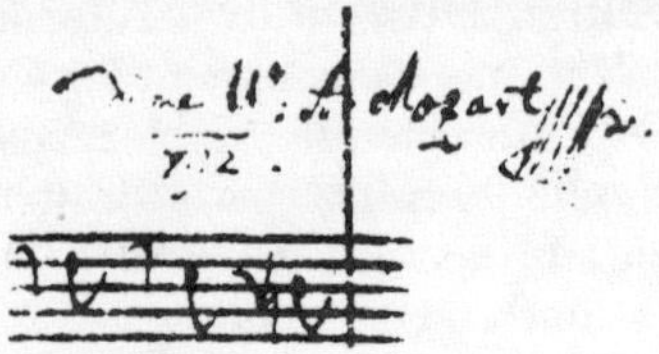

FIG. 10

FIG. 11

FIG. 15

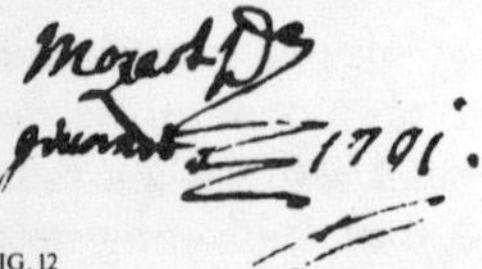

FIG. 12

FIG. 16

FIG. 13

FIG. 17

FIG. 14

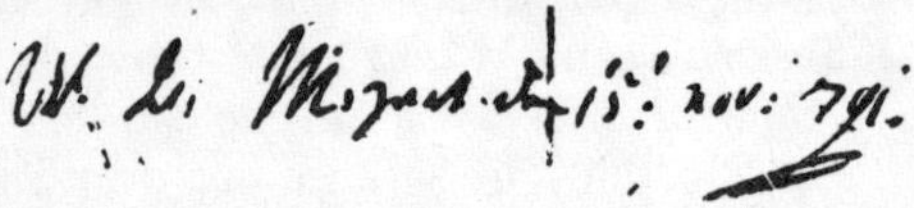

Mozart's signature on the autograph of the Requiem (FIG. 10) *was actually forged by Süssmayr – a discovery first published in the book* Mozarts Tod *(1971) – and dated 1792. Authentic Mozart signatures:* FIG. 11 *(1784)*, FIG. 12 (Ave, verum, *1791; also on jacket)*, FIG. 13 *(1790). Mozart's signature on the autograph of the* Kleine Freymaurer-Kantate K.623 (FIG. 14), *with the date 15 November 1791. Notice that in Süssmayr's Requiem forgery the letter 'M' was begun at bottom left, while Mozart's authentic signatures all begin in the middle of the letter.* FIGS. 15–17*: Süssmayr signatures from 1792/3.*

considering the matter a day or two returned it 'with beautiful excuses'. It is only a small point for Constanze to have forgotten. Or, alternatively. Eybler really took it home, completed the missing parts (instruments) of Mozart's autograph and decided it would be too difficult to compose the rest in a worthy manner.

Constanze then called in Süssmayr with whom she was annoyed (and surely he with her) and persuaded him (was money involved?) to finish the piece. She gave him everything she could find, and perhaps he helped her search; but he must have been piqued at not being the first choice, although Mozart had obviously discussed the Requiem with him and even sung through sections. Actually there is another much more convincing reason why he was piqued and Constanze 'annoyed' at him: *he was already in the Salieri camp*! It will be noticed that Constanze, when talking of Süssmayr to the Novellos, described the young man not as Mozart's friend but as Salieri's friend; and she did so in the context of Salieri's jealousy being explained by the extraordinary story of *Così fan tutte*: this was 'the first origin of his enmity and malice towards Mozart (Süssmayr a friend of Salieri).'

How did this come about? The answer lies, I think, in the archives of the Court Chapel (now in the Austrian National Library, Vienna):

> The undersigned declares herewith that he has been correctly paid from the cashier's office of the I.[mperial] R.[oyal] National Theatre for having done services in the I.[mperial] R.[oyal] Court Chapel, replacing Herr Franz Hofer, violinist, who at that time had service in Laxenburg [where the court spent the summers and enjoyed opera as well as church music]
>
> the 12th June: High Mass on Whitsunday 2.–f
> the 13th June: Again Mass on Whitmonday 2.–f
> Total 4.–f
>
> Vienna 30th July 1791 Franz Xaver Süssmayr

Seen by me
Ant. Salieri
C.[hapel] M.[aster][18]

In another, undated, letter Süssmayr recommends himself as 'questa mia creatura catholica' (my dear Catholic creature) to Salieri's protection.[19] Obviously Süssmayr thought the future looked brighter with Salieri than with Mozart, and by 1791 he appears to have had his foot well within the 'enemy's' camp. As a go-between he may not have been a brilliant success.

All this must be borne in mind when evaluating the documents of this turbulent period.

Writing about *The Magic Flute* in 1798, Rochlitz says that Mozart 'was rather fond of this opera, although he laughed about some of the numbers which received the most applause.'

> It was given in Vienna without cessation almost as often as earlier Beaumarchais's *Marriage de Figaro* had been played in Paris: but his [Mozart's] sickness worsened to the degree that he could only conduct [attend?] about the first ten performances. When it was no longer possible for him personally to be in the theatre, very sorrowfully he placed his watch next to him and heard the music in his imagination –
>
> 'Now they've finished the first act – now is the passage 'Dir grosse Königin der Nacht' [Scene 30 of Act II, just before the end] – and so on.[20]

My next extensive quotation is the famous letter that Sophie Haibel wrote to Nissen for inclusion in his biography (I have used the original letter and not Nissen's abbreviated transcript; I have also used Emily Anderson's beautiful translation). It was written from Diakovar, where Sophie's husband, Jakob Haibel, was choirmaster:

Sophie Haibel to Georg Nikolaus von Nissen, Salzburg

D[iakovar], 7 April 1825

Now I must tell you about Mozart's last days. Well, Mozart became fonder and fonder of our dear departed mother and she of him. Indeed he often came running along in great haste to the Wieden (where she and I were lodging at the Goldener Pflug), carrying under his arm a little bag containing coffee and sugar, which he would hand to our good mother, saying, 'Here, mother dear, now you can have a little *Jause* [afternoon coffee].' She used to be as delighted as a child. He did this very often. In short, Mozart in the end never came to see us without bringing something.

Now when Mozart fell ill, we both made him a night-jacket which he could put on frontways, since on account of his swollen condition he was unable to turn in bed. Then, as we didn't know how seriously ill he was, we also made him a quilted dressing-gown (though indeed his dear wife, my sister, had given us the materials for both garments), so that when he got up he should have everything he needed. We often visited him and he seemed to be really looking forward to wearing his dressing-gown. I used to go into town every day to see him. Well, one Saturday [3 December] when I was with him, Mozart said to me: 'Dear Sophie, do tell Mamma that I am fairly well and that I shall be able to go and congratulate her on the octave of her name-day.' Who could have been more delighted than I to bring such cheerful news to my mother, who was ever anxious to hear how he was? I hurried home therefore to comfort her, the more so as he himself really seemed to be bright and happy. The following day [4 December] was a Sunday. I was young then and rather vain, I confess, and liked to dress up. But I never cared to go out walking from our suburb into town in my fine clothes, and I had no money for a drive. So I said to our good mother: 'Dear Mamma, I'm not going to see Mozart today. He was so well yesterday that surely he will be much better this morning, and one day more or less won't make much difference.' Well, my mother said: 'Listen to this. Make me a cup of coffee and then I'll tell you what you ought to do.' She was rather inclined to keep me at home; and indeed my sister knows how much I had to be with her. I went into the kitchen. The fire was out. I had to light the lamp and make a fire. All the time I was thinking of Mozart. I had made the coffee and the lamp was still burning. Then I noticed how wasteful I had been with my lamp, I mean, that I had burned so much oil. It was still burning brightly. I stared into the flame and thought to myself, 'How I should love to know how Mozart is.' While I was thinking and gazing at the flame, it went out, as completely as if the lamp had never been burning. Not a spark remained on the main wick and yet there wasn't the slightest draught – that I can swear to. A horrible feeling came over me. I ran to our mother and told her all. She said: 'Well, take off your fine clothes and go into town and bring me back news of him at once. But be sure not to delay.' I hurried along as fast as I could. Alas, how frightened I was when my sister, who was almost despairing and yet trying to keep calm, came out to me, saying: 'Thank God that you have come, dear Sophie. Last night he was so ill that I thought he would not be alive this morning. Do stay with me today, for if he has another bad turn, he will pass away tonight. Go in to him for a little while and see how he is.' I tried to control myself and went to his bedside. He immediately called me to him and said: 'Ah, dear Sophie, how glad I am that you have come. You must stay here tonight and see me die.' I tried hard to be brave and to persuade him to the contrary. But to all my attempts he only replied: 'Why, I already have the taste of death on my tongue. And, if you do not stay, who will support my dearest Constanze when I am gone?' 'Yes, yes, dear Mozart,' I assured him, 'but I must first go back to our mother and tell her that you would like me to stay with you today. Otherwise she will think that some misfortune has befallen you.' 'Yes, do so,' said Mozart, 'but be sure and come back soon.' Good God, how distressed I felt! My poor sister followed me to the door and begged me for Heaven's sake to go to the priests at St Peter's and implore one of them to come to Mozart – a chance call, as it were. I did so, but for a long time they refused to come and I had a great deal of trouble to persuade one of those clerical brutes to go to him. Then I ran off to my mother who was anxiously awaiting me. It was already dark. Poor soul, how shocked she was! I persuaded her to go and spend the night with her eldest daughter, the late Josepha Hofer. I then ran back as fast as I could to my distracted sister. Süssmayr was at Mozart's bedside. The well-known Requiem lay on the quilt and Mozart was explaining to him how, in his opinion, he ought to finish it, when he was gone. Further, he urged his wife to keep his death a secret until she should have informed Albrechtsberger, who was in charge of all the services [at St Stephen's Cathedral]. A long search was made for Dr Closset, who was found at the theatre, but who had to wait for the end of the play. He came and ordered cold poultices to be placed on Mozart's burning head, which, however, affected him to such an extent that he became unconscious and remained so until he died. His last movement was an attempt to express with his mouth the drum passages in the Requiem. That I can still hear. Müller[21] from the Art Gallery came and took a cast of his pale, dead face. Words fail me, dearest brother, to describe how his devoted wife in her utter misery threw herself on her knees and implored the Almighty for His aid. She simply could not tear herself away from Mozart, however much I begged her to do so. If it was possible to increase her sorrow, this was done on the day after that dreadful night, when crowds of people walked past his corpse and wept and wailed for him.[22]

Sophie Haibel related the nightmarish story again, four years later, to the Novellos in Salzburg.[23] I have included the entire transcription in note 23, but here I wish to stress only two points: both Novellos quote Sophie as saying that Mozart had died in her arms; 'the Doctor persisted in his orders and Madame Haibl accordingly applied a damp towel to his forehead. Mozart immediately gave a slight shudder and in a very short time afterwards he expired in her arms. At this moment the only persons in the Room were Madame Mozart, the Medical Attendant and herself. The Room in which he died was the front one on the street on the first floor.' The second point is the precise listing of those present.

Nissen made a series of notes for his biography, using information from Constanze; here is one which was not used, and which gives us a vivid picture of the waning hours of Sunday, 4 December 1791:

> His death excited public attention. People halted down on the street in front of the windows of his apartment and waved their handkerchiefs. He asked his wife what the Physician Closset had said. She answered comfortingly. He contradicted: that's not true, and was very depressed: now I must die, when I could care for you and the children. *Ach*, now I leave you unprovided for.[24]
>
> Suddenly he began to vomit – it spat out of him in an arch – it was brown, and he was dead.

A young protégé of Mozart's, Ludwig Gall, related that the next morning he

> came into town from the Landstrasse to go to the music-dealer Lausch, and when I arrived he said, 'Imagine what a misfortune has happened to us: Mozart died this last night!' Quite appalled I rushed at once to the apartment, still doubting the Job's News, but alas I was soon convinced of its truth. – Mad. Mozart herself opened the door of the apartment and led me to a little room on the

left, where I saw the dead Master on the bier, lying in a coffin, in a black suit with a cowl down over his forehead, hiding his blond hair, with his hands folded over his breast . . .[25]

Later that day one of Mozart's patrons, Gottfried van Swieten, was dismissed by an Imperial memorandum from his powerful position as President of the Court Commission for Education. (He had played a leading role in matters of education and censorship under Joseph II, and Leopold's broom was sweeping with a wide arc.)[26] But Swieten found time to come to the Mozarts' apartment and began to arrange the funeral. Many years later Constanze told Nissen that she was taken away, first to 'Herr Bauernfeind'. Scholars have asserted that this was a misprint for Joseph von Bauernfeld, Schikaneder's 'silent partner'; but there was also a Joseph Bauernfeind who had been in 1785 an Entered Apprentice in the Lodge *Zur gekrönten Hoffnung*, on the membership list of which he is listed as a Clerk of the Imperial Royal Joint Court Chancellery.[27] (In another court record – the *Hof-Schematismus* of 1789 – he is again listed as a clerk in the Joint Bohemian–Austrian Court Chancellery: 'H[er]r. Joseph Bauernfeind, lives in the Leopoldstadt 232'.) Later Constanze was taken to the (in)famous 'Herr Goldhann', Joseph Odilio Goldhann (Goldhahn),[28] who figured prominently as one of Mozart's potential (and probably real) moneylenders, and who signed the official list of Mozart's effects[29] on 7 December as a witness 'but without my being put at disadvantage or being in any way responsible'. From this document, and from others which list Mozart's possessions and the contents of the apartment, it is clear that Constanze did not become ill at once and remained in the house for most of December (she was also there, specifically, on the 9th, 16th, 19th, and 20th, when official documents were presented to her and inventories taken).

It was at fifty-five minutes past midnight on Monday, 5

December that Mozart died: we have this precise information from an autograph letter by Maria Anna (Nannerl), Mozart's sister, written about April 1792.[30] Zinzendorf's Diary tells us that the weather was 'mild. Three or four patches of fog a day for some time now'; the unnaturally mild weather continued the next day: 'and frequent fog.' It was wind-still.[31]

In the City of Vienna's Registry of Deaths[32] for the December appears the following: 'Mozart, Wohledler [nobleman] H[er]r: Wolfgang Amadeus, I.[mperial] R.[oyal] Kapellmeister and Chamber *Compositeur*, born in Salzburg, in the Small *Kaiserh[aus]* No. 970 in the Rauhensteingasse, from acute miliary fever [*hitziges Frieselfieber*], [his corpse] examined, 36 years old [recte: 35].'

It was suggested to Constanze, in view of her financial situation, that Mozart be given the cheapest funeral possible. Hence she paid for a third-class funeral: 4 fl. 36 kr. parish fees; 4 fl. 20 kr. church fees; the wagon which took the corpse from the Rauhensteingasse to St Stephen's Cathedral and then to St Marx's cemetery cost 3 Gulden.[33]

This last journey of the Imperial Royal *Kapellmeister* has been reconstructed as follows (it is assumed that this all took place on 6 December, not later, because of the putrid state of the corpse):

> About 2:30 p.m. Mozart's corpse was taken from the apartment in the Rauhensteingasse, put into the funeral wagon on the street outside, and then taken to St Stephen's, where the funeral party was waiting. On the north side, in a chapel known [popularly but wrongly] as the 'Crucifix Chapel', at the old entrance to the crypt (and opposite the apartment of the gravedigger) the coffin was placed upon a bier; there could follow the first, so-called 'house' blessing by the priest, who approached with the cross-bearer and the ministrants. That would explain the otherwise curious version whereby Mozart is said to have received the benediction there

> in the open air [because of the putridity?] Then the little funeral party proceeded to enter the Cathedral, perhaps passing through the 'Sacristan's Portal' on the north side opposite the Prince-Archbishop's Palace, probably arriving at the real 'Crucifix Chapel' which was situated just inside; there, the ecclesiastical benediction was given. After the end of the ceremony, the little procession went outside again to the Capistranus Pulpit [again on the outer north side], where the funeral wagon had waited to carry the coffin on its last journey, to the Cemetery of St Marx.[34]

St Marx is a suburb of Vienna, a good hour's walk from the centre. None of the funeral party – we do not know the names of those who participated – wanted to accompany the corpse, and no one, for years, cared to find out where Mozart was buried: as a result, we know only the approximate section of the cemetery under which, somewhere, music's greatest genius lies.

Mozart kept a commonplace book (*Stammbuch*), in which Constanze – aged thirty – wrote the following notice:

> That which you wrote on this page to your friend,[35]
> I write now, in deep reverence, to you,
> Dearly beloved husband! Mozart, unforgettable to me and to the whole of Europe –
> Now you are well – well forever! –
> At one hour past midnight between 4th and 5th December of this year
> He left, in his 36th year – O! only too suddenly! –
> This good – but thankless world – O God!
> Eight years long we were joined in the most tender and in this world inseparable bond,
> O! Would I were soon joined to you forever.
> His most distressed wife
> Constance Mozart née Weber
> Vienna, 5th Decem: 1791

In the second edition (1808) of Niemetschek's biography, we read the following epitaph by one of Mozart's fellow composers in Vienna:

> A composer, by no means unfamous and living in Vienna, said to a colleague at Mozart's death, with much truth and uprightness: 'Of course it's too bad about such a great genius, but it's good for us that he's dead. Because if he had lived longer, really the world would not have given a single piece of bread for our compositions.'[36]

It has taken perhaps two hundred years for the world to realize fully and in all its aspects what this loss has meant to music – and to humanity. Haydn said: 'Posterity will not see such a talent again in 100 years!'[37] Posterity has not seen it in two hundred.

XII
Myths and Theories

Mozart's sudden death immediately gave rise to all sorts of speculations about its real cause, and very soon rumours were spreading about poison. As early as New Year's Eve of 1791, a Berlin newspaper reported:

> Mozart is – dead. He returned from Prague feeling sickly: it was thought he had contracted dropsy, and he died in Vienna. Because his body swelled up after death, people even thought he had been poisoned. . . .[1]

We have seen that Mozart's son, Carl Thomas, found the swelling of his father's corpse odd, if not downright suspicious, though his reference to poisoning remains slightly oblique. With the passage of time, however, this theory of poisoning was forgotten. Constanze never seems to have lent it any credence, although she quotes Mozart himself as having believed it (as in her conversations with the Novellos). Then in the 1820s, a dramatic event re-awakened the poisoning theory in a particularly lurid manner; and this theory, many years later, was to form the basis of Peter Shaffer's by now legendary play *Amadeus*, of which the principal protagonist is not Mozart but Antonio Salieri.

Salieri was already Court *Kapellmeister* by the time Mozart arrived in Vienna to live in 1781, and unlike Mozart, who still had his operatic career to make in Vienna, Salieri was an established darling of the court (and especially Joseph II) – hence also of the aristocratic public at the opera house. He was soon to make a profound impression in Paris with his new French opera *Les Danaïdes* (1784), first announced as a joint composition by Gluck and his pupil Salieri. Successfully revived in 1985, *Les Danaïdes* shows Salieri at his very considerable best. But at his worst, Salieri is commonplace and of course in no way comparable to Mozart. It took only a generation for Salieri's popularity to wane and finally to die, but in the decade 1781–91 Salieri and his music were very much in the foreground of operatic life in Vienna. The curious thing about Salieri is that, despite his success, he really seems to have been extremely jealous of Mozart, as many contemporary sources attest. In this chronicle, Salieri must of necessity take second place to the drama of Mozart's last year; but the Italian had been a thorn in Mozart's side for the last decade of his life and through his endless intrigues had made Mozart's operatic existence much more miserable than was necessary.

In October 1823, Ignaz Moscheles, Beethoven's pupil, was in Vienna, and decided to try to visit the ancient Salieri, who had meanwhile been transferred to the General Hospital in the suburb of Alservorstadt. Salieri was not only very old, he was also very ill; and Moscheles had to secure permission from Salieri's unmarried daughter and the authorities in order to visit him.

> The reunion was a sad one. His appearance already shocked me and he spoke only in broken sentences about his imminent death. But at the end he said: 'Although this is my last illness, I can assure you on my word of honour that there is no truth in that absurd rumour; you know that I am supposed to have poisoned Mozart. But no, it's malice, pure malice, tell the world, dear Moscheles, old Salieri, who will soon die, has told you.[2]

Shortly thereafter, in November 1823, Salieri tried unsuccessfully to commit suicide. Beethoven followed the events through friends writing for him in the Conversatio Books; Schindler, Beethoven's amanuensis, noted:

> Salieri is again in a very bad way. He is quite ruined. He has fantasies that he was responsible for Mozart's death and gave him poison. This is *true* – for he wants to confess it . . .

In another, slightly earlier entry, a Viennese journalist named Johann Schickh added, 'I'll wager 100 to 1 that Salieri's statement is true. Mozart's manner of death confirms that statement.' Beethoven's Conversation Books are full of the subject, on which the composer appears to have brooded frequently. At the beginning of 1824, Schindler wrote:

> You are again in such a black mood, great master – what is wrong? Where has your good mood gone these days? – Don't take it so much to heart, it's usually the fate of great men! There are many still alive who can bear witness how he [Mozart] died, whether symptoms [of poisoning] showed themselves. He [Salieri] will, however, have hurt Moz. more with his disparagement than Mozart hurt him.

Even after Salieri's death, Beethoven's nephew Carl wrote, 'They are still saying with great conviction that Salieri was Mozart's murderer.'[3]

Haydn's Italian biographer, Giuseppe Carpani, went vigorously to Salieri's defence in September 1824, publishing a long letter in an Italian journal,[4] where he wrote:

> Mozart was poisoned? Yes? Where is the evidence? Useless to ask. There is no evidence, and it is also impossible ever to find any, because Mozart caught an infectious rheumatic fever which not only attacked him but also slaughtered all those others who caught it during those days. The efforts and experience of the two most famous professors of medicine, Closset and Sallaba, were useless,

useless the children's tears, the wife's prayers and the hopes of the whole city of Vienna for the beloved maestro.[5]

Carpani had the good fortune to find a doctor who had been consulted about Mozart's illness and death, Court Councillor Eduard Vincent Guldener von Lobes, and procured from him a letter, indignantly denying any poisoning.[6] A letter was also sent to Haydn's pupil, Sigismund von Neukomm, then living in Paris, which in English translation reads:[7]

> It is with great pleasure, sir, that I hasten to communicate to you all I know relative to the illness and death of the great Mozart. In the autumn of 1791 he fell ill of an inflammatory fever, which at that season was so prevalent that few persons entirely escaped its influence. I was not applied to till some days after he had been labouring under the disorder; but I had received information of it from Dr Closset, who daily attended him. He considered Mozart's case as dangerous, and said that from the first appearance of the complaint he had feared a fatal result – viz., a determination to the head. One day he met Dr Sallaba, and observed to him that it was all over with Mozart – that it was not possible to prevent the determination to the head. Sallaba instantly acquainted me with this; and in fact Mozart died some days after the usual symptoms.
>
> His death excited very general interest, but never did it once occur to the mind of anyone to suspect, even distantly, that his death had been occasioned by poison. Numerous were the attentions shown him by his family; above all, so scrupulous was the watchfulness and care bestowed upon him by the worthy and experienced Dr Closset, who, during the whole of this painful period, displayed rather the solicitude of a friend than the attention of a medical man, that it is impossible the slightest trace of anything violent, of anything like poison, could

have escaped him. The disorder had its usual course and its ordinary term of duration. Dr Closset had watched its progress with so much attention that he predicted the result to the very hour. A great number of the inhabitants of Vienna were at this time labouring under the same complaint, and the number of cases which terminated fatally, like that of Mozart's, was considerable. I saw the body after death, and it exhibited no appearances beyond those usual in such cases.

Such is the substance of what I have to adduce relative to the death of Mozart. Nothing would prove more gratifying, or more satisfactory to my mind, than to know that the testimony I give is, in some degree at least, available to counteract this horrid imputation against the memory of the excellent Salieri. You will pardon me, sir, for not having returned so early an answer to your application as I should have wished; nothing but a severe indisposition could have prevented me.

But if Mozart was not poisoned, what did he die of? The standard medical opinion has hitherto been that Mozart died of *Rheuma inflammatorium*, or rheumatic fever, an acute non-infectious febrile disease marked by inflammation and pain in the joints. Dr Carl Bär, a Swiss physician, has written what was until recently the authoritative work on the subject. He dismisses the description in the Vienna City Death Register and Nissen's book (*hitziges Frieselfieber* or acute miliary fever) as amateurish – well meant but hopeless from a professional point of view. 'In any event,' he writes, 'almost all terminal cases as a result of rheumatic fever can be traced back to coronary defects.' And after they bled Mozart, 'the results, considering his small size and his cardiac condition, could only have been catastrophic.' Dr Bär's diagnosis is ultimately based on information handed down in a very complicated chain of circumstances, but deriving from Mozart's physician, Dr Closset (who also consulted another colleague, Dr Sallaba).

The rapid decline and short period of illness 'were not unusual for that age.'[8]

But since 1966, when Dr Bär published his epochal work, many other physicians and scientists have been at work on the difficult task of identifying not only Mozart's terminal illness but the previous illnesses in his short life that led up to the fatal three weeks in November and December 1791. It is useless for a non-medical man to enter into such a discussion, but from all appearances the final word on the subject has been said by Peter J. Davies.[9] All an amateur can do in the circumstances is to summarize Dr Davies's findings and express admiration for their lucid presentation.

The illnesses to November 1791

In 1762, Wolfgang contracted an infection in the upper respiratory tract due to streptococcal infection, the effects of which may be delayed for weeks, months and even years. Later, the boy contracted what his doctor thought was scarlet fever but which was *erythema nodosum*, 'almost certainly a streptococcal infection'. Later in that same year he 'contracted another streptococcal infection' and 'suffered a mild attack of rheumatic fever.' Still later, in Paris and London in the year 1764, Wolfgang contracted tonsillitis 'or even quinsy (paritonsillar abscess)', and again suffered from 'tonsillitis complicated by sinusitis' (1765).

In December 1765, when in The Hague, Wolfgang was in a coma and lost a great deal of weight. The appalling symptoms included 'severe toxaemia, slow pulse, delirium, skin rash, pneumonia, haemorrhagic exfoliation of the oral mucous membrane' and suggest endemic typhoid fever. In November 1766, Wolfgang was again ill, this time in Munich, 'with fever and rheumatism', and Dr Davies considers that 'this was a second attack of rheumatic fever . . . Both . . . attacks of rheumatic fever appear to have been mild and it seems unlikely that his heart was badly damaged.' In 1767, Wolfgang contracted smallpox and recovered in Olmütz (Olomouc). During his Italian trips he contracted frostbite (1770) and in 1771 'he suffered an upper respiratory tract infection and tracheo-bronchitis' in addition to what appears to have been yellow jaundice. Davies suggests a diagnosis of type A virus hepatitis.

In December 1774, Wolfgang suffered a severe dental abscess (he had gone through an earlier bout in 1770 when in Italy), and four years later, in Mannheim, he developed another illness which 'has the feature of a viral upper respiratory tract infection', but he recovered. While rehearsing *Idomeneo* in Munich in December 1780, he developed what again appears to have been 'upper respiratory tract infection complicated by bronchitis'. When he left Archbishop Colloredo's service in Salzburg (May 1781), Wolfgang developed a viral infection, but it was not until 1784 that he suffered such a major illness in Vienna that one can begin to look for clues as to the causes of his death seven years later. The symptoms were fearful attacks of colic which ended in violent vomiting and a rheumatic inflammatory fever. Dr Davies's opinion is that

> Mozart at this time suffered a streptococcal infection contracted during an epidemic, and that this was complicated by the development of Schönlein-Henoch Syndrome. Further, . . . immune complexes were deposited in Mozart's kidney during that illness so as to cause chronic glomerulonephritis, the disease which was eventually to cause his death. Intestinal colic is a common symptom in the Schönlein-Henoch Syndrome . . . This is an allergic hypersensitivity vasculitis in which immune complexes are deposited in the small blood vessels of the skin, joints, gastro-intestinal tract and kidneys, resulting in purpuric lesions and

oedema of the skin and inflammatory changes in the other three organs. About 10% of cases develop chronic renal disease, which, if untreated, can result in chronic renal failure and death.

In 1787, it appears that Mozart 'again contracted a streptococcal infection which caused a second bout of Schönlein-Henoch Syndrome, and furthermore that his already damaged kidneys received further insult at this time.' Hence, when the crucial year 1791 began, Mozart had already 'contracted kidney disease (chronic glomerulonephritis) as a complication of the Schönlein-Henoch Syndrome . . . and . . . he suffered further recurrences in . . . April to August 1790. In patients with chronic nephritis there is a gradual decline in kidney function, which in the earlier stages is asymptomatic.' In those days there were no laboratory tests to diagnose this pre-symptomatic phase. 'Commonly there develops an elevation of blood pressure (hypertension) and haemorrhages in the retina of the eye.' There was no knowledge of nephritis or hypertension in 1791. Mozart's depressions during that year (the 'paranoid features in his personality associated with a possessive jealousy and emotional lability') arose from his chronic renal failure or uraemia.

'Such depression, personality change and mental delusions in a young man are not uncommon in uraemic hypertensive disease' – hence the famous carriage-ride in the Prater, the preoccupation with the Requiem and his own death (being, as he thought, induced by acqua toffana). The fainting-fits (blackouts) referred to in the authentic biographies are 'common in patients with chronic renal failure and are sometimes related to sudden rises in blood pressure (hypertensive encephalopathy).'

The terminal illness

Dr Davies has an interesting theory: that Mozart contracted his final illness during his attendance at the Masonic Lodge on 18 November 1791 (there was an epidemic in Vienna at that time, as many sources state).[10] The painful swellings in Mozart's hands and feet 'would suggest a polyarthritis', and as the swellings became more widespread and pronounced they suggest oedema. From the patient's immobility, 'it may be concluded that Mozart at this time suffered a hemiparesis and was paralysed down one side of his body.'

Since there was no knowledge in those days 'of chronic renal failure . . . [Dr Closset] reasonably suspected that Mozart had a growth within his brain . . . In my view, Closset was puzzled by the recent symptoms of fever, painful joint swellings and skin rash, which was why he called in the senior physician at the hospital, Dr Mathias von Sallaba . . . Sallaba diagnosed *hitziges Frieselfieber* [acute miliary fever], which is the diagnosis in the Register of Deaths . . . [It] is entirely non-specific and refers to an illness associated with fever and exanthem (skin rash) . . .' Speaking of Dr Bär's diagnosis of acute rheumatic fever, Dr Davies says that 'exanthem is rare in rheumatic fever, and such a diagnosis does not account for the chronic ill-health of 1791; nor does a diagnosis of rheumatic fever explain the neurological symptoms of the fatal illness . . .'

Summing up, in what is a particularly moving account of Mozart's death – the truth is often more gripping than even the most carefully conceived and delicately executed fantasy – Dr Davies writes:

> Mozart died from the following: streptococcal infection – Schönlein-Henoch Syndrome – renal failure – venesection(s) – cerebral haemorrhage – terminal broncho-pneumonia.
>
> Mozart contracted yet another streptococcal infection

while attending the lodge meeting on 18 November 1791, during an epidemic. The streptococcal infection caused a further exacerbation of Schönlein-Henoch Syndrome and renal failure, which manifested as fever, polyarthritis, malaise, swelling of the limbs, vomiting and purpura. The later, more generalized swelling of his body, was probably due to additional salt and fluid retention from renal failure. One or more venesections were performed and these would have aggravated his renal failure and contributed to his death. The Schönlein-Henoch Syndrome caused an exacerbation of his hypertension, which contributed to his nocturnal vomiting and caused a stroke. His partial paralysis was a hemiplegia (paralysis of one side of his body) due to a cerebral haemorrhage. About two hours before Mozart died, he convulsed and became comatosed. Then, an hour later, he attempted to sit up, opened his eyes wide and fell back with his head turned to the wall; his cheeks were puffed out. These symptoms suggest paralysis of conjugate gaze and facial nerve palsy, consistent with a massive cerebral haemorrhage. On the evening before his death Mozart had suffered with fever and drenching sweats. Bronchopneumonia is frequently the immediate cause of death in patients with uraemia and usually develops when the patient is already moribund.

* * *

Side by side with the lurid hypothesis that Mozart was murdered came a number of legends about his involvement with women at this final stage of his life. In one case there was a disgusting attack by a friend and Lodge-brother of Mozart's, Franz Hofdemel, on his pregnant wife, Magdalena, one of the composer's piano pupils. The attack took place the day after Mozart died, and in the blood-bath that followed Hofdemel maimed his wife for life with razor attacks on her face and throat and then killed himself.

Beethoven's conduct once again provides a hint of the

gossip circulating in Vienna.[11] He was asked to play (improvise) before Magdalena Hofdemel but was reluctant because he thought she had been Mozart's mistress (what a prude Beethoven was!). But there is absolutely no evidence that the Hofdemel tragedy can be connected either directly or indirectly with Mozart. The Empress Maria Luisa immediately took a personal interest in Magdalena's circumstances, which she would hardly have done if the court had considered the forthcoming child to be Mozart's. (The child, Johann Alexander Franz, was born at Brünn [Brno] on 10 May 1792 and was hence probably conceived in August 1791, when Constanze Mozart had just brought into the world her last child, Franz Xaver Wolfgang.)[12] It is also hardly likely that Hofdemel was commissioned by the Masons to poison Mozart, as has been suggested.

It has further been alleged that one of Mozart's mistresses in 1791 was his first Pamina, Anna Gottlieb, then aged seventeen (she had made her début at the age of twelve as Barbarina in *Le nozze di Figaro*). There is no evidence that she was (as has been proposed) Mozart's pupil, much less that their relationship was anything but that of a composer and a willing interpreter. It has been suggested that at the end of 1791 or the beginning of 1792 she lost her voice and retired from the stage as a singer, securing a position as actress in the rival Marinelli Company (in the Leopoldstadt Theatre). Mozart's death, in other words, broke her heart – and voice.

What actually happened is entirely different. Anna Gottlieb did in fact transfer to the Marinelli Company but she went on acting *and* singing, just as she and the others had done for Schikaneder in the Freyhaustheater. Christopher Raeburn has discovered interesting contemporary criticisms of her singing all through the 1790s, and she continued to sing and act well into the new century. Thus another Mozartian tradition may be summarily dismissed as a myth.[13]

Myths will continue to pursue Mozart. *Amadeus*, play

and film, has already created another, and it may prove difficult to dissuade the public from the current Shafferian view of the composer as a divinely gifted drunken lout, pursued by a vengeful Salieri.

By the same token, Constanze Mozart, she (in the film) of extraordinary *décolleté* and fatuous giggle, needs to be rescued from Shaffer's view of her.

XIII
Constanze: A Vindication

Constanze Mozart is perhaps the most unpopular woman in music history. For the last hundred years or so she has been subjected to an increasingly slanderous series of attacks: she was a sex kitten, she was a superficial, silly woman incapable of understanding Mozart, she mismanaged the household finances and encouraged him to live a scatterbrained, if not absolutely dissolute, life. These attacks were mounted for the most part by German musicologists and have recently reached the zenith of nastiness.

How did musicology arrive at this conclusion? Are there facts, or documents, of which we are ignorant? In fact there are not, and in this chapter it is proposed to examine the relevant authentic documents about Constanze Mozart and to see if there is any basis for this slander.

We have seen that on 5 December 1791 Constanze Mozart was herself in a state of near hysteria; that she tried to crawl into her husband's bed to catch the (as she thought) infectious illness; and that she was not even in a state to attend the funeral. Readers will have formed their own conclusions about the quality of the Mozarts' marriage – as far as it is revealed to us in the correspondence – and the couple's relationship. I shall now continue this investigation, starting immediately after Mozart's death on 5 December 1791.

Our first witness is Niemetschek:

> Mozart's enemies and slanderers became so vehement, particularly towards the end of his life and after his

death, that some of the rumours even reached the Emperor's ears.

These stories and lies were so shameless, so scandalous, that the monarch, not being informed to the contrary, was quite indignant. In addition to disgraceful inventions and exaggerations of excesses which they said Mozart had committed, it was maintained that he had left debts to the value of no less than thirty thousand florins – at which the monarch was absolutely astounded.

The widow had just decided to ask the monarch for a pension. A noble-minded woman, who had been an excellent pupil of Mozart's, informed her how her husband's name was being slandered at court, and advised her, when she obtained an audience, to tell the benevolent Emperor the real facts.

The widow soon had an opportunity of following this advice:

'Your Majesty, everybody has enemies,' she said with feeling at the audience, 'but nobody has been more strenuously and continuously attacked and slandered by his enemies than my husband, merely because he had such great talent! People have had the audacity to tell Your Majesty many lies about him; the debts he left behind him have been exaggerated tenfold. I vouch with my life that three thousand florins would liquidate all his debts. And these debts have not been rashly incurred. We have had no fixed income; we have had many children, and I suffered a serious and costly illness lasting a year and a half. Your Majesty, can you not make allowance, you with your kind heart?'

'If it really is as you say', said the monarch, 'then there is still time to do something for you. Let a concert be given of the works he left, and I will support it.'[1]

On 11 December 1791 – perhaps the day of the audience described above – Constanze submitted an application for a pension.[2] In order to be eligible for this pension, the late husband had to have been in Imperial Royal service for at least ten years, whereas Mozart had filled his position for only four.

On 30 December 1791, the application had reached the man responsible for music at court, Johann Wenzel, Count Ugarte, who wrote the now famous passage explaining how Emperor Joseph II had engaged Mozart in the first place. Ugarte suggested granting Constanze a yearly 200 Gulden and the orphans 50 Gulden each 'as a special *ex gratia* salary'. But this sum was found to be unacceptable to the authorities (the *Obersthofmeisteramt*).

On 5 January 1792, a month after Mozart's death, these authorities suggested to Constanze that she re-apply with a sworn affidavit stating that she had no right to a pension from the *Tonkünstler-Societät* (Society of Musicians). (We have seen that Mozart had never been an official member of the Society because he could not or would not produce a birth-certificate.) The Society provided Constanze with the affidavit and on 25 February the file was re-submitted. On 5 March 1792, the director of the court's financial section, Johann Rudolph, Count Chotek, wrote that 'the widow . . . according to the strict interpretation of the pension procedures has no right to a pension but only to a severance payment consisting of a quarter's salary, *i.e.*, the sum of 200 Gulden.' But it seemed that the court was highly embarrassed 'to provide the widow of a man of such talents who had been in royal service with a beggar's staff.' Therefore, Chotek suggests, 'in this special case and without setting a precedent', that Constanze and her children receive one-third of her late husband's salary, *viz.* 266 fl. 40 kr., back-dated to 1 January 1792. This was the definitive and final suggestion for the pension.

Leopold II had died on 1 March and the new Emperor, Francis, was presented with the petition on 12 March. He signed it forthwith: 'Placet–Franz m.p.' On 13 March, Constanze's pension was sent to the proper office for registration and implementation.

It was not a generous pension, but it was certainly a 'basis'; and Constanze had meanwhile found herself with many friends and well-wishers. First there were benefit and memorial concerts – one in Prague was especially impressive. It took place in the Parish Church of St Nicholas on 14 December, and Mozart's beloved orchestra of the National Theatre under Joseph Strobach and a choir with Josepha Duschek as soprano solo – a total of 120 musicians – gave a performance of Rosetti's Requiem. 'On the day itself', wrote the *Pressburger Zeitung*,

> All the bells of the Parish church were rung, and almost the entire city streamed towards the square, so that the Wälscher Platz could hardly accommodate all the carriages nor could the large church, which can house nearly 4000 persons, contain all the admirers of the transfigured [Mozart] . . .[3]

And only the *Pressburger Zeitung* reports on a concert given in Vienna in the Burgtheater on 23 December 1791, to which the court contributed 150 ducats (675 Gulden) and which altogether brought in 1500 Gulden.[4] (That the *Pressburger Zeitung* sometimes tended to go overboard on the subject of Mozart may be seen in the following report, dated 21 December: '. . . the widow of the late Herr *Kapellmeister* Mozart has now been provided for. H.M. the Emperor has granted her the entire salary of her husband, and her son has been taken in custody by Baron van Swieten.'[5] Neither had in fact happened.)

Constanze received a present from Archduke Maximilian Franz, Elector of Cologne and Beethoven's patron, who sent the widow 24 ducats (108 Gulden). By 7 February 1792, Friedrich Wilhelm II of Prussia had ordered his Ambassador, Baron von Jacobi (a Freemason in Mozart's Lodge), to purchase several of Mozart's compositions at 100 ducats each, including the Requiem – for a total of 800 ducats (3600 Gulden).[6] This was a huge sum and a great financial help to Constanze. All this suggested that she was really quite a clever manager (though it took Mozart's death to enable her to display this side of her personality), and that she now commanded much personal sympathy.

Constanze's next move was to commission a performance of the Requiem. Baron von Swieten made the necessary arrangements, and on 2 January 1793 the work was first performed at the Jahn Rooms[7] (where Mozart had given his last public concert some two years earlier). The Hungarian paper *Magyar Hirmondó* reported:

> Mozart, who has made an immortal name for himself in music, left behind a widow and two orphans in a state of poverty. Many noble well-wishers are helping this unhappy woman. The day before yesterday Baron von Swieten arranged a public concert with a sung Requiem as a memorial to Mozart. The widow received the box-office receipts of over 300 gold ducats [1350 Gulden].

Early in February 1794, another memorial concert was put on in Prague (in the Konviktsaal of the University)[8] at which Constanze and her two children were present (Carl was now boarding with the Niemetscheks) – in tears, like most of the audience. An orchestra played the 'Linz' and 'Prague' Symphonies, and the D minor Piano Concerto (K.466); Josepha Duschek sang the great Rondò *Non più di fiori* from *Tito*.

Then Constanze had a brilliant idea: Vienna had not yet heard Mozart's last opera in its entirety, and she persuaded the authorities to allow her to perform it as a benefit concert in the Kärntnerthortheater on 29 December 1794.[9] Aloysia Lange sang the part of Sextus.

Constanze had now moved to more modest quarters in the 'House at the Blue Sable', No. 1046, Krugerstrasse (a house where Haydn was to live in 1798 during preparations for *The Creation*). *Tito* was such a success that she repeated the whole operation in Lent 1795[10] – again with Aloysia Lange and other, equally celebrated artists (Giuseppe Viganoni sang Titus, Marianna Sessi was Vitellia, and

Publius was sung by Johann Michael Vogl, later a friend of Schubert). Between the acts Beethoven played Mozart's D minor Piano Concerto (K.466), probably improvising the famous cadenzas which he later wrote down (WoO 58).[11]

On 1 May 1795, Constanze proposed an even bolder idea: the publication of Mozart's *Idomeneo* (one of his particular favourites) by subscription.[12] But in this noble undertaking she failed; the opera had been totally forgotten and not enough subscribers could be found. The world was not quite ready for Mozart's lesser-known operas, but within a year or two a publisher for the piano score was found in Germany (Schmid & Rauh of Leipzig), and gradually this first fruit of Mozart's mature operatic genius began to appear in the repertoire.

In September 1795, Constanze took *Tito* to Graz as a benefit for herself and her two sons.[13] Apparently fired by the success of this still neglected work in all these benefit concerts, Constanze now decided to take *Tito* on tour in Germany with herself (as Vitellia)[14] and Aloysia Lange among the singers. The first stop was Leipzig, where she gave *Tito* in extracts and other pieces in the famous Gewandhaus (11 November 1795). She then went on to Berlin, where she applied to Mozart's old admirer, Friedrich Wilhelm II of Prussia, for permission to give a benefit concert with *Tito* as the feature. The King granted permission to mount the concert in the great opera house, using the royal orchestra, and the notable event took place (without Madame Lange, who was, apparently, singing in the Hamburg Opera House) on Sunday, 28 February 1796. On her return journey Constanze gave a second concert in Leipzig (April 1796) with the Requiem, and it was such a success that a third concert was given (25 April 1796) in which Aloysia Lange again participated and the entrance chorus of *Thamos* (in the arrangement as a Latin motet) was performed. Dresden followed in May – again with *Tito*. In late December 1796 she was back in Graz, to arrange (with her own participation) a benefit concert with selections not only from that opera but also, in the first part of the concert, from *Idomeneo*, awaiting its rediscovery. In all this Constanze displayed an interesting flair for her husband's lesser-known works, always making sure to include operas (which always attract the mundane public) as well as other pieces, both instrumental and vocal.

* * *

Constanze remembered that Prague had always maintained a special love and veneration for Mozart; hence it was in the Bohemian capital that she decided to begin the musical career of her son, Franz Xaver Wolfgang. He had been in Prague since 1796, at first with Josepha Duschek and later with Niemetschek. On 15 November 1797, in the historic National Theatre – the scene of so many of Mozart's triumphs (and of the ignominious première of *Tito* in 1791) – Constanze launched her second son on what she hoped would be a musical career as a *Wunderkind*:

Part One

The beginning is a symphony by Mozart.

1. Mad. Campi sings a bravura aria by Mozart.
2. Mr Witassek (pianoforte) plays a grand, powerful concerto by Mozart.
3. Mad. Mozart, Messrs Campi and Benedetti sing a posthumous Trio ['Mandina amabile', insertion in Bianchi's *La villanella rapita*], an excellent work by Mozart.
4. Mr Campi sings a bass aria by Mozart.
5. By gracious request the small, just six-year-old *Wolfgang*, Mozart's younger son, will be presented to the admirable public of Prague, which displayed such manifold affection for his father. He will proffer a small token of thanks for this, and will attempt to follow the great example of his father, singing the Aria 'Der Vogelfänger bin ich' ['I am the bird-catcher'] from *The Magic Flute*, accompanied on the pianoforte.

One asks for forbearance at this first attempt to display his gentle talents.

Second Part

1. An Overture and the subsequent Quartet from an unfinished opera by Mozart [*Lo sposo deluso*].
2. Mad. Campi sings an aria by Mozart.
3. Mad. Mozart, Messrs Benedetti, Zardi and Campi sing a quartet finale by Mozart ['Dite almeno', insertion in Bianchi's *La villanella rapita*].
4. The conclusion is a German scene with a final chorus, celebrating the joyous return of peace [in the Napoleonic Wars: the treaty of Campo Formio, October 1797]. The poetry is specially written for the occasion by the famous poet and university professor, Mr A. Meissner.

   The music of the recitative is by Mr Witassek, the chorus from Mozart's *La clemenza di Tito*; the latter was chosen because it is hoped that on such a joyous occasion the public will join in the festive chorus.

   The printed text can be obtained at the box-office for 7 kr. and the income will be given to the Poor-house.

   N.B. All these pieces, except the chorus, are new and have not yet been performed [in Prague] . . .[15]

Mozart's second son pursued a very modest career as composer and musician, and died in 1844. The elder son, Carl Thomas, studied music in Italy but later became a government official, dying as a bookkeeper for the Austrian government in Milan in 1858. There are no surviving members of the immediate family.

In 1797, the Danish Secretary of Legation, Georg Nikolaus (later von) Nissen, who had been in Vienna since 1793, became Constanze's lodger. They became friends and, later, lovers. They married in 1809 before moving to Copenhagen.[16] Nissen took an active part in Constanze's attempt to salvage Mozart's legacy and to sell his musical manuscripts to two German publishers – Breitkopf & Härtel in Leipzig and J. A. André in Offenbach. Nissen actually wrote most of Constanze's business correspondence and helped her enormously.

By now, it is clear that Constanze regarded *La clemenza di Tito* as Mozart's most neglected work, and her production of it became an annual, even a semi-annual, event in Vienna's musical life. In 1798 she gave it on 27 April (Carl Joseph Rosenbaum, a friend of Haydn's and an Esterházy court official, heard it and reported the event in his diary);[17] on 8 December she gave it again, with her sister Josepha Hofer as Servilia and Josepha's second husband, Friedrich Sebastian Mayer, as Publius, in Schikaneder's Freyhaustheater.[18] The great impresario printed, in the textbook, the note that 'Mozart's work is noble beyond any praise; when one hears it, as with any of his music, one feels too keenly what Art has lost.'

* * *

What was Constanze like in 1798? She had suffered terribly and made a brilliant comeback; the year before, she had lent the Duscheks in Prague 3500 Gulden at 6 per cent interest. During this period, the Swedish diplomat F. A. Silverstolpe was in Vienna, and recorded his impressions of Constanze,[19] whom he invited to dinner with Nissen and with whom he played billiards. When he left Vienna in 1803 for another post, he noted, 'She is an *estimable person*, I shall miss her company as long as I live.' Another reliable description of Constanze Mozart is in Niemetschek (1798), who wrote:

> Mozart was happy in his marriage to Constanze Weber. He found in her a good and loving wife, who was able to fall in with his every mood, and thereby win his complete confidence and exercise great influence over him. This, however, she used only in preventing him from making hasty decisions. He loved her dearly, confided everything in her, even his petty sins – and she

forgave him with loving-kindness and tenderness. Vienna was witness to this and his widow still thinks nostalgically of the days of her marriage.*[20]

His greatest pleasure was music. If his wife wanted to give him a special surprise at a family festivity, she would secretly arrange a performance of a new church composition by Michael or Joseph Haydn.

He was very fond of billiards, probably because it gave him physical exercise. He had a billiard table at home. There he and his wife played every day.

But Constanze was not without enemies, even at this period. Leopold Mozart and Maria Anna (Nannerl), Wolfgang's sister, had not liked her, as can be surmised from the following remarks made in a letter written by Maria Anna in 1792 for the future biography of Friedrich Schlichtegroll:

> Both Mozart's parents were in their time the handsomest couple in Salzburg; and in her younger years the daughter was considered to be a regular beauty. But the son Wolfgang was small, thin, of pale complexion, and quite without any remarkable aspects in his outward appearance and frame. Except for his music he remained *a child*; and this is the main aspect of the dark side of his character: he always required a father, a mother, or some attendant; he could not manage money, married against his father's will a girl not at all suitable for him; and hence the great disorder in his household during and after his death.[21]

We have seen that Vincent and Mary Novello went to visit Constanze in Salzburg (where, ironically, both she and Wolfgang's sister, now Frau von Berchtold zu Sonnenburg were living). This was in 1829; Constanze had met, married,

*This worthy woman conducts herself in a seemly way in her widowhood, and is a good mother to both her children. She lives in Vienna on her pension and a small income from the money her husband left. [original footnote.]

and lost Nissen, whose imperfect but nonetheless vital Mozart biography had been published in 1828, a year after his death. The Novellos' diaries give us a vivid impression of Constanze, certainly the most accurate and interesting ever recorded.

> M.N. We have just seen Mozart's widow – oh what a world of sensations has this interview excited – the woman that was so dear to him, whom he has so often fondly caressed, for whom his anxiety and tender solicitude urged on [*sic*] to such great and glorious efforts of his genius, next to seeing himself it was the nearest approach to his earthly remains, and I felt during the whole interview as if his spirit were with us; how could it be otherwise as I held his portrait in my hand which breathes of life and of him. When I first entered I was so overcome with various emotions that I could do nothing but weep and embrace her. She seemed also affected and said repeatedly in French 'oh quelle bonheur pour moi, de voir les enthousiastes pour mon Mozart'. She speaks French fluently though with a German accent, in Italian she thinks better but as I do not converse in that language she politely continued in French. She is indeed completely a well bred Lady, and though no remains of beauty appear except in her eyes such as the engraving prefixed to her biography of Mozart would indicate, yet she keeps her figure and a certain air, well, for a woman of her age, which I suppose must be 65. She is charmingly lodged in the Nun's street half way up a cliff from which a most extensive and charming view is gained scarcely to be equalled in the world. The apartments, like most foreign ones, are not encumbered with furniture and the room she received us in opened to a cabinet which contained her bed, but it was tastefully covered with a bright green silk counterpane forming a nice unison with some flowers round the room. . . .

V.N. Description of Madame Nissen. In youth her Eyes must have been very brilliant and are still fine. Her face does not resemble the portrait given of her in the Biography. It is thin and has the traces of great care and anxiety in it, but when her features relax into a smile, the expression is a remarkably pleasant one. She is of a rather small stature, slim figure, and looks much younger than what I expected to find her. Her voice is low and gentle, her manners well-bred and prepossessing, unconstrained like a person who has lived much in society and seen a good deal of the world, and the way in which she spoke of her illustrious Husband (though not quite so enthusiastic as I should have expected in one 'so near and dear' to him) was tender and affectionate, and I could perceive a little tremor in her voice whilst she was looking with me at his portrait and on two or three occasions when she was alluding to some of the last years of his Life, which was not the less affecting or pathetic, from its being involuntary, unobtrusive and partly repressed. Nothing could be more kind, friendly and even cordial than her behaviour to me during the whole visit. Altogether this Lady is, to me, one of the most interesting Persons now in existence. . . .

M.N. She told us that Mozart when he finished an opera brought it to her and begged she would study it, after which he would play it over and sing with her, so that not only the songs but the words she knew by heart, but one air in the 'Idomeneo' he preferred to hear her sing and on that account she prefers it also, 'Se il Padre perdei' . . . The most happy time of his life was whilst at Munich during which he wrote Idomeneo which may account for the affection he entertained towards the work.

V.N. The widow seemed pleased when I mentioned so many pieces out of his operas – 'Oh, I see you know them all by heart as I do' – she knows all the words by memory as well as the music . . . told me that 'Non so più' in 'Figaro' was a great favourite with Mozart, also 'Riconosci a questo amplesso' [Sextet from *Figaro*].

In 'Così fan tutte' she remarked that in 'Di scrivermi' (which I guessed was one of his favourites) you could actually fancy the sobs and tears of the performers – also noticed the extraordinary *difference* of the melodies he has assigned to the various characters and the wonderful appropriateness of them – the passages of the Ghost part of Don Giovanni made one's hair stand on end . . . She does not admire the plot of 'Così fan', but agreed with me that such music would carry any piece through . . .

M.N. The son [Franz Xaver Wolfgang] said, when I was remarking how much younger his Mother looked than she really was, she is my Mother but it must be allowed that she has great qualities to secure the esteem of two such husbands as she has had . . . she is really a delightful woman. When we left she would accompany us for a little walk – and behold Vin and I supporting the wife of Mozart. It was a delicious recompense for my dear Vin after all his exertions in behalf of Mozart's music to render this token of respect to this relic of the divine man. Our walk was most delightful. Great respect is shown to her by the inhabitants of Salzburg although she seldom quits home, having such a delicious house and garden, where she can quietly enjoy the air without fatigue.

Madame declares she could not bear to hear either the Requiem or 'Idomeneo' performed, the last time she heard 'Il Don Giovanni', she was not calm for a fortnight afterwards. At Prague she thinks the operas have been best performed, and very well sometimes at Vienna, but at present whilst the Italian singers are there, there is no chance of hearing Mozart's operas, when they leave, they are performed.[22]

Here we have, without question, the most accurate description of Constanze we shall ever find. She was a cultivated lady with three languages and polished manners, extremely musical (she sang to the Novellos the part in the minuet of the String Quartet in D minor (K.421), where Wolfgang had written into the score her cries when she was in labour)[23] and obviously very likable even in old age.

* * *

'Side by side in the long line of mourners' at the funeral of Felix Mendelssohn in the afternoon of 7 November 1847 in Leipzig, two acquaintances moved slowly towards the church. They grieved at another 'early loss' for music, and the talk 'turned to the more particular consideration of music in itself, and to the great masters of the past.' It was a period when Beethoven had all but obliterated appreciation for Haydn's music and even Mozart's star now shone less brightly on the musical horizon than previously. 'At a certain period of our mental development Mozart's music had seemed cold and unintelligible to our restless spirits, ever soaring into the unknown, and incapable of appreciating a master whose passions in their workings are not laid bare to view . . . We agreed . . . that [nevertheless] minds which are able to receive and appreciate art for its own sake, must yield themselves captive to Mozart, but without sacrificing their freedom to recognize all that is grand and beautiful elsewhere.'

From that conversation the first 'modern', scientific biography of Mozart was born, for one of the two men in that funeral procession was Otto Jahn (the other was Gustav Hartenstein), whose monumental study in four volumes began to appear in 1856, the centenary of Mozart's birth, and was concluded three years later.[24] In it we have the following long footnote on the subject of Constanze's character, taken from the official English translation by Pauline Townsend of 1882:

I cannot undertake to give anything like a comprehensive description of Mozart's wife, although I have received many communications from trustworthy persons who have known her personally. Their knowledge is of her later years only, and their accounts are often inconsistent. This inconsistency arises from the conflict in the widow's mind between pride in the fame of the husband, of whose greatness she was fully aware only after his death, and a painful remembrance of the hardships of their married life. These hardships she was inclined to ascribe solely to his want of capacity for practical affairs, and an injured feeling was often mingled with her unbounded pride in Mozart's artistic achievements and her belief in his love for her. The peculiarities of her second husband, Nissen, a business man, painfully accurate and precise, tended no doubt to intensify the contrast. Nissen's was an honourable, although a commonplace nature, and he had earned Constanze's gratitude by his care for her in her widowed and destitute condition, and by placing her in a good worldly position as his wife; so that it is not surprising that Mozart's memory should have passed into the background, with the exception of his musical fame, which Nissen could not rival. At any rate, we find Constanze continually posing as a patient martyr, suffering from the thoughtlessness of a man of genius, who remained a child to the end of his days. This is unjust to Mozart, but it would be equally unjust to Constanze to make her mainly responsible for the family difficulties.

I propose to show that the prejudice against Constanze Mozart originated with Leopold Mozart, and in turn that Leopold's prejudice had its roots in Wolfgang's early relationship with the Weber family. To trace this first encounter with the Webers we must go back to 1778 and the ill-fated trip that Mozart and his mother made to Paris. En route they spent four and a half months in Mannheim

(30 October 1777–14 March 1778), where Mozart hoped, vainly as it turned out, to secure a position with the Elector; and where he fell in love with Aloysia, daughter of Fridolin Weber (1733–79) – uncle of the composer Carl Maria von Weber – and Maria Cäcilie. The father had a very modest position as a bass singer at the Mannheim court and supplemented his meagre salary by music-copying and prompting. He had little more than a year to live by the time Mozart was courting his daughter. Weber's daughters included two who were to become spectacular coloratura sopranos – the eldest, Josepha (Mozart's first Queen of the Night) and the second, Aloysia. Mozart proposed accompanying Aloysia and Josepha with their father to Italy and merrily suggested visiting Salzburg en route to Italy with this entourage, saying that 'my sister will find a friend and companion' in Aloysia.[25] Maria Anna wrote to her husband, 'You will have seen . . . that when Wolfgang makes new acquaintances, he immediately wants to cede his life and property to them.'[26]

Leopold Mozart was, rightly, horrified. He stayed up the whole night before answering and explained at great length and with considerable patience that the Italian scheme was ill-planned: no German prima donna was launched in Italy before having sung many times in her native country. 'As for your proposal (I can scarcely write when I think of it) . . . it has nearly put me out of my mind . . . Your letter reads like a romance . . .'[27] Wolfgang had meanwhile reflected and, with considerable reluctance, and under constant pressure from Leopold, mother and son set off for Paris. There, on 3 July, Mozart's mother died, and Wolfgang's next scheme was to import Aloysia and her father to Paris for the coming winter,[28] but this plan came to naught, not least because Wolfgang's own attempts to conquer the French capital were, to put it mildly, unsuccessful. Leopold wrote in a letter of 3 September 1778 that 'as for Mslle. Weber, you shouldn't think that I would be opposed to this acquaintance. All young people have to bang their heads against the wall. You can go on writing [to each other] as before ...'[29] But he was beginning to be extremely suspicious of the Webers. In another letter (23 November 1778) he writes, 'Herr Weber is a man like most of his kind. ... He flattered you when he needed you ...'[30]

Mozart arrived in Munich on Christmas Day 1778[31] and, dressed in his French suit of mourning (red coat and black buttons), he found Aloysia in a room with other people. 'She seemed ... not to know him any more.' So Mozart sat down at the piano and with a heart 'full of tears' bravely sang, 'I'll gladly leave the girl who doesn't love me any more.'[32] The Nissen biography continues:

> From now on her sister *Constanze*, who was perhaps more attracted by his talent than by his person, and was sympathetic to his betrayal by Aloysia, sought to entertain him. He taught her pianoforte and, as she was a willing pupil, with pleasure. Later they saw each other again in Vienna and discovered that *Constanze* made more impression on Mozart than had Aloysia previously.

One can imagine Leopold's deep suspicion when Wolfgang, in December 1781, broke the news to his father that he had fallen in love with Constanze (the Weber family, like Wolfgang, had meanwhile moved to Vienna). Here, in a letter to his father of 15 December 1781, is Mozart's extraordinarily level-headed and even coldly dispassionate description of the daughters:

> The eldest [Josepha] is a lazy, crude perfidious woman, as cunning as a fox. – Mme Lange [Aloysia had meanwhile married a court actor, Joseph Lange in 1780] is a false, malicious person and a flirt. – The youngest [Sophie] is still too young to be anything special – she's just a good-natured but scatterbrained creature! God protect her from seduction! – But the middle one, my good, dear Konstanze [a few lines earlier he spells her 'Costanza', the Italian form] ... has the kindest of hearts, is the

cleverest and in short the best of the lot . . . She is not ugly, but also far from beautiful. – Her whole beauty consists in two little black eyes and a pretty figure. She has no wit, but enough common sense to enable her to fulfil her duties as wife and mother . . . – She understands housekeeping, and has the best heart in the world – I love her and she loves me dearly . . .'[33]

But tongues were already wagging, and Leopold received sinister tales of the conniving Weber family. They had insisted on a marriage contract with Wolfgang, who, despite his immense talents, was, when all was said and done, only a freelance musician with limitless prospects but no fixed salary. The family required Wolfgang to sign a statement saying that 'I bind myself to marry Mlle Constanze Weber within the period of three years and if it should prove impossible because I were to change my mind, she should be entitled to claim three hundred Gulden p.a. from me.' As soon as Constanze's guardian was gone, she called for the document and tearing it up said, 'Dear Mozart! I need no written assurance from you. I believe your word without it.'[34]

Despite the apparent sincerity of the lovers, however, Leopold suspected the worst: that Madame Weber and Constanze's guardian were 'seducers of youth' and ought to be made to sweep the streets like prostitutes in Maria Theresa's time. Leopold also heard that Madame Weber took a drop too much and Wolfgang (in a letter of 10 April 1782) had to admit that 'she [does] drink and more – than a woman should'[35]

Constanze was, like her elder sister Aloysia, something of a flirt – a Viennese habit which has not changed in 200 years – and in a letter of 29 April 1782, Wolfgang remonstrates with her for letting a young blade 'measure the calves of your legs. – No woman who holds her honour dear can do such a thing.'[36] Constanze had meanwhile left her mother's apartment and had gone to live with Baroness

Waldstätten who, separated from her husband, befriended the newly engaged couple. Constanze apparently retorted that the Baroness had done the same at the party. 'The case is quite different,' said Mozart firmly, 'for she is a woman beyond her prime (who can't possibly attract any longer) – and moreover she's altogether inclined to be fond of *et cetera* . . .' He hopes, even if Constanze does not marry him, that she will 'never lead a life like that.' (The fact that Constanze kept all these letters shows that she did not consider her action in the least damaging. She and Nissen suppressed certain letters and passages within letters, mainly to protect persons still living, when publishing them in the Nissen biography.)

Wolfgang was longing for parental approval: he did not receive it at once, but finally Leopold sent his unwilling blessing, after Wolfgang had been united with his Constanze at St Stephen's Cathedral on 4 August 1782. In a letter to Salzburg on 7 August, we read:

> When we had been joined together, both my wife and I began to weep. – All those present, even the priest, were touched. – And all wept to see how much our hearts were moved.[37]

In a letter ten days later Mozart adds:

> For some time before we were married we had always attended Mass and gone to confession and received Communion together; and I discovered that never had I prayed so ardently or confessed and received Communion so devoutly as by her side; and she felt likewise. In short we are made for one another; and God who orders all things and hence this too, will not forsake us.[38]

Not God but German musicology forsook that marriage. It is hard to know precisely when it started. In the great biography by Hermann Abert of 1919–21, we read a then new approach.[39] Constanze started her marriage with Mozart as a silly and irresponsible girl, but under his tactful guidance, and even more under the wise diplomatic eye of Nissen, she improved and became, towards the end of her life, a good citizen and mother. She is pictured by Abert as coming from a family of 'a widespread moral degeneracy', to which she 'certainly contributed her part'. This 'consisted in particular in a total lack of inner breeding, of morals in a higher sense.' Constanze did not tear up the marriage contract 'because of an inner tact of the heart but simply in a sudden wave of sentimentality.' German musicology knows better. 'It is beyond question that as Mozart's bride, under the mother's influence, she was a real "Weberische" in Leopold's sense . . . [she had] not the faintest conception of the moral principles of her future marriage.' And so forth.

Arthur Schurig's biography of 1913 set the pattern for portraying Constanze as a scheming, brainless sex-symbol. During 'the whole of her life [Constanze] never had an inkling of Mozart's deeply isolated inner life.' Her sexuality was particularly repellent to German scholars: it 'robbed the marriage of the intensity of its artistic productivity.'[40]

Wolfgang Hildesheimer, whose Mozart biography of 1977 has ultimately led to Peter Shaffer's *Amadeus* and a five-part French television documentary on Mozart (written by Beatrice Rubenstein and Marcel Bluwal), has this to say on the subject:

> Constanze had an easy-going but withal pushing nature; she granted Mozart – and perhaps not only him – erotic, or at least sexual satisfaction, but was unable to grant him that happiness that a lesser man would have required for his self-satisfaction . . . It is unlikely that she ever really suffered physically and in her physical difficulties we may see a more than welcome excuse to take the waters . . .[41]

Hildesheimer's book had an interesting side-effect. It was favourably reviewed in the *New York Review of Books* by Alan Tyson,[42] a highly regarded scholar. In that review, Tyson proposed that the father of Constanze's youngest son, Franz Xaver Wolfgang, born on 26 July 1791, was Süssmayr (hence the shared first two Christian names); and that Mozart was fully aware of the situation: a charming little *ménage à trois*, in fact. Tyson took this remarkable and bizarre idea from a scholarly article by Dieter Schickling.[43] From Hildesheimer's attitude to Schickling's proposal, that Constanze slept regularly with Mozart's pupil Süssmayr and agreed to name the child of their illicit union with the adulterer's Christian names, seemed to be a logical step.

The young German scholar, Volkmar Braunbehrens (1986), is the first to take serious objection to this wicked defamation of Constanze's character. He writes that she deserves a great deal better than she has received. He notes that Leopold Mozart, although thoroughly disapproving of the whole Weber family, could find nothing of which he could disapprove during his stay in Vienna with Constanze and Wolfgang.[44] 'Nonetheless this aversion to Constanze, which continues unabated until the present day, probably has its origin in him [Leopold] . . .'

All other German scholars have preferred to start their investigations into the character of Constanze from Leopold's standpoint. But for that, Constanze would have appeared in an entirely different light. Braunbehrens sums up:

> If we therefore adhere to the little we know about Constanze Mozart from the first period of her marriage, and if we candidly admit that this little is insufficient to establish a complete picture of her personality, we must agree that there is not the least reason for any kind of negative opinion.

But I believe another, and perhaps higher, precept obtains in the case of Constanze and Wolfgang Mozart; it needs to be presented with peculiar force:

> 'Those whom God hath joined together let no man put asunder.'

Appendix A

AN ILLUSTRATED STUDY OF MOZART'S APARTMENT AND WARDROBE
by Else Radant

The bourgeois dwelling-house in eighteenth-century Vienna took its general form largely from the size and shape of messuages laid out in the Gothic period. Property was expensive, hence the individual lots were long and narrow, often only forty feet in width. The house in which Mozart lived for the final year of his life corresponded to this type. No. 970[1] is, because of its jutting façade, clearly identifiable on the bird's-eye plan by Daniel Huber of 1769–74 (ill. 14) as the third house on what was by then known as the Rauhensteingasse.[2] The owner of the house from 1775 to 1795 was Elisabeth Dabokur (*recte* d'Abocur); most houses in Vienna bore a name, and Madame d'Abocur's was 'das kleine Kaiserhaus' (small, imperial house).

In 1806, the house was to have been rebuilt, and the master-builder Adam Hildwein submitted his plan to the authorities. The plan was in two forms, both of which exist now only in copies of 1873 by Emil Hütter: an elevation of the façade (ill. 12) and a groundplan of the first (US second) floor, including, of course, the apartment of which Constanze (in Mozart's absence) took possession in 1790. Valuable as the plan is, it does not entirely correspond with the layout of the apartment in Mozart's day. We see the street front (at the bottom of the plan) with (to the left) one window opening towards the Himmelpfortgasse and the small line which shows the façade of the neighbouring house, set back from the street (Rauhensteingasse). The left-hand corner room with the three windows was, according to tradition, Mozart's study, and the list of furniture in the Suspense Order (the effects listed after his death) bears this out (see p. 220); behind this room are four other rooms, a stairwell and a rectangular space which, if we examine the Huber plan, might have been a transverse wing. We also see, in the middle, the well of a large, rectangular courtyard, and, to the right, a second apartment which was reached by a spiral staircase. The walls indicated by the lighter shading on the sketch are marked in red on the original and show the planned additions and/or transformations. On the right was to be a second large stairwell, and in the centre a second courtyard and a chimney big enough for a sweep, with outlets for four

12 *Elevation by Adam Hildwein (1806) of the Rauhensteingasse house. It has now been established that – contrary to earlier supposition – only the two left-hand windows on the 1st (US 2nd) floor belong to Mozart's apartment. Entrance was by the large archway on the ground floor.*

13 *Detail from a bird's-eye perspective of Vienna and its suburbs by Joseph Daniel von Huber (engraving, 1769–74). The house in the Rauhensteingasse is arrowed.*

stoves, indicated on the plan by small circles. In the third room on the left was to be a chimney and also a ventilation space opposite the new courtyard. Between the third and fourth rooms is a wall that, curiously, appears to be of variable thickness, so that one may assume there was, in Mozart's day, a connecting door in the wall. The firewall on the right also shows red shading; if the bird's-eye perspective is accurate, the neighbouring house was in 1806 lower than ours and these red sections indicate opening which were walled up. In the nineteenth century, the house was demolished, three lots were amalgamated and a large apartment house was erected which, after World War II, was rebuilt entirely. Today the department store Steffel is on the site of Mozart's house; on the third floor of Steffel can be found various objects commemorating the composer.

What do we actually know about Mozarts apartment? It is said that it was not well lit: Mozart's pupil Süssmayr described it as a dark apartment, but added that one room had windows onto the well of the courtyard. The Suspense Order gives us an exact list of the furniture, room by room, and hence we know that the apartment consisted of four rooms, with a vestibule which also served as the kitchen. Taken together, this information strongly suggests that the Mozarts lived in the apartment which consisted of four rooms on the left-hand side of the building, aligned from front to back. Dr Alfred Lechner of the Technische Hochschule in Vienna has kindly undertaken to reconstruct the whole first (US second) floor of the house and has also attempted to place the

Neue
Markt
Francisc
Platzel

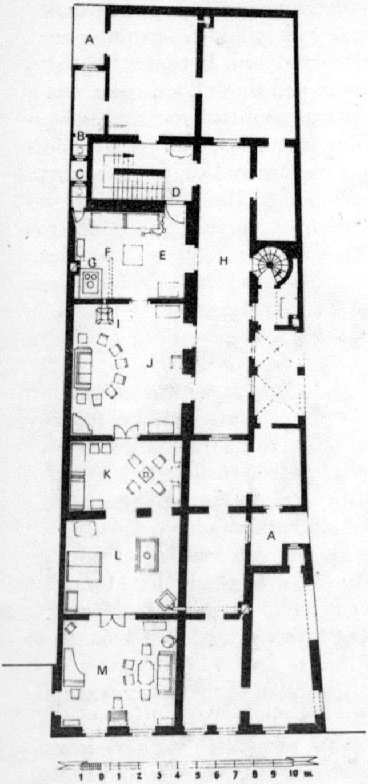

Items listed in the Suspense Order of December 1791

In the vestibule and kitchen [E]:
2 tables of soft wood, 1 old ditto wardrobe, 1 Spanish wall [screen], 2 bedsteads of soft wood, 1 closet with doors, remaining small quantity of kitchen utensils
(listed separately) 1 ordinary servant's bed

Furnishings in the first room [J]:
2 chests of drawers in hard wood, 1 sofa and 6 chairs upholstered in canvas, 2 small stools, 1 corner cupboard in soft wood, 1 commode, 1 set of Venetian blinds, 2 curtains

In the second room [K]:
3 tables of hard wood, 2 divans and 6 chairs upholstered in stiff linen material, 2 lacquered cupboards with doors, 1 mirror in gilt frame, 1 ordinary central chandelier, 1 set of panels with wallpaper, 3 porcelain figures, 1 ditto box

In the third room [L]:
1 table of hard wood, 1 billiard table with green felt and 5 balls, 12 cues, 1 lantern and 4 candlesticks, 1 iron stove with stove-pipe
(listed separately) 1 matrimonial bed and 1 children's cot

In the fourth room [M]:
1 table of hard wood, 1 couch and 6 chairs upholstered in old damask, 1 roll-top desk, 1 clock, wheel-work movement in a gold case, 1 forte-piano with pedal, 1 viola in its case, 1 lacquered writing cupboard [a kind of filing cabinet], 2 bookcases in soft wood, 60 pieces of various porcelain, 1 brass pestle, 3 brass candlesticks, 2 coffee-grinders, 2 glass candlesticks, 1 tin teapot, 1 lacquered serving tray, some ordinary glasses

14 (OPPOSITE)
Groundplan of Mozart's apartment in a reconstruction by Dr Alfred Lechner (1987), showing the apartment as it was in Mozart's day and the probable position of the furniture possessed by him.

A small courtyard
B toilet (next floor)
C toilet
D entrance and staircase to Mozart's apartment
E vestibule and kitchen
F chimney
G oven
H courtyard
I stove and smoke-funnel
J living-room
K sitting-room
L billiard-room
M study

furniture as indicated in the Suspense Order. We publish here Dr Lechner's reconstruction (ill. 14).

One evidently entered Mozart's apartment via the stairwell at the back and arrived in the vestibule/kitchen. In the corner of the kitchen was a large chimney, with a smoke-funnel for the stove in the living-room, which was the one Süssmayr described as dark and with windows opening onto the courtyard. Between the living-room and the billiard-room was a sitting-room that received light only from those two rooms; hence it was dark and contained a central chandelier. The billiard-room was perhaps separated from Mozart's study by a large glass door. The study had the most light and was the airiest. The other, windowless rooms were a heritage of the Gothic period, which architecturally continued well into the seventeenth century. It was to improve this situation that the plan of 1806 included a second courtyard, so that all the rooms would have windows.

A very different layout was previously assumed for Mozart's apartment. In 1887, the *Wiener Extrablatt* reproduced a sketch of Mozart's study (ill. 15) and a groundplan of the apartment (ill. 16) by Johann Peter Lyser, from whose fertile pen we have many sketches of Beethoven (probably all posthumous). Lyser's sketch, which was based on his examination of the house before its destruction in 1849, is notable for its inclusion of a piano of the period 1825! By the time Lyser examined the property, the layout had evidently been altered. We can see, in his plan, the second courtyard planned by Hildwein, around which the apartment was now grouped, and the new chimney with the stoves. The

15, 16 *Sketch of Mozart's study and groundplan of apartment by J. P. Lyser (1847), showing incorrect disposition across the house.*

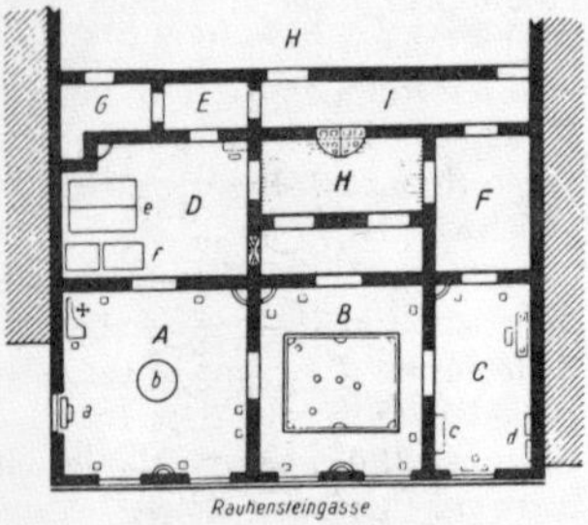

A music-room, in which Mozart died
a) his last desk
b) table
B billiard-room
C study
c) spinet
d) wall cupboard
D bedroom
e) double bed
f) children's cot
E dressing-room
F vestibule
G kitchen
H courtyard
I passage

shaded section outside the house (above) shows where the neighbouring house, set back, began. In Lyser's sketch, Mozart's 'last desk' is placed in front of this side window.

The furnishings of a bourgeois rented flat in eighteenth-century Vienna were very simple. The furniture of the Josephinian period, during which Mozart married and set up house, was characterized by straight lines (avoiding the curves of the Rococo), excellent craftsmanship and a marked ability to deal with all kinds of wood. The item shown in ill. 19 is typical of the furniture that would have stood in his apartment.

The upholstery was extremely simple, mostly chequered cotton with the following combinations: blue and white, green and white, red and white, brown and white. Divans were covered with canvas which had its own 'rhythmic' pattern, with quiet colours. It was not until the Austrian Biedermeier period that more extravagant colours came into general use. The 'set of panels' mentioned in the Suspense Order were wallpapered panels that could be detached when required.

Mozart's wardrobe seems to have been purchased according to the very latest fashion: probably he had to provide himself with stylish clothes for the Frankfurt coronation in 1790, where he appeared in both public concerts and private salons. Some idea of fashions of the time may be obtained from a contemporary journal, which informs its readers:

> . . . For knee-breeches, people have now for some time been using . . . worsted (for daily usage) and in the summer straw-coloured, also ash-grey and *couleur sur couleur* striped (this is the very latest in fashion) nankeen, also whitish, greenish-, or brimstone-coloured cloth. . . . Waistcoats have been very much in use here. . . . They are beginning to be worn in plain, striped, or in a chequered-pattern Manchester [cotton]. . . . Now boots are beginning to be worn . . . if

17 *Furniture of the type owned by Mozart, cast iron stove with brass base and legs; south German region,* c. *1780–90, total height 63″.*

18 *Formal dress of the type worn by Mozart,* justaucorps *or jerkin, Austrian,* c. *1780–90.*

> shoes are worn it is with . . . steel-grey silk stockings. [The warm great-coat] is worn so long that it almost reaches the shoes and they appear in every colour.

An 'elegant German in the latest fashion' is illustrated and his suit described: 'The fine gentleman is a combination of an Englishman and a Frenchman.'[3]

Mozart owned a nankeen frock-coat (the 'latest fashion') and one of 'Manchester' (cotton), as well as others of white, blue and red material; he also had a long great-coat and three pairs of boots. He was thus – whatever his financial circumstances – clearly aware and abreast of contemporary fashion.

SOURCES
Dissertation: Dipl.-Ing. Johannes Daum; *Das Wiener städtische Mietwohnhaus in der Zeit von 1700–1859*, Vienna, 1957. Marianne Zweig, *Wiener Bürgermöbel*, Vienna, 1920. Archives of the Technische Hochschule, Vienna: Dipl.-Ing. Dr Alfred Lechner. Historisches Museum der Stadt Wien: Dr Adalbert Schusser, Frau Dr Sylvia Wurm. Modeschule der Stadt Wien, Schloss Hetzendorf: Frau Dr Regine Forstner. Kunsthistorisches Museum, Vienna: Hofrat Dr Georg Kugler. Hofkammerarchiv, Vienna: Dr Christian Sapper. *Journal des Luxus und der Moden*, V (1790) ('For knee-breeches . . .'); IV (1789) ('elegant German').

Appendix B

DANCE MUSIC FOR THE VIENNESE COURT

Mozart's thematic catalogue for 1791 lists the following dances:

23 January: Six Menuetti for the Redoute – with all the parts [K.599]

29 January: Six German Dances – with all the parts [K.600]

5 February: Four Minuets and four German Dances [K.601, 602]

item Two Country Dances [designated *'kontertänze'* by Mozart. These are K.603, of which no. 1, in D, is for full orchestra with trumpets and kettledrums]

12 February: Two Minuets and Two German Dances [K.604, 605, nos 1 and 2; no. 3, with its delightful posthorn soli and the tuned sleigh-bells, was entitled *Die Schlittenfahrt* (The sleigh ride), and immediately became popular; it has remained one of Mozart's best loved pieces of dance music.]

28 February: One Country Dance. *Il Trionfo delle Donne* [K.607] and six Ländler [K.606] [The Country Dance was based on motifs from the opera *Il trionfo delle donne* by Pasquale Anfossi, which was popular in Vienna at the time; its original title was *La forza delle donne*. The Ländler, K.606, were for small orchestra.]

6 March: 1 Contredanse 'Les filles malicieuses' (K.610 or in a slightly different orchestration, K.609, no. 5], 1 German Dance with leyerer Trio [K.611, for large orchestra with trumpets and kettledrums; the word *Leyerer* means a kind of hurdy-gurdy, an instrument with a drone bass; the Trio of K.611 has something of the listless poignancy* of those French paintings of old men or beggar boys playing the hurdy-gurdy, such as the famous blind player painted by De La Tour (Musée des Beaux-Arts, Nantes)]

*See also the final song in Schubert's *Die Winterreise*.

Appendix C

DANCE MUSIC PUBLISHED BY ARTARIA & CO.

The following Mozart works were published by the Viennese firm of Artaria & Co. in 1791:

K.585: 12 Minuets for large orchestra (December 1789); first edition for piano, Artaria, Pub. no. 345* (announced in the *Wiener Zeitung*, 10 August 1791. There were no less than three issues of this edition.)

K.586: 12 German Dances for large orchestra (December 1789); first edition for piano, Artaria, Pub. no. 348 (same date, three issues).

K.599, 601, 604: 12 Minuets for large orchestra (1791); first edition for piano, Artaria, Pub. no. 344 (same date as K.585, four issues).

K.600, 602, 605: 12 German Dances for large orchestra (1791); first edition for piano, Artaria, Pub. no. 345 (same date as K.585, four issues. Actually there were 13, not 12, dances.)

*Publishers at this time numbered their pieces consecutively, thus providing a useful method of dating.

Appendix D

ANALYSIS OF PAPER TYPES USED FOR *LA CLEMENZA DI TITO*

In his examination of the paper types used by Mozart for the composition of *La clemenza di Tito*,* Alan Tyson provides the following breakdown:

Type I. Watermark: in both moulds, CS over c, in reverse, is on the left; three moons, over REAL in reverse, are on the right. TS† = 182.5–183 mm.

Type II. Watermark: in both moulds, FC in reverse is on the left; three moons are on the right. TS = 186.5, 187, 187.5 mm.

Type III. Watermark: in mould 'a', three moons over REAL in reverse are on the left; a cross-bow pointing left over AM is on the right; in mould 'b', a cross-bow pointing left over the letters MA is on the left: three moons over REAL are on the right (thus the two moulds are neither identical nor mirror-images of each other). TS = 184, 184.5, 185, 185.5 mm.

Type IV. Watermark: in both moulds, three moons are on the left; a crown over G over RA is on the right. TS = 188.5 mm.

Type V. Watermark: a moon facing *outwards* is on one side; a star with six points is on the other. There are two moulds which the symmetry of the design makes it hard to distinguish. TS = 21 mm (2 staves) × 6.

*'*La clemenza di Tito* and its chronology', in *Musical Times*, CXV (1975), 221–7.

† TS = abbreviation for 'total span', the measurement between the staves. This stave-ruling, or rastrology, is a new and precise science: the staves were ruled either by hand or by a little machine with claw-like abilities. TS, then, is [to quote Tyson] 'the distance in millimetres from the highest line of the first stave to the lowest line of the bottom stave'.

Type I	No. 1 (duet): Vitellia, Sextus
	No. 7 (duet): Servilia, Annius
	No. 10 (terzet): Vitellia, Annius, Publius
Type II	No. 3 (duettino): Sextus, Annius
	No. 5 (chorus)
	No. 6 (aria): Titus
	No. 15 (chorus with solo): Titus
	No. 18 (terzet): Sextus, Titus, Publius
	No. 19 (aria), up to Allegro (3 leaves): Sextus
	No. 20 (aria), first 4 leaves: Titus
	No. 24 (chorus)

	No. 26 (sextet), all parts except wind: all soloists and chorus
Type III	No. 9 (aria): Sextus
	No. 13 (aria): Annius
	No.14 (terzet): Vitellia, Sextus, Publius
	No. 16 (aria): Publius
	No. 17 (aria): Annius
	No. 19 (aria), from the Allegro (last 6 leaves): Sextus
	No. 20 (aria), last 4 leaves: Titus
	No. 21 (aria): Servilia
	No. 22 (accompanied recitative), except for last 6 bars: Vitellia
	No. 23 (aria), first 2 leaves: Vitellia
	No. 26 (sextet), wind parts
Type IV	No. 23 (aria), last 8 leaves: Vitellia
Type V	See below

Paper type I appears to have been a kind that Mozart happened to have to hand: he had used it in pieces such as *Così fan tutte* (1789) and other works completed in 1790. Before Mozart knew that the part of Sextus was going to be sung by a castrato, he wrote it for a tenor: early versions of nos. 1 (Duet) and 3 (Duettino) in the Library of the Royal Music Academy, Stockholm, have the tenor notation, and all are on type I; this paper is also used for a draft of Terzet no. 14 from Act II (Deutsche Staatsbibliothek, Berlin). Type II, according to Tyson, was the next kind of paper Mozart used, still unwilling to tackle any solo arias except for Baglioni's arias nos. 6 and 20. Type III must have been used for numbers written after Guardasoni had been to Italy and returned to Vienna with detailed information about the cast – mostly the crucial arias which Mozart hardly wished to approach before that information was to hand.

The usefulness of this kind of paper examination for scholarly investigations is seen graphically in the problem of the Terzet no. 14. There is no reason why this concerted number could not have been drafted before Mozart knew the identity of the cast, as he had done with other ensembles. But Christopher Raeburn and Robert Moberly have suggested that no. 14 is a kind of afterthought, replacing arias for Vitellia and Sextus; hence Mozart used type III for this revision.

The music composed at a late stage in Prague itself included the following: the Overture; the March, no. 4; Titus's aria no. 8, *Ah, se fosse intorno al trono*; the accompanied recitative (*NMA*, II/5, Band 20, *La clemenza di Tito*, Kassel, etc., 1970, pp. 204–7), Scene 8 in Act II, *Che orror! che tradimento!;* and the final half-a-dozen bars of Vitellia's accompanied recitative no. 22, preceding the famous rondo no. 23, *Non più di fiori* (see *NMA* p. 264). The fact that this lead-in had to be, at least, rewritten in Prague, again suggests that some kind of change was necessary, perhaps a modulation, to accommodate the insertion – even if the *Larghetto* part had been altered in Vienna. But maybe this was some of the type III paper that Mozart had taken with him to Prague (*i.e.* he made some kind of widespread change from bar 31 of the preceding recitative right up to the *Allegro* section of the rondo, using Prague paper for the end of the recitative and type III paper brought from Vienna for the rondo's opening).

Abbreviations of Bibliographical Sources

Abert	Hermann Abert, *W. A. Mozart*, 7th edn, 2 vols Leipzig, 1955; Vol. III (index), ed. Erich Kapst, Leipzig, 1956
AMZ	*Allgemeine Musikalische Zeitung*, Leipzig, 1798 *et seq*.
Bär	Carl Bär, *Mozart: Krankheit, Tod, Begräbnis*, Salzburg, 1966.
Chailley	Jacques Chailley, *The Magic Flute, Masonic Opera: An Interpretation of the Libretto and the Music*, translated by Herbert Weinstock, New York, 1971.
Da Ponte, *Memoirs*	*Memoirs of Lorenzo da Ponte*, translated by Elisabeth Abbott, ed. and annotated by Arthur Livingston, with a new preface by Thomas G. Bergin, New York, 1929, reprinted 1967.
Deutsch, *Dokumente*	*Mozart: die Dokumente seines Lebens*, ed. Otto Erich Deutsch, Kassel etc., 1961. Vol. II, *Addenda und Corrigenda*, ed. Joseph Heinz Eibl, Kassel etc., 1978.
Deutsch, *Freihaustheater*	Otto Erich Deutsch, *Das Freihaustheater auf der Wieden*, Vienna, 1937.
Freimaurer und Geheimbünde	*Freimaurer und Geheimbünde im 18. Jahrhundert in Mitteleuropa*, ed. Helmut Reinalter, Frankfurt am Main, 1983.
Gould	Robert F. Gould, *The History of Freemasonry*, 3 vols, Edinburgh, n.d. [1886].

Köchel	The edition of Köchel to which reference is made is, unless stated otherwise: Ludwig Ritter von Köchel, *Chronologischthematisches Verzeichnis sämtlicher Tonwerke Wolfgang Amadé Mozarts* . . . , 8th edn, Wiesbaden, 1983. In the main text, the 'old' (*i.e.*, customary) Köchel number is given, e.g. *Maurerische Trauermusik* (k.477), In the index, its latest Köchel number has been added in parentheses (K.479a).
Komorzynski	Egon Komorzynski, *Emanuel Schikaneder, Ein Beitrag zur Geschichte des deutschen Theaters*, Vienna, 1951.
Landon, *Masons*	H. C. Robbins Landon, *Mozart and the Masons. New Light on the Lodge 'Crowned Hope'*, London and New York, 1982.
Mozart, *Briefe*	*Mozart: Briefe und Aufzeichnungen*, ed. Wilhelm A. Bauer and Otto Erich Deutsch. Letters: 4 vols, Kassel etc., 1962–3. Commentary (ed. Joseph Heinz Eibl): 2 vols, Kassel etc., 1971. Indexes (ed. Eibl): 1 vol., Kassel etc., 1975.
Mozarts Tod	Johannes Dalchow, Gunther Duda, Dieter Kerner, *Mozarts Tod 1791–1971*, Pähl, 1971.
NMA	*Neue Mozart Ausgabe*, the collected edition of Mozart's works begun in 1955 and in progress. Individual titles are given for each volume, as they appear in the text.
Nettl	Paul Nettl: *Mozart in Böhmen*, Prague, 1938, revised and enlarged edn of R. Procházka: *Mozart in Prag*, Prague, 1899.
Niemetschek	*Life of Mozart . . . by Franz Xaver Niemetschek*, translated by Helen Mautner with an introduction by A. Hyatt King, London, 1956.

Nissen	Georg Nikolaus Nissen, *Biographie W. A. Mozarts nach Originalbriefen*. Photographic reprint of the original edn, Leipzig, 1828, Hildesheim, 1972.
Novello	*A Mozart Pilgrimage, Being the Travel Diaries of Vincent and Mary Novello in the year 1829*, transcribed and compiled by Nerina Medici di Marignano, ed. Rosemary Hughes, London, 1955.
Rochlitz	Friedrich Rochlitz, 'Verbürgte Anekdoten aus Wolfgang Gottlieb Mozarts Leben: ein Beytrag zur richtigeren Kenntnis dieses Mannes, als Mensch und Künstler', *Allgemeine Musikalische Zeitung* beginning in its issue no. 2 (10 October 1798) and continuing serially until December 1798.
Schenk	Erich Schenk: *Wolfgang Amadeus Mozart: eine Biographie*, Zurich etc., 1955.
Zinzendorf	MS. Diaries of Count Carl Von Zinzendorf, in the Haus-, Hof- und Staatsarchiv, Vienna.

Notes

CORONATION IN FRANKFURT (pp. 1–12)

1 Nissen, p. 683, and Mozart's letter of 28 September 1790; Mozart, *Briefe*, IV, pp. 112f., VI, pp. 397f.

2 For more on general Habsburg history see C. A. Macartney, *The Habsburg Empire 1790–1918*, London, 1968; for Joseph II see catalogue: *Österreich zur Zeit Joseph II*, Melk Monastery, 1980; for Leopold II the standard biography is Adam Wandruszka, *Leopold II, Erzherzog von Österreich, Grossherzog von Toscana, König von Ungarn und Böhmen, Römischer Kaiser*, 2 vols, Vienna–Munich, 1964–65; see also E. Wangermann, *From Joseph II to the Jacobin Trials: Government Policy and Public Opinion in the Habsburg Dominions in the Period of the French Revolution*, London, 1969.

3 Otto Michtner, *Das alte Burgtheater als Opernbühne*, Vienna etc., 1970, pp. 315, 425.

4 Mozart, *Briefe*, IV, pp. 112f.

5 Mozart, *Briefe*, IV, p. 118.

6 On title pages of both editions of these concertos published by J. J. André (Offenbach-am-Main, 1794) we read: 'Ce concerto a été exécuté par l'auteur à Francfort sur le Main à l'occasion due Couronnement de l'Empereur Leopold II.' See Köchel; Mozart, *Briefe*, VI, p. 207 (830). The entry in Mozart's thematic catalogue for K.459 includes, at the end, '. . . 2 Corni, 2 Clarini, timpany e Basso'. The trumpets and kettledrum parts have not survived. Diary of Bentheim-Steinfurt: Deutsch, *Dokumente*, pp. 329f.

7 The French original is *brune de marine* (*i.e.* navy-blue); I suggest this was the dress-suit listed in Mozart's effects as *braun*, which was probably the Viennese equivalent of *brune de marine*.

8 For more on the Rauhensteingasse apartment, see Appendix A, pp. 217–25.

9 Mozart, *Briefe*, IV, p. 121.

10 Mozart, *Briefe*, III, pp. 378f., 380.

11 On the sale of quartets to Artaria see Leopold Mozart to his daughter, 22 January 1785; Mozart, *Briefe*, III, p. 368. On *Don Giovanni* in Vienna (1788) see C. Bitter, '*Don Giovanni* in Wien 1788', *Mozart-Jahrbuch 1959*, pp. 146ff; for Da Ponte on the subject: *Memoirs*, p. 180.

12 Letter of 12 July 1789; Mozart, *Briefe*, IV, pp. 92f. Mozart's correspondence with Puchberg has only partially survived in autograph. String quintets

offered to subscribers: Deutsch, *Dokumente*, pp. 280f.

13 A. van Hoboken, *Joseph Haydn: Thematisch-bibliographisches Werkverzeichnis*, 3 vols, Mainz, 1957, 1971, 1978, I, pp. 419f.

14 That these quartets were actually intended for Berlin may be seen in the entry in Mozart's own thematic catalogue for K.575: 'Ein Quartett für 2 violin, viola et violoncello, für [*sic*] Seine Mayestätt dem König in Preussen', Mozart, *Briefe*, IV, p. 91. For publication of Mozart's works, see Köchel.

15 For Salomon's arrival in Vienna and the meal with Mozart and Haydn, see H. C. Robbins Landon, *Haydn: Chronicle and Works: Haydn at Eszterháza 1766–1790*, II, London and Bloomington, Ind., 1978, pp. 751ff., where may be found details of references to the biographies of Dies and Griesinger. See also Novello, pp. 170ff.; Nissen, pp. 536ff.; *Harmonicon: A Journal of Music*, VIII, London, 1830, p. 45.

In another account in *Harmonicon* (V, 1827, p. 7 n.), we read: 'Salomon having determined to embark in the speculation of subscription concerts, went in 1790 to Vienna, for the purpose of engaging either Haydn or Mozart to come to London . . .'

In Nissen (pp. 536f.) we have an extraordinary addition to this meeting between Haydn, Mozart and Salomon. Nissen relates that Mozart returned to Vienna after the trip to Berlin and the court of Friedrich Wilhelm II in 1789. 'He knew that here he could again expect jealousy, cabals of various kinds, suppression, lack of understanding, and poverty, since from the Emperor he received nothing certain in those days [in the way of commissions for operas, etc.] His friends encouraged him [to accept Friedrich Wilhelm's offer of a position at the Berlin court] – he began to waver. *A certain circumstance* [footnote:] This circumstance was Salomon's appearance in Vienna to engage J. Haydn and Mozart for his concerts in London. [end footnote] which I shall not relate [meanwhile Salomon had died and Nissen thought he could now tell the story] . . . finally changed his mind. He went to the Emperor and prayed to be dismissed. *Joseph*, this much misunderstood and maligned prince, whose mistakes were forced upon him, and pressed out of him, by his subjects – he loved music and had taken Mozart's music to his heart. He allowed Mozart to speak his piece and then answered: Dear Mozart, you know what I think of the Italians; and you still want to leave me?

Mozart looked at his face, full of expression, and said, touched: Your Majesty – I – recommend myself to Your Grace – *I shall stay!* And with that he went home.

But Mozart, said a friend, whom he met and to whom he related the occurrence, why didn't you use the opportunity and secure at least a regular salary? [Nissen uses the familiar *Du* form here.]

The devil think about it in such a moment, said Mozart unwillingly.' The chronology of this is, of course, all wrong. Joseph II had died on 20 February 1790. Moreover, Nissen continues (after the above quotation) by saying that 'Emperor Joseph later came upon the idea . . . of conferring a proper salary' on Mozart.

The interesting parts of this confused story are: 1. Constanze remembered that Salomon came to Vienna to engage Mozart as well as Haydn; 2. The Mozart household was definitely pro-Josephinian; 3. Mozart had once, *before* December 1787 (when Joseph conferred title and salary on Mozart), wanted to leave Vienna and his unofficial imperial position.

16 For Neukomm see *Mozarts Tod*, p. 227.

MOZART'S VIENNA
(pp. 13–24)

1 Hans Wagner, 'Das Josephinische Wien und Mozart', *Mozart-Jahrbuch 1978–79*, pp. 1–13, esp. p. 5; Volkmar Braunbehrens, *Mozart in Wien*, Munich and Zurich, 1986, pp. 50ff.; Marcel Brion, *Daily Life in the Vienna of Mozart and Schubert*, London, 1961; H. C. Robbins Landon, 'Vienna and its Musical Life in 1795', in *Haydn: Chronicle and Works: Haydn: The Years of 'The Creation' 1796–1800*, IV, London and Bloomington, Ind., 1977, pp. 19ff.

2 C.-G. Stellan Mörner, *Johan Wilkmanson und die Brüder Silverstolpe*, Stockholm, 1952, p. 321.

3 Joseph Farington, *The Farington Diary*, 8 vols, ed. James Greig, London and New York, 1922–28, II, p. 261.

4 J. F. Reichardt, *Vertraute Briefe geschrieben auf einer Reise nach Wien, etc.*, 2 vols, ed. Gustav Gugitz, Munich, 1915, I, p. 318.

5 Karl Pfannhauser, 'Epilogomena Mozartiana', *Mozart-Jahrbuch 1971/72*, pp. 284f.

6 Deutsch, *Dokumente*, p. 495.

7 Mozart wore this at his concert in Frankfurt on 15 October 1790. Deutsch, *Dokumente*, p. 329 ('wearing a navy-blue satin suit richly émbroidered . . .')

8 Later renumbered no. 934.

9 Groundplan and engraving of outside of house in *NMA*, X/32, *Mozart und seine Welt in zeitgenössischen Bildern*, Kassel, etc., 1961, p. 239.

10 Deutsch, *Dokumente*, pp. 502–4.

11 Two books known to have been owned by Mozart are missing from this inventory: 1. The Italian-German dictionary signed by Mozart twice, once in Italian ('Questo Dizionario appartiene à me / Wolfgango Amadeo Mozart, 1785.') and once in German ('dieses Wörterbuch gehört mir. Wolfgang / Amadé Mozart, 1785.') – facsimile in *NMA*, X/32, *Mozart und seine Welt in zeitgenössischen Bild-*

ern, Kassel, etc., 1961, p. 190; 2. *Wochenblatt für Kinder zur angenehmen und lehrreichen Beschäftigung in ihren Freystunden*, ed. Joseph May and Johann Strommer, Vienna, 1787 and 1788, of which Mozart was a subscriber – see Deutsch, *Dokumente*, pp. 251f.

12 This was a family joke: the caterer Joseph was called 'Primus', as in Emperor Joseph I (*Josephus Primus* in Latin) of Austria. There is no evidence to connect this Joseph with Joseph Deiner, concierge of the house *Zur silbernen Schlange* (The Silver Snake), no. 1074 in the Kärntnerstrasse; see Mozart, *Briefe*, VI, p. 417 (line 2) and VII, p. 602 (1172). Deiner, who died in Vienna on 29 May 1823, is supposed to have provided the information for one of the greatest frauds in Mozart scholarship, the infamous article printed in the Vienna *Morgan-Post* (28 January 1856) to celebrate the centenary of Mozart's birth, which contains a clever pastiche of truth and fiction about Mozart's last days as seen through the affectionate eyes of Joseph Deiner. See Deutsch, *Dokumente*, pp. 477–80. Even Deutsch was taken in by this gigantic hoax and used information from the article in the main body of his text, *e.g.*, the entry for 28 November 1791 (p. 361). The fictitious account of the weather at the time of Mozart's death comes from Deiner ('the night of Mozart's death was dark and stormy, and at his funeral it began to storm and blow. Rain and snow fell at the same time, as if nature wished to growl . . .')

13 Else Radant has been doing some research into those infamous gambling dens in Vienna, where people lost fortunes playing illegal games (*Chance*). It is hoped to publish this material elsewhere, but she assures me that only very rich people could possibly afford to play (or indeed even to enter the doors of such establishments).

CONCERT LIFE IN THE AUSTRIAN CAPITAL (pp. 25–36)

1 Alan Tyson, 'New Dating Methods: Watermarks and Paper-Studies' in *Neue Mozart-Ausgabe, Bericht über die Mitarbeitertagung in Kassel, 29.–30. Mai 1981*, Kassel, 1984, p. 67.

2 Otto Biba: 'Grundzüge des Konzertwesens in Wien zu Mozarts Zeit', *Mozart-Jahrbuch 1978–79*, pp. 132ff.

3 Mozart, *Briefe*, IV, p. 65; VI, pp. 367–9.

4 On the Tonkünstler-Societät, see C. F. Pohl, *Denkschrift aus Anlass des 100-Jährigen Bestehens der Tonkünstler-Societät*, Vienna, 1871.

5 Mainly put together from the Kyrie and Gloria of the unfinished Mass in C minor (K.427).

6 For the symphonies K.543, 550 and 551, see *NMA*, IV/11, *Sinfonien*, Band 9, ed. H. C. Robbins Landon, Kassel, etc., 1957.

7 Mozart's customary method of

composition was to complete the first violin, the second violin if necessary, the bass line and such other parts, usually of a soloistic nature, as he considered necessary to 'prod' his memory. Interested readers may examine the first part of the Credo of the Mass in C minor (K.427), which is easily available both in the Eulenburg miniature score and in *NMA*, I/1, *Geistliche Gesangswerke*, Band 5, Kassel, etc., 1983, pp. 100ff., to see what a large-scale *particella* (as it is termed by scholars) looked like. In the case of a large vocal work of this kind, Mozart sketched in the chorus, the *basso continuo* and the ritornello sections of the orchestra – again usually the first violin, complicated polyphonic or canonic entries of string parts or woodwind solo sections. Using such a *particella*, Mozart could lay aside even a substantial work for as much as three years, as was the case with the Piano Concerto K.595, in order to take it up and 'flesh it out' when the time came.

8 See entry in Mozart's catalogue, Mozart, *Briefe*, III, p. 363; for Leopold's letter of 22 January 1785 see *ibid.*, p. 368. For a case in which the date of the entry in Mozart's catalogue is ambiguous, see the *Maurerische Trauermusik* (K.477), entered under date 'im Monath July [1785]' with the following note: '. . . bey dem Todfalle der Brbr: Mecklenburg und Esterhazy . . .' The deaths of the two Brothers Mecklenburg and Esterházy occurred in November, and the *Trauermusik* was performed in that month in Vienna. For an explanation of July as a possible date for an earlier version, see Philippe A. Autexier: 'L'Ode funèbre maçonique (Musique de Maitrîse, K.477)) et le cantus firmus des Lamentations', *Studia Mozartiana*, I, 1983, p. 1 and Autexier's reconstruction of the original version with vocal parts published by Breitkopf & Härtel, Wiesbaden, 1985.

9 Deutsch, *Dokumente*, p. 339.

10 Mozart conducted the first parts of *The Magic Flute* later in the year.

11 For K.595 see Deutsch, *Dokumente*, p. 350.

12 A graphic description of Mozart's changing audience may be seen by examining the list of the composer's subscribers which he sent to his father in March 1784: on it were the names of 176 persons, who paid 6 Gulden each for the series of three concerts (total: 1056 fl.), and most of them were from the nobility. In a letter to his father of 3 March 1784, Wolfgang describes the other 'academies' in which he participated (Mozart, *Briefe*, III, pp. 303f.)

Thursday, 26 February: Gallizin [Dimitrij Michajlović Prince Golicyn]

Monday, 1 March: Joh: Esterhazy [Johann Nepomuk, Count Esterházy, a member of the Masonic Lodge *Zur gekrönten Hoffnung*

(Crowned Hope), to which Mozart also belonged in 1791]
Thursday, 4th: Gallizin
Friday, 5th: Esterhazy
Monday, 8th: Esterhazy
Thursday, 11th: Gallizin
Friday, 12th: Esterhazy
Monday, 15th: Esterhazy
Wednesday, 17th: my first private academy concert
Thursday, 18th: Gallizin
Friday, 19th: Esterhazy
Saturday 20th: Richter [Georg Friedrich Richter (*c* 1759–89), a popular teacher and pianist, who also gave a series of concerts that year]
Sunday, 21st: my first academy concert in the *theatre* [etc., etc.]

By 1789, as we have seen, Mozart could no longer command that kind of public for subscription concerts, and the same applied in 1790 and 1791.

13 For the Quintet K.614 see Mozart *Briefe*, IV, p. 128. For Tost, see H. C. Robbins Landon, *Haydn: Chronicle and Works: Haydn at Eszterháza 1766–1790*, II, London, 1978, pp. 81f. For Constanze's letter to André of 26 November 1800: Mozart, *Briefe*, IV, p. 388.

14 For K.612 see Mozart, *Briefe*, IV, p. 128; for K.613 *ibid.*, IV, p. 128; VI, p. 407.

15 As Imperial Royal Chamber Composer.

16 Mozart, *Briefe*, IV, p. 129.

17 Apparently Joseph Orsler (1722–1806), cellist in the court orchestra; see Mozart, *Briefe*, VI, p. 408.

18 Mozart, *Briefe*, IV, p. 130.

19 On Greiner, see Maria Hörwarthner, 'Joseph Haydns Bibliothek–Versuch einer literarhistorischen Rekonstruktion' in *Joseph Haydn und die Literatur seiner Zeit*, ed. H. Zeman, Eisenstadt, 1976, pp. 157ff.; Roswitha Strommer, 'Wiener literarische Salons zur Zeit Joseph Haydns' in *ibid*, p. 98; Alfred Arneth, *Maria Theresia und der Hofrath von Greiner*, Vienna, 1859.

20 *Österreichische Biedermanns-Chronik*, I, Freiheitsburg [Vienna?], 1784, pp. 66f.

21 Joseph von Hormayr, *Taschenbuch für die vaterländische Geschichte*, 34, 1845, p. 115.

22 *Allgemeine Theaterzeitung*, Vienna, 15 July 1843; Caroline Pichler, *Denkwürdigkeiten aus meinem Leben*, ed. E. K. Blümml, 2 vols, Munich, 1914; I, pp. 49, 293ff.

23 On the Tukish campaign see Karl Gutkas, 'Kaiser Josephs Türkenkrieg', in catalogue *Österreich zur Zeit Kaiser Josephs II*, Melk Monastery, 1980, pp. 274ff. with further list of sources.

24 On the Genzinger family see Landon, *op. cit.*, II, pp. 720ff. For *Arianna: ibid.* p. 738.

25 Among the commissions of Mozart's last year were three for mechanical organ (or musical clock), of which the first, chronologically, was composed for a curious Austrian aristocrat, Count Joseph Deym von Stržitež. He had been forced to flee the city as a result of a youthful duel, but he later returned as Herr Müller and founded the Müller *Kunstkabinett* (a kind of

art gallery) in the Rotenturmstrasse, Vienna, where were displayed, *inter alia*, wax masks of Joseph II and (after his death) Mozart. Deym also owned some curious mechanical organs, powered by clockwork mechanisms, one of which was constructed to play funeral music for the monument of Field-Marshal Laudon (Loudon). The Count was later (1790) married to Countess Josephine von Brunsvik, with whom Beethoven was to fall in love after her husband's death in 1804.

Laudon died on 14 July 1790 and Count Deym commissioned Mozart to compose the funeral music (K.594), which he did not like having to do ('it is a job which I much hate' and 'the little pipes are all high and . . . too childish for me') (Mozart, *Briefe*, IV, pp. 115f.). In a description of the gallery published in 1797 we read:

> Every hour one hears a suitable funeral music [for the Field-Marshal] which the unforgettable composer Mozart wrote especially for it, and which lasts for eight minutes; it surpasses, in precision and clarity, everything which was ever attempted or designed for this kind of artistic product.

This music was K.594 (completed at the end of 1790) and was followed by two other pieces for mechanical organ: K.608 (entered in Mozart's catalogue on 3 March 1791) and K.616 (catalogue entry: 4 May 1791). On 31 May 1800 Constanze wrote to the German publisher Johann André concerning various works, including K.608, stating that it was 'supposed to be owned by . . . Count v. Deym here' (see Mozart, *Briefe*, IV, p. 356); the suggestion that K.616 was also commissioned by the Count seems possible, although Pater Primitiv Niemecz, Haydn's clockmaker, had at least two works by Mozart on an organ which existed in 1801.

A final work in this series of commissioned pieces for out-of-the-way instruments was the Adagio and Rondeau for glass harmonica, flute, oboe, viola and violoncella K.617, which Mozart wrote for the blind harmonica-player Marianne Kirchgessner (Kirchgäßner), entering the work in his catalogue on 23 May 1791. He also wrote another work for glass harmonica alone, the Adagio K.356 (617a), the undated autograph of which, in the Bibliothèque nationale, Paris, shows that it was composed at this period.

Mademoiselle Kirchgessner performed Mozart's ethereally beautiful Quintet at a benefit concert first announced for 10 June – the concert had for some reason to be postponed – following it with another at the Kärntnerthortheater on 19 August. She later went to London and performed what appears to have been the Mozart Quintet at a Haydn-Salomon concert, Hanover Square, on 17 March 1794, the programme of which included 'Quintetto on the harmonica, Mademoiselle Kirashgessner [*sic*] (being her first appearance in this ceuntry [*sic*].' The *Morning Chronicle* thought:

> Her taste is chastened, and the dulcet notes of the instrument would be delightful indeed, were they more powerful and articulate; but that we believe the most perfect execution cannot make them. In a smaller room, and an audience less numerous, the effect must be enchanting. Though the accompaniments were kept very much under, they were still occasionally too loud.

For a portrait of Count Deym and his wife, see H. C. Robbins Landon, *Beethoven: A Documentary Study*, London, 1970, illustrations 120 (p. 180) and 122 (p. 181). Laudon's funeral music in the 1797 booklet: Köchel, p. 681. For Niemecz and the Mozart pieces see H. C. Robbins Landon, *Haydn: Chronicle and Works: The Late Years (1801–1809)*, V, London and Bloomington, Ind., 1977, p. 30. Mademoiselle Kirchgessner and K.617: see Köchel, pp. 703f.; Deutsch, *Dokumente*, pp. 350f.; Mozart, *Briefe*, VI, p. 409; Landon, 'Morning Chronicle' in *Haydn: Chronicle and Works: Haydn in England (1791–1795)*, III, London and Bloomington, Ind., 1976, p. 243.

DANCE MUSIC FOR THE IMPERIAL COURT
(pp. 37–44)

1 I have consulted the original of this letter in the Hofkammerarchiv. It is reproduced in Deutsch, *Dokumente*, p. 388.

2 Zinzendorf's manuscript reads: 'Dela chez moi, puis au *bal de cour*. Le tourbillon m'ennuya. La Reine de Naples me salua gracieusement. L'Imperatrice jouoit.' On 10 January, we read: '. . . Dela au *bal d'enfans* de Mr de Kinsky, ou etaient la reine de Naples', and on 9 February: 'Le soir au *Spectacle*. Le nozze di figaro. Dela au bal de *Colloredo*.' It is not possible to estimate the size of these private balls at the houses of the great nobles in Vienna, but we know that Haydn's dance music for the Esterházy house was for his full orchestra; there is no reason to doubt that Princes Kinsky and Colloredo engaged a full orchestra. Mozart may have written some of his dance music for private balls (that would explain the smaller orchestration for some of the minuets and German dances of 1791).

3 For Haydn's dance music of 1792 and Beethoven's of 1795 see H. C. Robbins Landon, *Haydn: Chronicle and Works: Haydn in England 1791–1795*, III, London and Bloomington, Ind., 1976, pp. 205ff.; and *The Years of 'The Creation' 1796–1800*, IV, London, 1977, pp. 56ff., where may be found the details for the Italian guidebook, 'His Majesty's Admonition', etc.

4 Gianluigi de Freddy, *Descrizione della città, sobborghi, e vicinanze di Vienna*, Vienna, 1800, pp. 276–9.

5 A. van Hoboken, *Joseph Haydn: Thematisch-bibliographisches Werkverzeichnis*, 3 vols, Mainz, 1957, 1971, 1978, I, p. 119. This was the first (authentic) edition of Haydn's Symphonies nos. 76–78.

6 Size of orchestras derived from the records of the Pensionsgesellschaft bildender Künstler Wiens; see also Landon, *op. cit.*, III, p. 206.

7 Deutsch, *Dokumente*, p. 340. *Così* copy: Dr Alan Tyson, London.

8 A bifolium is a double sheet, or four pages.

9 Mozart, *Briefe*, IV, pp. 124–7. For K.599, see the only known set of manuscript parts by a Viennese copyist which the author discovered in the Franciscan Monastery of Brunn near Mari-Enzersdorf: 'Eine neue Mozart Quelle', *Österreichische Musikzeitung*, 9, 1954, pp. 42f. Mozart entered these dances in his catalogue in small groups, but the copyists sold them in large gatherings: '13 Deutsche, 13 Trio und Coda, Aus dem k.k. kleinen Redoutensaal 1791. 2te Abtheilung . . . Del Sig[re] Mozart', a Viennese manuscript (parts, Gesellschaft der Musikfreunde) derived from K.600(1–6), 602(1–4), and 605(1–3). A manuscript piano score marketed by Lorenz Lausch, and dedicated to the Archduchess Maria Theresa (Leopold II's eldest daughter, born in 1767), of the same collection was announced in the *Wiener Zeitung* in March 1791 – copy in the Nationalbibliothek, Vienna. The Gesellschaft der Musikfreunde owns contemporary manuscript parts produced by various Viennese scriptoria of K.602, 603 (with K.106 [588a]), 604 and 605: see Köchel for the details. These copies are all designated 'Aus dem k.k. [kleinen bzw. grossen] Redoutensaal 1791 . . .' and attest to the music's distinct popularity. The Viennese public hardly attended the expensive court operas or Mozart's subscription concerts (or indeed any of the others such as the Tonkünstler-Societät's), but it flocked to the Redoutensaal masked balls and – as all this scribal activity attests – loved Mozart's latest dance music. There are indications that K.605 no. 3 (with piccolo flute, two posthorns and the sleighbells) was a special favourite then as it is today. A Viennese new year's card has survived (engraved by one Neuhauser) with the Trio of no. 3 arranged for two violins and bass. This card is reproduced in facsimile in Robert Haas, *Mozart*, Potsdam, 1933, p. 132.

10 Six piano trios 80 ducats (360 fl.), 'But for you he will let them go for 70 ducats' (315 fl.).

11 For Haydn's letter of 10 August 1788 see H. C. Robbins Landon, *Haydn: Chronicle and Works: Haydn at Eszterháza 1766–1790*, II, London and Bloomington, Ind., 1978, pp. 708f.; January 1789: *Joseph Haydn: Gesammelte Briefe und*

Aufzeichnungen, ed. Dénes Bartha, Budapest etc., 1965, p. 199; March 1789: Landon, *ibid.*, p. 718; January 1790: Landon *ibid.*, p. 735, n. 2 (the German originals in Bartha); Receipt January 1790: Bartha, *ibid.*, p. 225; Dances 1792: Bartha, *ibid.*, pp. 293ff.

12 Mozart, *Briefe*, IV, pp. 110f.

13 See Köchel.

14 Bartha, *op. cit.*, pp. 293f.; Landon, *op. cit.*, III, p. 206.

15 Nissen, p. 539.

NEW DIRECTIONS
(pp. 45–53)

1 Mozart, *Briefe*, IV, p. 131; VI, p. 408.

2 The first reference to what is evidently a serious misdating of this work is in Alan Tyson, 'The Mozart Fragments in the Mozarteum, Salzburg: A Preliminary Study of Their Chronology and Their Significance', *Journal of the American Musicological Society*, 34, 1981, pp. 491f.

3 Mozart, *Briefe*, IV, pp. 132f.; VI, pp. 409f.

4 See Chapter IX, Coronation diary, pp. 103ff.

5 Alan Tyson, 'New Dating Methods: Watermarks and Paper-Studies', in *Neue Mozart-Ausgabe, Bericht über die Mitarbeitertagung in Kassel, 29.–30. Mai 1981*, Kassel, 1984, p. 54. The date on the autograph used to be read as 1797 (even in Köchel); but Good Friday in 1792 was in fact on 6 April. See *NMA*, V, 14 (1987).

6 Mozart, *Briefe*, IV, pp. 133f. The letter begins:

> Ma tré cher [*sic*] Epouse! J'écris cette lettre dans la petite Chambre au Jardin chez Leitgeb [*sic*] ou j'ai couché cette Nuit excellement – et j'espére que ma chere Epouse aura passé cette Nuit aussi bien que moi, j'y passerai cette Nuit aussi, puisque j'ai congedié Leonore, et je serais tout seul à la maison, ce qui n'est pas agréable. –
>
> J'attends avec beaucoup d'impatience une lettre qui m'apprendra comme vous avés passée le Jour d'hier; – je tremble quand je pense au baigne du st: Antoin; car je crains toujours le risque de tomber sur l'escalier, en sortant – et je me trouve entre l'esperance et la Crainte – une Situation bien desagreable! – si vous n'etiés pas grosse J'en craignerais moins – mais abbandonons cette Jdée triste! – le Ciel aura eu certainement soin de ma Chere *stanzi-Marini*, – Mad:me de Schwingenschu [Anna von Schwingenschuh, wife of an official in the court mint office] m'a priée de leur procurer une Loge pour ce soir au theatre de Wieden ou l'on donnera, la cinquième partie D'Antoin [the fifth part, or fourth continuation of *Der dumme Gärtner*, with the title *Anton bei Hofe oder Das Namensfest*, Mozart,

Briefe, VI, p. 411] et j'etais si heureux de pouvoir les servir; j'aurai donc le plaisir de voir cet Opera dans leur Compagnie. [Mozart's orthography etc. has been left unaltered.]

In another affectionate letter to Constanze written the very next day we hear that Mozart 'lunched yesterday with Süssmaier [*sic*] at the Ungarische Krone [The Hungarian Crown] because I had things to do in town at 1 o'clock and – S . . . [dots original] had to eat early and the S . . . s, who would have liked to have me for lunch one of these days, were already engaged to go to Schönbrunn – today you already know that I eat at Schicaneder [*sic*] because you were invited there, too.

'No letter from Mad. Duschek yet but I'll go and ask today. – About your dress I can't know because I haven't seen the Wildburgs for some time. If all else fails, I shall certainly bring the hat with me. – Adieu, darling – I can't tell you how much I look forward to tomorrow.'

7 The first part of Mozart's letter of 11 June reads: '. . . Criés avec moi contre mon mauvais sort! Mad[selle] Kirchgessner ne donne pas son Academie Lundi! par consequent j'aurai pu vous posseder, ma chère, tout ce jour de Dimanche – mercredi je viendrai sûrement. –

8 'Tod und Verzweiflung war sein Lohn' (said in jest, of course).

9 Wenzel Müller's *Kaspar der Fagottist*, running at the Leopoldstädtertheater. Mozart had seen it on the 11th.

10 Johann Martin Loib(e)l, an official in the Hungarian-Transylvanian court bookkeeping department, Master of the Lodge *Zum Palmbaum* and Master of Ceremonies of the Austrian Grand lodge.

11 Ludwig Franz, Markgrave Montecuculi, Maltese Knight, one of Mozart's subscribers to the 1784 concert series.

12 These letters, which reveal a certain amount of Mozart's dealings (for a loan?) with Goldhahn, and the other matters are to be found in Mozart, *Briefe*, IV, pp. 133–8.

13 Köchel, p. 705; Mozart, *Briefe*, VI, p. 414. A handsome facsimile of the 'Ave, verum corpus' was printed for private circulation by the Austrian Government, Vienna, 1956.

MIDNIGHT FOR THE MASONS (pp. 54–65)

1 The standard work on Mozart and Freemasonry is O. E. Deutsch, *Mozart und die Wiener Logen, zur Geschichte seiner Freimaurer-Kompositionen*, Vienna, 1932. For the entire 1790 list of members of Mozart's last Lodge, *Zur gekrönten Hoffnung*, and the identification of a picture of this Lodge (containing Mozart and Prince Esterházy) see Landon, *Masons* (with a list of manuscript sources on the subject in the various Vienna archives). A

new book with much useful information is Philippe A. Autexier, *Mozart et Liszt sub. Rosa*, Poitiers, 1984, also with much additional literature, including some hitherto unknown Lodge songs by Mozart. For a useful summary of Masonry in Austria, see Hans Wagner, 'Das Josephinische Wein und Mozart', *Mozart-Jahrbuch 1978/79*, pp. 1–13, esp. p. 8f.

2 Mozart, *Briefe*, IV, p. 41.

3 Deutsch, *Dokumente*, p. 253.

4 Nissen, p. 686.

5 On the subject of Mozart's finances I am much indebted to Dr Gottfried Mraz and Dr Christian Sapper of the Vienna Hofkammerarchiv, who have permitted my wife and me to examine all the important papers relating to Mozart in the archives of which they are the curators. For Mozart's tax and other matters relating to his finances the *Hofzahlamtsbücher* (HZAB) may be consulted. A few other salaries from this source: as organist, Albrechtsberger received 300 fl. net, Salieri, in 1792, 1200 fl. before taxes (so he did not earn that much more than Mozart). In 1802 during the inflation caused by the Napoleonic Wars, Leopold Koželuch received 1500 fl. before taxes, 1425 fl. net. In 1787 a *Kammerdiener* (court servant) received 800 fl. p.a., as did the Schlosshauptmann (Castle captain) at the Belvedere – it was an income of the middle range. The fiscal year ran from November to the following October. Mozart's service began on 1 December 1787 and he received 63 fl. 20 kr. a month, but the payments were usually made quarterly. In April 1788 he received 126 fl. 40 kr., in July 193 fl. 45 kr., in October 192 fl. 30 kr. and a back-payment of 193 fl. 45 kr. For eleven months, therefore, he earned 706 fl. 40 kr. (HZAB 184, fol. 159, 2/4v; 118v). In 1789 he received a quarterly 190 fl. (January, April, July, October) making 760 fl. (HZAB 185, fol. 117r); in 1790 the same (HZAB 186, fol. 128); in 1791 the same until October (HZAB 187, fol. 186), *viz* 760 fl.; for November-December Constanze received 126 fl. 40 kr. (until 31 December 1791) (HZAB 188, fol. 225). For Constanze's loan of 3500 Gulden in 1797, see Deutsch, *Dokumente*, p. 422.

6 Mozart, *Briefe*, IV, pp. 139f.

7 See Chapter VIII, A journey to Prague, p. 96.

8 See note 5 above for explanation.

9 H. C. Robbins Landon, *Haydn: Chronicle and Works: Haydn in England 1791–1795*, III, London and Bloomington, Ind., 1976, pp. 104f.

10 *Ibid., loc. cit.* Haydn prudently banked these earnings in Vienna in sterling. For the figure of 24,000 Gulden, see *ibid.*, p. 319 (from Haydn's biographer Griesinger).

11 Finances at Mozart's death: from the Suspense Order, Deutsch, *Dokumente*, pp. 493ff.; Leopold II and the 30,000 Gulden debts: Nissen, p.

580 (taken from Niemetschek, p. 48).

12 For Constanze's activity after Mozart's death, see Deutsch, *Dokumente*, pp. 412, 416 *passim*.

13 *Ibid.*, p. 406.

14 *Ibid.*, p. 407.

15 *Ibid.*, p. 385f. See also Köchel.

REQUIEM FOR A COUNTRY HOUSE
(pp. 66–78)

1 Niemetschek, pp. 41f. [in Nissen, pp. 554f.]

2 Rochlitz published his anecdotes in the *AMZ* in 1798 (December, pp. 149–51 for this quotation).

3 On 2 January 1793. The occasion was organized by Baron van Swieten.

4 Letter to Breitkopf & Härtel of 15 June 1799: Mozart, *Briefe*, IV, p. 246.

5 Deutsch, *Dokumente: Addenda & Corrigenda*, pp. 101–7; *Mozarts Tod*, pp. 78ff.; O. E Deutsch, 'Der Graue Bote', *Mitteilungen der Internationalen Stiftung Mozarteum*, August 1963, pp. 1–3; Mozart, *Briefe*, VI, 391 (1118).

6 Carola Oman, *Nelson*, London, 1947, p. 633.

7 Otto Biba, 'Par Monsieur François Comte de Walsegg', *Mitteilungen der Internationalen Stiftung Mozarteum*, September 1981, pp. 34–50.

A JOURNEY TO PRAGUE
(pp. 79–100)

1 Ulrich Tank, *Studien zur Esterházyschen Hofmusik von etwa 1620 bis 1790*, Regensburg, 1981.

2 For the festivities at Eszterháza, see Mátyás Horányi, *The Magnificence of Eszterháza*, trans., London, 1962, pp. 153f.

3 See *Pressburger Zeitung*, Summer 1791; repeated reports on *Installationsfest* at 'Esterház'; Leopold unable to come because of 'überhäufte Geschäfte' (overwhelming work).

4 *Haydn Yearbook*, XV, pp. 153–7.

5 The term used to describe the governing body of Bohemia, with its permanent seat in Prague. The Estates were responsible to the Austrian government in Vienna, where they maintained a chancery.

6 Something like 'Lord Protector of Prague'.

7 See Tomislav Volek, 'Über den Ursprung von Mozarts Oper *La clemenza di Tito*', *Mozart-Jahrbuch 1959*, pp. 281f.

8 Mozart, *Briefe*, IV, p. 80.

9 Volek, *op. cit.*, p. 280.

10 *Ibid.*, p. 282.

11 Rudolph Angermüller, *Antonio Salieri*, Teil II, I, Munich, 1974, pp. 211f.

12 Otto Michtner, *Das alte Burgtheater als Opernbühne*, Vienna and Graz, 1970, pp. 317, 334.

13 V. J. Sýkora, *František Xaver Dušek: život a dílo*, Prague, 1958, p. 47 (facsimile, p. 49); Volek, *op. cit.*, p. 275 *passim*.

14 Haydn's 'Aria di Rosina': *Joseph*

Haydn Arien: Revisionberichte (ed. H. C. Robbins Landon), Haydn-Mozart-Presse, Salzburg, 1963, p. 6.

15 Helga Lühning, 'Zur Entstehungsgeschichte von Mozarts *Titus*', *Musikforschung*, XXVII, July-September 1974, pp. 300ff.

16 Volek, *op. cit.*, p. 279.

17 Metastasio, *Opera*, II, Venice, 1783, p. 93.

18 His arrival was noted by the Prague *Oberpostamtszeitung* as 'Mr. Matzola [*sic*], poet, from Dresden, in the Blue Star [Tavern]'.

19 The move from Mazzolà to Bertati was accompanied by the usual scandal and gossip: on 11 June 1791 Antonio Zaguri wrote from Venice to the retired libertine Casanova, quietly staying with Count Waldstein in Dux Castle in Bohemia, 'How can Mazzolà be the successor to Da Ponte, when here [in Venice] they are congratulating Bertati, the author of the bad pieces for the Teatro San Moisè? (*G. Casanova chevalier de Seingalt, Gesammelte Briefe* (German translation), 2 vols, Berlin, 1970; II, p. 217.)

20 'Caesar' is Latin for 'Emperor', hence 'in Caesarian service'.

21 Lühning, *op. cit.*, pp. 307f.; Volek, *op. cit.*, p. 279.

22 '*La clemenza di Tito* and its chronology', *Musical Times*, CXV, 1975, pp. 221–7.

23 Used in the Terzet No. 14, a replacement for discarded arias (see Appendix D, pp. 227–9). See also C. Raeburn and R. Moberly, 'The Mozart Version of *La clemenza di Tito*', *Music Review*, XXXI, 1970, pp. 285–94, esp. 288. One of the discarded arias, *Se mai senti spirati sul volto* (Act II, Scene 15 in the 1734 libretto) was offered by Constanze to Breitkopf & Härtel in 1799: see her letter of 25 February, Mozart, *Briefe*, IV, p. 229, item 13. This aria is lost. Vitellia's aria, which originally ended Act II of the 1734 version, was *Tremo fra' dubbi miei*.

24 Volek, *op. cit.*, p. 283.

25 Nissen, p. 555 (from Niemetschek, pp. 42f.).

26 H. C. Robbins Landon, *Haydn: Chronicle and Works: The Early Years 1732–1765*, I, London and Bloomington, Ind., 1980, p. 325.

27 For the post-coach schedule, see *Topographisches Post-Lexikon aller Ortschaften der k. k. Erbländer*, ed. Christian Crusius, I, Vienna, 1798, pp. xl, lxxii; K. N. Pisarowitz, 'Mozart auf den Reisen nach Prag', *Mitteilungen der Internationalen Stiftung Mozarteum*, December 1960, p. 18. For the description of the route taken, see Karl Baedeker, *Austria-Hungary . . . Handbook*, 11th edn, Leipzig, 1911, pp. 349ff.

28 Nissen, pp. 555f. (from Niemetschek, pp. 41, 64). In Nissen, the section dealing with *Tito* (pp. 556f.), which is principally concerned with the value and stylistic content of the work, is taken from Rochlitz, *AMZ*, December 1798 (pp. 151f.), on the whole, word for word. But there is one significant change: in Rochlitz, the trip to Prague occurs not only after Mozart's receiving the commission to

write a Requiem from a mysterious messenger, but actually after beginning to compose it and being in a state of exhaustion by the time of the invitation to go. Then we read:

> [Anecdote] 21.
> Meanwhile the time was approaching for Leopold to leave for his coronation in Prague. The opera direction, which did not decide until late to fill to the point of overflowing the already full programme of festivals and ceremonies with a new opera, turned for that reason to Mozart. That was very pleasing for his wife and his friends, because it forced him to a different work and to distractions. On their encouragements, and because it flattered his sense of honour, he took on the composition of the proposed opera, *Clemenza di Tito*, by Metastasio. The text was chosen by the Bohemian Estates . . .

Later, Rochlitz (*ibid.*, p. 177) adds, 'He [Mozart] left for Prague feeling very sickly. The amount of work once again excited the powers of his spirit and concentrated it on one point; the many distractions raised his courage, his spirit was enlivened to the point of lightheartedness – the little lamp flamed brightly once more before it was extinguished: but precisely through this effort he was even more exhausted and returned even more sickly to Vienna . . .'

In the Niemetschek-Nissen version, however, it is clearly stated, 'Shortly before the coronation of Emperor Leopold, even before Mozart had received the order to travel to Prague, a letter without signature was brought him by an unknown messenger . . .' (Niemetschek, pp. 41f.; Nissen, p. 554. This latter version, chronologically and from other standpoints as well, has seemed to me the more plausible.

29 On the choice of *Tito* and previous history, see *NMA*, II/5, Band 20, *La clemenza di Tito*, ed. Franz Giegling, Kassel, etc., 1970, foreword (edition used throughout present discussion); Nettl, pp. 183ff.

30 Nettl, p. 180, Volek's counter-suggestion, that except for Count Künigl, 'no member of the commission was a Mason', is untrue; since Masonry is forbidden in all Communist countries, we may consider this a statement made because it was impossible for Volek to gain access to the sources that would have revealed to him that men like Canal and Thun were famous Masons (there were actually five Counts Thun in the Craft). it is also, of course, the Communist Party's official 'line'.

31 For the quintet finale see Lühning, *op. cit.*, pp. 309f. For Mozart's letter see *Briefe*, III, pp. 163f.

32 Nettl, p. 184, n. 3.

33 On the function of the Overture, see D. Heartz, 'Mozart's Overture to Titus as Dramatic Argument', *Musical Quarterly*, LXIV, 1978, pp. 29ff. On the

psychological aspects of *Tito*, see B. Brophy, *Mozart the Dramatist: a New View of Mozart, his Operas and his Age*, London, 1964; see also D. Heartz, 'Mozart and his Italian Contemporaries: "La clemenza di Tito", *Mozart-Jahrbuch 1978/79*, pp. 275ff.

CORONATION DIARY
(pp. 101–123)

1 K. Baedeker, *Austria-Hungary . . . Handbook*, 11th edn, Leipzig, 1911, pp. 293ff.
2 Nettl, *passim*; V. J. Sýkora, *František Zaver Dušek: život a dílo*, Prague, 1958.
3 Nettl, p. 190.
4 Karl Pfannhauser, 'Mozarts *Krönungsmesse*', *Mitteilungen der Internationalen Stiftung Mozarteum*, 11, Salzburg, 1963, pp. 3–11, esp. 4f.
5 Ignaz, F. E. von Mosel, *Über das Leben und die Werke des Anton Salieri . . .*, Vienna, 1827, p. 142.
6 The original French of this document, not previously quoted in full, reads as follows: 'On se rassembla dans *l'antichambre* de l'Imp[ce] on dina à 100. *personnes* dans le salon de courronement . . . Je me trouvois presque au bout de la table entre les Charwunscher Lisette Schoenborn et Auguste Sternberg. Le dîner bon . . . Des spectateurs sans nombre . . . La musique de Don Juan. Après table on s'arreta longtemps dans le salon malgré la mauvaise odeur de l'auditoire.'
7 Nissen, pp. 559f.
8 Nettl, p. 190.
9 Nettl, p. 190; Deutsch, *Dokumente*, p. 524 (also *Oberpostamtszeitung* notice of 6 Sep.).
10 *Pressburger Zeitung* (copy consulted held by the Österreichische Nationalbibliothek, Vienna).
11 Nettl, pp. 192f.
12 P. Nettl, 'Prager Mozartiana', *Mitteilungen der Internationalen Stiftung Mozarteum*, December 1960, p. 3.
13 *Ibid.*, pp. 3f.
14 Nettl, pp. 194f.; Tomaschek's autobiography appeared in the periodical *Libussa*, 1840, p. 367.
15 Nettl, p. 191.
16 K. Pfannhauser, *op. cit.*, pp. 5, 6.
17 Mozart, *Briefe*, IV, p. 154 (with facsimile).
18 Nissen, p. 556.
19 C. Raeburn, 'Mozarts Opern in Prag', *Musika*, XII, 1959, pp. 158f.
20 Nettl, p. 191.
21 K. Pfannhauser, *op. cit.*, pp. 5, 6 *passim*.
22 Nettl, p. 201.
23 *NMA* II/5, Band 20, *La clemenza di Tito*, ed. Franz Giegling, Kassel, etc., 1970.
24 Deutsch, *Dokumente: Addenda & Corrigenda*, p. 70.
25 Zinzendorf.
26 Deutsch, *Dokumente*, pp. 355, 545, 525.
27 Volek, 'Über den Ursprung von Mozarts Oper *La clemenza di Tito*', *Mozart-Jahrbuch 1959*, p. 284.
28 *Ibid.*, p. 285, n. 33.

29 P. Nettl, *op. cit.*, pp. 4f.
30 K. Pfannhauser, *op. cit.*, p. 9.
31 Nettl, p. 191; Deutsch, *Dokumente*, p. 355.
32 Nettl, p. 209.
33 Deutsch, *Dokumente*, p. 355.
34 H. C. Robbins Landon, *Haydn: Chronicle and Works: Haydn in England 1791–1795*, III, London and Bloomington, Ind., 1976, p. 113.
35 J. Cuthbert Hadden, *George Thomson, the Friend of Burns: His Life and Correspondence*, London, 1898, pp. 292ff.
36 Wilhelm Hitzig, 'Die Briefe Franz Xaver Niemetscheks und der Marianne Mozarts an Breitkopf & Härtel', *Der Bär*, Leipzig, 1928, pp. 101ff., esp. 105f.

THE MAGIC FLUTE
(pp. 124–53)

1 Da Ponte, *Memoirs*, pp. 193f.
2 The theatre was on land owned by Count Starhemberg. Komorzynski, pp. 152ff.
3 *Ibid.*, pp. 160f. From manuscript notes by Leopold von Sonnleithner, 'Materialien zur Geschichte der Oper und des Balletts in Wien', Gesellschaft der Musikfreunde, Vienna. Sonnleithner notes that in 1796 Schikaneder's orchestra was enlarged from thirty-five to thirty-seven by the addition of one first and one second violin. Another publication, *Das Jahrbuch der Tonkunst von Wien und Prag* of 1796, gives a much smaller orchestra 'Auf der Wieden', with three first and three second violins, two violas, one cello and two double basses. Komorzynski gives plausible reasons for preferring Sonnleithner's statistics. The orchestras in the court theatres (Burgtheater, Kärntnerthor) employed six first and six second violins, four violas, three cellos and four or three double basses, apart from the usual complement of woodwind, brass and a kettle-drummer.
4 Nissen, pp. 547ff. In this particular case, the whole tale has been adapted from Anecdote no. 11 in Rochlitz's *Anekdoten aus Mozarts Leben*, which appeared serially in *AMZ* (in this case in the issue of November 1798, pp. 83f.) As noted before, Rochlitz maintained that Constanze was a principal source of his information – he probably came to know her personally when she made her concert tour through Germany to Berlin in 1796; and as before, the fact that the tale was incorporated, in this case almost wholesale, into Nissen's biography suggests that it did, indeed, originate with her. Since he was still alive, Schikaneder is not named but referred to as 'a certain impresario'.

Compared with Nissen's version, the differences in Rochlitz's original are as follows: Rochlitz starts his text with Nissen's paragraph (in my translation 'He composed *The Magic Flute* . . . ') but phrased thus:

A certain impresario, who,

however, deserves to be known – was, partly through his own fault . . . [etc., word for word as in Nissen.] . . . Write an opera . . . [instead of 'Viennese' Rochliz has '–'] . . . When Mozart heard of this person's deceit . . . [added by Nissen, but using material from the end of Anecdote no. 17, published in *AMZ* a month later, in December 1798 (p. 147), where we read: 'When he heard of the theatre director's deceit, which I have published under no. 11, all he said was . . .', etc.]

5 Komorzynski, pp. 170ff.' Schenk, p. 756; Chailley, pp. 11ff. *passim; Mozarts Tod*, pp. 38ff.; Alfons Rosenberg, *Die Zauberflöte: Geschichte und Deutung*, Munich, 1964, pp. 152ff.

6 A Roman Catholic religious order.

7 A. W. Thayer, *Ludwig van Beethovens Leben*, 5 vols, Leipzig, 1901–11, IV, p. 211.

8 *Schauspielerleben im 18. Jahrhundert*, Munich, 1912, I, pp. 363–5.

9 On numerology in the opera, see *Mozarts Tod*, pp. 38ff.; Chailley, *passim*.

10 Facsimile of 1524 edition in Chailley, p. 144; for Chailley's explanation of why Mozart used the melody, see p. 277.

11 See Köchel 453b (p. 454); transcribed in *NMA*, II/5, Band 19, *Die Zauberflöte*, p. 377 (as a_3).

12 For 1725 booklet, see Gould, III, pp. 475–7; for 1723 print, *ibid.*., pp. 487f.

13 Gould, III, p. 162.

14 Zinzendorf, 19 June 1792.

15 *Freimaurer und Geheimbünde*, pp. 35f., 56.

16 *Ibid.*, p. 55.

17 *Ibid.*, pp. 55f.

18 Catalogue of the Exhibition, *Freimaurerei und Joseph II: Die Loge Zur Wahren Eintracht*, Schloss Rosenau, near Zwettl, 1980. For general questions about this period see Edith Rosenstrauch–Königsberg, *Freimaurer im Josephinischen Wien*, Vienna and Stuttgart, 1975.

19 Deutsch, *Freihaustheater*, p. 18.

20 Komorzynski, p. 151.

21 H. C. Robbins Landon, *Haydn: Chronicle and Works: Haydn in England 1791–1795*, III, London and Bloomington, Ind., 1976, p. 59.

22 I. F. Castelli, *Memoiren meines Lebens*, 2 vols, Munich, 1913, I, pp. 232ff., 46.

23 Mozart, *Briefe*, IV, pp. 154f.

24 Deutsch, *Dokumente*, pp. 356f.

25 Abert, II, p. 620, n. 2.

26 For Mozart's letters of 7–14 October, see *Briefe*, IV, pp. 157–63 and commentary, *ibid*, VI, pp. 423–6.

27 Mozart, *Briefe*, VI, p. 422.

28 'A 6½ au Théatre *de Starhemberg* au faubourg de la Vienne dans la loge de M. et M[e] d'auersperg, entendre la 24me representation von der Zauberflöte. La musique et les decorations sont jolies, la reste une farce incroyable. Un auditoire immense, Mr de Seilern et de Kinsky dans notre loge . . .' (Zinzendorf). First published by Christopher Raeburn in his

article on *The Magic Flute*, Glyndebourne Festival Programme, 1956, p. 53.

THE FINAL ILLNESS
(pp. 154–82)

1 Rochlitz, pp. 177f.
2 See Mozart's letter to his father, Linz, 31 October 1783 (*Briefe*, III, p. 291): 'On Tuesday 4 November I shall give an academy in the theatre here – and since I didn't have a single symphony here with me, I am writing a new one head over heels, which must be ready by then . . .' Mozart arrived at 9 a.m. on 30 October.
3 Leopold Nowak, 'Wer hat die Instrumentalstimmen in der Kyrie-Fuge des Requiems von W. A. Mozart geschrieben? Ein vorläufiger Bericht', *Mozart-Jahrbuch 1973/74*, pp. 191 ff.; also *Mozarts Tod* (with report from a handwriting expert, Herbert Peter), pp. 284ff.
4 *NMA*, I/2, *Requiem*, Teilband, 1, ed. Leopold Nowak; see also the facsimile edition: *Mozarts Requiem. Nachbildung der Originalhandschrift Cod. 17561 der k.k. Hofbibliothek in Wien in Lichtdruck*, ed. and with commentary by Alfred Schnerich, Vienna, 1913 which also includes reproduction of watermarks.
5 The theft occurred when the autograph was on loan at the Brussels Exposition.
6 For the dates 27 or 28 October and the weather for this whole period, see: *Mozarts Tod*, p. 86 (from A. Geusau, *Geschichte Wiens*, Vienna, 1793); Deutsch, *Dokumente: Corrigenda & Addenda*, pp. 73f.; Bär, pp. 105–7.
7 See Köchel, 6th edn (Wiesbaden, 1964). Entry of work in Mozart's thematic catalogue: Mozart, *Briefe*, IV, p. 163 (with facsimile).
8 Niemetschek, pp. 42ff.; Nissen, pp.563ff. The order has been slightly rearranged here.
9 Novello, pp. xxi, 124–8.
10 Wolfgang Plath, 'Requiem-Briefe. Aus der Korrespondenz Joh. Anton Andrés 1825–1831', *Mozart-Jahrbuch 1977/78*, pp. 174–203.
11 *Mozarts Tod*, p. 231.
12 Zinzendorf and Bär, pp. 105–7.
13 Karl Pfannhauser, 'Epilogomena Mozartiana', *Mozart-Jahrbuch 1971/72*, pp. 291f.
14 Süssmayr's falsification of Mozart's signature was first revealed by the graphologist Herbert Peter in *Mozarts Tod*, pp. 284ff. (with important facsimiles of Mozart's, Süssmayr's and Eybler's handwriting); see also Agnes Ziffer, *Kleinmeister zur Zeit der Wiener Klassik*, Tutzing, 1984, where Freystädtler's, Süssmayr's, and Eybler's handwriting are all analysed (with many facsimiles).
15 Pfannhauser, *op. cit.*, p. 276.
16 Mozart, *Briefe*, IV, pp. 491f.
17 Facsimile in *Mozarts Tod*, p. 91 (with transcription); it is now thought that this handwring is perhaps that of Sophie Haibel, Mozart's sister-in-law.
18 Rudolph Angermüller, 'Süssmayr, ein Schüler und Freund Salieris', *Mitteilungen*

der Internationalen Stiftung Mozarteum, February 1973, pp. 19–21.

19 *Ibid., loc. cit.*

20 Rochlitz, pp. 148ff.

21 Count Joseph Deym von Střžitež (*c.* 1752–1804), alias Müller; see above, p. 217, n. 25.

22 *The Letters of Mozart and His Family*, ed. Emily Anderson, London, 1938; 2nd edn, ed. A. Hyatt King and Monica Carolan, 2 vols, London, 1966, II, pp. 975–7.

23 For Sophie Haibel's report to Vincent (V.N.) and Mary (M.N.) Novello, see Novello, pp. 214f., 220. The Novellos had been to Vienna and were now on the return trip to England; they naturally took the opportunity to visit Salzburg again, this time having an extensive talk with Sophie who was living with Constanze:

> (M.N) In the course of conversation Madame Haibl told us that Mozart was about the same size and figure as his son, but rather shorter. (Madame Mozart told me that both sons are like their father, but especially the younger one). She also told me that *Mozart had died in* HER *arms*. On the very day that he had died he had been writing a part of the Requiem, and had given directions to a friend (this must have been Süssmayr) how he wished certain passages to be filled up. He afterwards said to her, 'My dear Sophy, I wish you to stay here with your sister tonight for her sake, as I feel that I am dying.' She said she endeavoured to the best of her power to console and encourage him, to remove the sad impression from his mind, but he repeated his conviction that he was fast sinking, and said that 'he already perceived the earthy taste of Death on his tongue.'
>
> He also bitterly expressed his regret at leaving his wife and family so ill provided for. Madame Haibl accordingly obtained permission from her mother to remain all night with her Sister and Brother-in-law. Towards evening they sent for the Medical person who attended Mozart, but he merely said that he would come 'as soon as the opera was over.' On his arrival he ordered Madame Haibl to bathe the temples and forehead of Mozart with vinegar and cold water. She expressed her fears that the sudden cold might be injurious to the sufferer, whose arms and limbs were much inflamed and swollen. But the Doctor persisted in his orders and Madame Haibl accordingly applied a damp towel to his forehead. Mozart immediately gave a slight shudder and in a very short time afterwards he expired in her arms. At this moment the only persons in the Room were Madame Mozart, the Medical Attendant and herself.
>
> The Room in which he

died was the front one on the street on the first floor.

On my inquiring of Madame Mozart (who soon after arrived and received us with even more cordiality, if possible, than on our previous visit) how it happened that l'Abbé Stadler had only a part of the Requiem, and that the last part was in the possession of Eybler, she said that, although both the gentlemen declared they obtained the MSS from her, yet that she was so agitated and confused at the time that she has not the least recollection of the circumstances.

(V.N.) (*Private*) Young Mozart's [the Mozarts' youngest, Franz Xaver Wolfgang (1791–1844)] mistress in Poland is a countess who is, unfortunately, married to a man she does not esteem. He is so much attached to her that his mother feared he would never leave Poland for any length of time without her and as he cannot take her with him on account of the husband Madame Mozart begins to despair of his ever establishing himself in Vienna or other large capital where his parts [talents] might be better known and appreciated.

In the evening visited La Mozart. The sister [*i.e.*, Sophie Haibel] who received us at first told us that the son is a little taller than his father but much like him in face, though the forehead resembled the mother. Mozart died in this sister's arms, and lamented bitterly his approaching death on account of the poverty he would leave his wife in; he requested Sophie to stay with him all night saying he was sure he should die. 'No, no, she said, you will not die' – 'Yes, he said, I feel the taste of death on my tongue' – yet this day he called for the Requiem and dictated to Süssmayr what should be done.

24 Manuscript in the Mozarteum, Salzburg; facsimile in *Mozarts Tod*, p. 31 (transcription p. 30).

25 Pfannhauser, *op. cit.*, p. 284.

26 Deutsch, *Dokumente*, p. 368 (note to 6 December).

27 Printed *Verzeichnis der sämmtlichen Brüder und Mitglieder der gerechten und vollkommenen St Johannis □ genannt Zur gekrönten Hoffnung im Orient von Wien im VIIten Monath des Jahres 1785*, entry 104 (Haus-, Hof- und Staatsarchiv, Vienna, Vertrauliche Akten).

28 Both names from Nissen, p. 572.

29 Deutsch, *Dokumente*, pp. 493–508; for Goldhahn, *ibid.*, p. 493.

30 Mozart, *Briefe*, IV, p. 198.

31 Zinzendorf.

32 Deutsch, *Dokumente: Corrigenda & Addenda*, p. 73. In the Hummel Archives (formerly in Florence, now held by the Goethe-Institut, Düsseldorf) is the following, largely unknown document: 'Herr Wolfgang

Mozart K. K. Kapelmeister u. Kam̃er Compositeur a[us] Salzburg. gebürt. alt 36 J[ah]r, d. 5^{tn} Xbr $\overline{791}$ gesorben /Infections Wundarzt/ H. Birner' – important because it shows that Mozart's corpse was examined by a doctor responsible for infectious diseases. See also Dieter Kerner: 'Das Requiem Problem', *Neue Zeitschrift für Musik*, August 1974, p. 477.

33 Bär, p. 131.

34 Deutsch, *Dokumente: Addenda → Corrigenda*, p. 73 (from K. Pfannhauser, *op. cit.*, p. 290).

35 A doctor, Sigmund Barisani, had written a note in Mozart's book on 14 April 1787. Mozart then added the following lines: 'Today on the third Sept. of this same year I was so unfortunate as to lose this noble man, dearest friend and the man who saved my life, quite unexpectedly, by his death. – He is now well! – but I – we – and all those who knew him well – we shall *never* be well again until we shall be fortunate enough to see each other in a better world – again – and *never separated*'. Constanze added her note to this one, referring to it. Mozart, *Briefe*, IV, p. 175.

36 F. X. Niemetschek, *Leben des k.k. Kapellmeisters Wolfgang Gottlieb Mozart nach Originalquellen beschrieben*, Reprint of the enlarged second edition, Prague, 1808, Leipzig, 1978, p. 81.

37 Letter to Maria Anna von Genzinger, London, 20 December 1791: H. C. Robbins Landon, *Haydn: Chronicle and Works: Haydn in England 1791–1795*, III, London and Bloomington, Ind., 1976, p. 118.

MYTHS AND THEORIES (pp. 183–94)

1 *Musikalisches Wochenblatt*, Berlin, report dated Prague, 12 December 1791. Deutsch, *Dokumente*, p. 380.

2 About Salieri, see the new multi-volume work (still unfinished) by Rudolf Angermüller, *Antonio Salieri: sein Leben und seine weltlichen Werke . . .* , Munich, 1971 *et seq.* (three volumes published so far); also *Mozarts Tod*, pp. 191ff.

3 Salieri quotations all from Friedrich Kerst, *Die Erinnerungen an Beethoven*, 2 vols, Leipzig, 1913, II, pp. 282ff.

4 Quoted in *Mozarts Tod*, pp. 198ff.

5 For more on this subject see O. E. Deutsch, *Schweizerische Musikzeitung*, January 1957.

6 Deutsch, *Dokumente*, p. 449.

7 'Mozart Supplement', *Musical Times*, XXXII, 1891, p. 20.

8 Bär, pp. 91, 116f.

9 P. J. Davies, 'Mozart's Illnesses and Death', *Musical Times*, CXXV, 1984, pp. 437–41, 554–61. This includes details of articles concerning the various aspects of the composer's illnesses.

10 Bär, pp. 105ff.

11. A. W. Thayer; *Ludwig van Beethovens Leben*, II, 2nd edn, Leipzig, 1910, pp. 150f.

12 For a long account of the Hofdemel tragedy and Mozart's

supposed involvement with Magdalena, see Francis Carr, *Mozart and Constanze*, London, 1983.

13 For the conventional romantic view of Gottlieb, see Alfons Rosenberg, *Die Zauberflöte*, Munich, 1964, pp. 67–70; for an accurate account of her life, and a newly discovered, and rather unflattering, portrait, see O. E. Deutsch, 'Ein Kostümbild Anna Gottliebs', *Studien aus Wien 5, 1957*, pp. 89ff.

CONSTANZE: A VINDICATION (pp. 195–215)

1 Niemetschek, pp. 48f.

2 With reference to Constanze's pension I have consulted the original documents (see above, pp. 245, n.5); see also the very useful article by J. E. Eibl: 'Zum Pensions-Gesuch Konstanzes vom 11. Dezember 1791', *Mitteilungen der Internationalen Stiftung Mozarteum*, August, 1966, pp. 4ff.

3 *Pressburger Zeitung*, 103, 24 December 1791, p. 1093.

4 Deutsch, *Dokumente*, p. 379.

5 *Ibid.*, p. 375 (*Pressburger Zeitung*, 102, p. 1085).

6 For Archduke Maximilian Franz and Baron von Jacobi, see Eibl, *op. cit.*, pp. 6f.

7 Deutsch, *Dokumente*, p. 409.

8 *Ibid.*, p. 411.

9 *Ibid.*, pp. 412f.

10 *Ibid.*, p. 414.

11 Georg Kinsky (completed by Hans Halm), *Das Werk Beethovens: Thematisch-bibliographisches Verzeichnis seiner sämtlichen vollendeten Kompositionen*, Munich and Duisburg, 1955, p. 504.

12 Mozart, *Briefe*, IV, pp. 204f., and VI, p. 447.

13 Deutsch, *Dokumente*, p. 415.

14 *Ibid.*, pp. 416–19.

15 *Ibid.*, p. 421.

16 *Ibid.*, p. 422.

17 Else Radant, 'The Diaries of Joseph Carl Rosenbaum', *Haydn Yearbook*, V, 1968, English version, p. 41.

18 Deutsch, *Dokumente*, p. 423.

19 C.-G. Stellan Mörner, *Johan Wikmanson und die Brüder Silverstolpe*, Stockholm, 1952, pp. 335, 396.

20 Niemetschek, p. 72.

21 Mozart, *Briefe*, IV, pp. 199f.

22 Novello, pp. 73f., 82f., 94, 101f.

23 'She confirmed the truth . . . of his writing the Quartet in D minor while she was in labour with their first child; several passages indicative of her sufferings especially the Minuet (a part which she sang to us)', *Ibid.*, p. 112. The most suggestive description of labour pains are possibly in the *Andante*, bars 31ff. and 47ff.

24 Otto Jahn, *Life of Mozart*, trans. from the German by Pauline D. Townsend, with a preface by George Grove, 3 vols, London, 1882, I, pp. iif.; II, 265n.

25 Mozart, *Briefe*, II, pp. 253f.

26 *Ibid.*, p. 255.

27 *Ibid.*, pp. 272–6.

28 *Ibid.*, pp. 414–19.

29 *Ibid.*, p. 465.

30 *Ibid.*, p. 513.

31 Nissen, pp. 414f.

32 Mozart, *Briefe*, II, p. 529.

33 Mozart, *Briefe*, III, p. 181.

34 *Ibid.*, p. 186.
35 *Ibid.*, p. 200.
36 *Ibid.*, p. 206.
37 *Ibid.*, pp. 218f.
38 *Ibid.*, pp. 220f.
39 Hermann Abert, *W. A. Mozart*, 7th edn, 2 vols, Leipzig, 1955, I, pp. 813ff.
40 Arthur Schurig, *Wolfgang Amadé Mozart: Sein Leben, seine Persönlichkeit, sein Werk*, 2nd edn, Leipzig, 1923, II, pp. 131, 379.
41 Wolfgang Hildesheimer, *Mozart*, Frankfurt-am-Main, 1977, pp. 253f.
42 'Amadevious', *New York Review of Books* XXIX/18 (18 Nov. 1982), pp. 3–7.
43 Dieter Schickling, 'Einige ungeklärte Fragen zur Geschichte der Requiem-Vollendung', *Mozart-Jahrbuch 1976/77*, pp. 265ff.; see also J. H. Eibl's reply in the same issue, 'Süssmayr und Constanze', pp. 277ff. Peter J. Davies in his article 'Mozart's Illnesses and Death' (*Musical Times*, CXXV, 1984, pp. 560ff.) notes: 'Mozart's left ear lacked its usual convolution or concha (this rare congenital malformation is known in medical literature today as "Mozart Ear"); the fact that Mozart's younger son was born with the same deformity is a trump card for Constanze's innocence, for it provides the strongest possible proof of his paternity.'
44 V. Braunbehrens, *Mozart in Wien*, Munich and Zurich, 1986, pp. 104ff.; esp. 107.

APPENDIX A (pp. 217–24)

1 The house in Mozart's time bore the conscription number Stadt (City) No. 970; in earlier times it had been numbered, variously, 875 and 932, and after 1849 it became No. 934.
2 Formerly the Gassl bei dem Himmelpfortkloster.
3 The description continues as follows:
   1 His hair-style *en Grecque carré à dos d'âne* [frizzed hair, swept back in many small curls ending in a ponytail; Mozart's hair-style as in the unfinished Lange portrait of 1789–90 (see ill. 11)]
   2 A heavy English neckerchief of muslin
   3 An Anglo-French frock-coat
   4 A waistcoat *en fond filoche* [with a silk tissue base]
   5 Closely fitting knee-breeches of *bleu mignon* or bright blue worsted
   6 Two large watch-chains
   7 Blue-and-white chequered silk stockings
   8 Black shoes are still worn
   9 In the hand, a hat *à l'Andromane*, with rose-coloured lining, because the hat is for the hand rather than the head.

Select Bibliography

A good bibliography is to be found in the Mozart article in The New Grove Dictionary of Music and Musicians, ed. Stanley Sadie, London, 1980. This is reproduced in Sadie, Stanley: *The New Grove Mozart*, London, 1982. Articles and books of special interest published subsequently include:

BRAUNBEHRENS, Volkmar: *Mozart in Wien*, Munich and Zurich, 1986. A sensible re-examination of many aspects of Mozart's life in Vienna with some new interpretations of his last years.

DAVIES, Peter J.: 'Mozart's Illnesses and Death', *Musical Times*, CXXV, 1984, pp. 437ff., pp. 554ff. The authoritative new study on the subject, superseding all previous studies, great and small.

DAVIES, Peter J.: 'Mozart's Manic-Depressive Tendencies', *Musical Times*, CXXVII, 1986; part 1, pp. 123–6, part 2, pp. 191–6.

EISEN, Cliff: 'Contributions to a New Mozart Documentary Biography', *Journal of the American Musicological Society*, XXXIX/3 (Fall 1986), pp. 615–32. This important article arrived too late for consideration in the present work.

LANDON, H. C. Robbins: *Mozart and the Masons: New Light on the Lodge 'Crowned Hope'*, London and New York, 1982. Mozart identified in a group picture of the Lodge 'Crowned Hope', in 1790, with documentation, partly unpublished, of Lodge membership lists.

MORROW, Mary Sue: 'Mozart and Viennese Concert Life', *Musical Times*, CXXVI, 1985, pp. 453ff. Re-examination of the evidence.

STEPTOE, Andrew: 'Mozart and Poverty', *Musical Times*, CXXV, 1984, pp. 196ff. The subtitle is, again 'A re-examination of the evidence'.

Further attention should be drawn to the complete recordings of Mozart's symphonies on original instruments (L'Oiseau Lyre), by the Academy of Ancient Music, conducted by Christopher Hogwood, with notes by Neal Zaslaw, in the course of which vital new textual information has been gained (*e.g.*, the bassoon parts in the 'Paris' Symphony); and to the recording, also by Christopher Hogwood, of Richard Maunder's new reconstruction of the Requiem (L'Oiseau Lyre) with Maunder's essential notes – a brilliant operation from every viewpoint.

List of Illustrations

Index

Acknowledgments

Albertina, Vienna; Archiv der Stadt Wien; C. Bednarczyk (Antique Gallery), Vienna; Gesellschaft der Musikfreunde, Vienna (Dr Otto Biba); Glas Galerie Kovacek, Vienna; the late Ernst Hartmann, Vienna; Historisches Museum, Vienna (Dr Adalbert Schusser); Hofkammerarchiv, Vienna (Dr Christian Sapper); Reinhold Hoffstätter (Antique Gallery), Vienna; Kunsthistorisches Museum, Vienna (Hofrat Dr Georg Kugler); Kunstsalon Kovacek, Vienna; Modeschule der Stadt Wien, Schloss Hetzendorf (Frau Dr Regina Forstner); Mozarteum, Salzburg; Ingo Nebehay (Wiener Antiquariat), Vienna; Österreichische Nationalbibliothek, Vienna (Bildarchiv and Musiksammlung); Dr William B. Ober, Tenafly, New Jersey; the late Professor Hans Swarowsky, Vienna; Technische Universität (Hochschule), Vienna (Dipl.-Ing. Dr Alfred Lechner). Chief photographers: Piero Malvisi (Popolonia), Josef Vouk (Vienna). We wish to express particular thanks to Dr Alfred Lechner for his valuable assistance with the research on Mozart's last apartment and for drawing a groundplan of our reconstruction of the flat and the furniture contained therein.